COUNTY LI

Exploitation and Drug among Urban Street Gangs

Simon Harding

BRISTOL
UNIVERSITY
PRESS

First published in Great Britain in 2020 by

Bristol University Press
University of Bristol
1–9 Old Park Hill
Bristol
BS2 8BB
UK
t: +44 (0)117 954 5940
www.bristoluniversitypress.co.uk

North America office:
Bristol University Press
c/o The University of Chicago Press
1427 East 60th Street
Chicago, IL 60637, USA
t: +1 773 702 7700
f: +1 773-702-9756
sales@press.uchicago.edu
www.press.uchicago.edu

British Library Cataloguing in Publication Data
A catalogue record for this book is available from the British Library

Library of Congress Cataloging-in-Publication Data
A catalog record for this book has been requested

ISBN 978-1-5292-0307-3 hardcover
ISBN 978-1-5292-0308-0 paperback
ISBN 978-1-5292-0311-0 ePub
ISBN 978-1-5292-0309-7 ePdf

Cover design by blu inc
Front cover image: Alamy/Banter Snaps

*La crisi consiste appunto nel fatto che il vecchio muore
e il nuovo non può nascere: in questo interregno si
verificano i fenomeni morbosi piú svariati.*

The crisis consists precisely in the fact that the old is
dying and the new cannot be born; in this interregnum
a great variety of morbid symptoms appear.

Antonio Gramsci, *Selections from the Prison Notebooks*, 1971

Contents

List of Figures and Tables

Figures

Tables

Acknowledgements

I want to offer my sincere thanks to all those who contributed to this book. Having given a commitment of anonymity, I realise, of course, I cannot place their names here in print. However, without their help and assistance the book would be much impoverished. Thanks therefore are gratefully offered to all those who gave freely of their time, including various stakeholders such as local council staff, substance misuse teams, charity workers, housing staff, local police officers of all ranks, teaching staff and others.

Special thanks go to those gang-affiliated and ex-gang affiliated respondents, those who once ran, and those who continue to run or manage county lines, for their fascinating insight into this life. I hope you stay safe.

Thanks too to all the users, their carers and parents, who participated so openly and gave their time and thoughts, often with great humour, even through ill-health. I truly appreciate your contributions. Your insights greatly informed my work and I hope I have done justice to you in articulating your voices. I wish you all well.

My thanks too to the executive staff at the University of West London who graciously granted me the time, latitude and ethical approval for this study. Without their support, this work would never have moved from the starting blocks.

I am indebted to my family and friends who no doubt often wondered if I would ever emerge from my office. I thank them for their patience and understanding throughout the research and writing process.

Finally, my thanks too to the editors and publishing staff at Bristol University Press for their guidance, precision, dedication and encouragement to get this into print, and for their commitment to ensuring high quality as always.

The Structure of the Book

Overview

The aim of this book is to present the findings from two years of research undertaken in London and the south-east of England focussing on the evolution of urban street gangs and their involvement with changing drug markets. The reason for the study was to explore widely reported but under-researched changes in the presentation of street gangs and drug markets; their apparent movement from traditional inner-city locations to suburban/provincial settings; to help explain the alarming rise in violence linked to these phenomenon; and to better understand these emerging trends and their interconnectivity.

Since the year 2000, UK urban street gangs have grown in number, in visibility and in prominence, evolving into a significant presence in some urban areas. In recent years they have further rapidly evolved through the development and expansion of county lines drug supply networks and now exhibit a presence in non-metropolitan areas. The impact of county lines and changes to drug markets are further evidenced by Dame Carol Black (Black, 2020) in her wide-ranging Review of Drugs report.

County lines drug supply networks, or simply 'county lines' as we now commonly refer to them, are a recently evolved model of drug distribution in the UK involving the transportation and distribution of drugs from urban metropolitan centres to provincial, local or rural towns.

Concomitant with both these phenomena has been the steady development of social media and information technology with its continuing impact upon all aspects of social life.

I propose that all three phenomena; the evolution of street gangs, the evolution of drug markets and the evolution of social media, all converge and interact to influence, shape, alter and promote adaptive opportunities for criminal activity. The focus here is to consider how these elements converge in the process known as 'county lines' drug distribution networks.

Structure

The Introduction sets out how this research study was conducted, detailing the number, type and characteristics of the various respondents. The terminology around CLs can vary from one scholar to another so the terms used in this study are set out here. The methodological challenges of the research are discussed here including ethics, limitations, negotiating access and the usefulness of participant observation.

Chapter 1 sets the scene of the emergence of CLs, noting operational and cultural shifts in drug supply and distribution. It establishes the various definitions used throughout the book for CLs and street gangs. This chapter summarises emerging academic perspectives surrounding CLs before focussing on exploring the UK context for county lines. I establish the principle of flux and turbulence in the social field of the gang before considering CL via the prism of marketing, business enterprise and entrepreneurialism. Here I centre CLs within a transactional framework of customer relationship management and business decisions, and I establish the central premise of building competitive advantage which is further established throughout the book.

Chapter 2 develops the scene-setting further and proposes a theory of change offering an overarching narrative for the emergence of county lines. I establish how street gangs have evolved, leading the social field of the USG into a state of flux. Contributing to this flux are new affiliates with new aspirations to seek out and create competitive advantage by locating and exploiting dormant domestic drug markets in new locations. The push–pull factors which make a CL host location attractive are itemised. I establish the Evolutionary Models of CL Networks, creating a typology of different UK CL models increasingly adopting business modes of professionalisation and sophistication.

Chapter 3 asks: who joins a CL? Where do they come from? Why do they join? Here I establish the concept of the Pool of Availability – a conveyor belt of young people for entry into the Game. This chapter offers the first of a series of deeper case study insights from respondents articulating their lived experience of involvement and life inside a county line. Options for entry and types of role are explored alongside the prerequisites for joining a CL crew, managing a line and the logistics of getting staff to customers.

Chapter 4 considers the reality and internal dynamics of running a CL in more detail – a process known as 'grinding'. The internal dynamics of this is then unpacked to reveal life inside a trap house, managing staff, role differentiation and the marketing principles of customer relationship management. The management risks of CLs are set out and options for CL expansion are tabled.

Chapter 5 considers how CL managers now employ strategic and tactical actions to control their lives and their staff in the pursuit of competitive advantage. Two key areas are developed – criminal exploitation and the CL Control Repertoire. The role of gender is explored, with detailed insight into the exploitation, intimidation and violence now ever-present in CLs via issues such as debt bondage.

Chapter 6 delves more deeply into the exploitative practice of cuckooing – taking control of the domestic environment of vulnerable people in order to deal drugs from their property. Definitions of cuckooing are reviewed. A new typology of cuckooing is offered, detailing how it works in practice, highlighting the often nuanced relationships between 'vulnerable' users and dealers. I identify how local users can employ greater agency in their interactions with the dealers than previously thought. Again, respondent case studies are utilised to illustrate the lives of users and to illuminate the skills and techniques they employ to survive both addiction and multiple interactions with dealers.

Chapter 7 moves the focus to the families of those involved in CLs, looking at how violence and intimidation often reverberates back into families. I also consider the range of potential responses available to local youth once a CL emerges in their town, noting emergence can offer either opportunity or threat. I offer a spectrum of local adaptations employed by local youth before establishing a new theory of asymmetric clash and the gang Sprouting model – both detailing how CL emergence can dramatically impact host locations generating violence and fear.

Chapter 8 concludes the book by reflecting upon the unique contributions offered by the study while drawing out the key learning.

Introduction

Researching county lines and urban street gangs

In this research study I sought to examine how London-based USGs establish county line (CL) drug supply networks into the Home Counties. Specifically to:

- investigate localised drug markets, offending patterns, strategic action and the local economy of substance misuse;
- generate different CL models and explore how they are employed;
- examine the behaviours and dynamics of social actors;
- generate a typology of social control mechanisms and strategic action;
- review impacts and make policy recommendations to help tackle county lines.

In so doing, I draw upon two principle theoretical perspectives with great explanatory value regarding street-gang dynamics: social field analysis (Bourdieu 1984, 1985; Fligstein and McAdam, 2012; Martin, 2003); and street capital theory (Harding, 2012a, 2014; Sandberg, 2008; Sandberg and Pederson, 2011).

I have elected to keep the study locations anonymous. Location sampling was determined by key factors: – the county was identified in Home Office Ending Gang and Youth Violence (EGYV) reports (Home Office, 2013b; HM Government, 2016b) as having CL alongside emergent gang issues; – one town was the subject of an EGYV in-depth peer review. Following initial overtures it was recommended I focus on specific towns widely recognised as experiencing multiple challenges from county lines. Initial scoping included discussions with local stakeholders to ascertain the viability of further research. Secondary analysis of local datasets suggested high volumes of CL drug supply networks. Agreement was given by the Chief Superintendent to support the study. Final locality selection was determined by data availability, CL presence, presence of pre-existing contacts (May et al, 2005), and their agreement to assist with research.

This study sought to access those related to county lines via: professional stakeholders working locally: the local police, in particular, Divisional Detectives working on USGs and drug markets; active participants in CLs using a third-party gang consultant. Such work naturally leans heavily upon non-random, purposive sampling techniques (Green and Thorogood, 2004) for accessing and interviewing USGs, drug users and CL operatives.

Further contacts were made via snowballing (Gilbert, 2008; Griffiths et al, 1993). Respondents were viewed as being experts in their own social setting (Gilbert, 2008) offering a degree of validity to their comments/observations and their lived experiences. Statutory stakeholders, charities and local agencies were approached professionally via email/telephone with a short brief outlining the research and reassuring them of anonymity, confidentiality and data security. Stakeholders included public health, social work, Missing Children, Social Care, Youth Offending, substance misuse, youth diversion, community safety, and local voluntary sector agencies and charities. No incentives were paid. Interviews, conducted in professional settings, averaged one to two hours.

Active participants in CLs were interviewed in one-to-one qualitative interviews, shorter street-based interviews, or short focus groups. All were aged over 16 and the study acknowledged their status as victim, offender, or both (Walklate, 2018).

All accounts were cross-examined, triangulated (Denzin, 1978). Transcribed interviews were categorised thematically and a coding framework emerged from repeated and emphasised topics which generated headings (Ritchie and Lewis, 2003. General observations, draft findings and emerging opinions were shared during iterative discussions with respondents.

This research follows on from previous Doctoral research into the social field of violent USGs in south London (Harding, 2012a). It further builds upon contractual research for the Home Office (HO) (Harding and Cracknell, 2016), during which similar research methods were piloted. This HO study successfully generated over 50 qualitative interviews, now used to underpin this research.

Data collection included mixed methods (Bryman, 2004) to triangulate findings (Gilbert, 2008). Research instruments included qualitative semi-structured interviews which offered opportunities to probe personal understandings of complex social worlds (Rubin and Rubin, 2005); participant observation (Kawulich, 2005); Media review/analysis (Jewkes, 2004); document analysis and secondary data analysis (Creswell, 2007; Gilbert, 2008). Qualitative semi-structured interviews were conducted with the groups and individuals illustrated in Tables 0.1, 0.2, 0.3 and 0.4.

Show Cards were used for some ex-gang-affiliate interviews due to longer interview times and to promote deep reflection. Here a typology

Table 0.1: Study respondents

Type of respondent	Number of respondents
Police officers	18
Stakeholders	16
Drug users	12
Local CL runners	9
Urban street gang CL operators	12
Other	1
Focus groups/meetings	136

Table 0.2: Stakeholder interviews

Stakeholders	Number of respondents
Serving police officers	18 male
Recognised gang specialists	2 male
Local school staff	1 female
Local authority staff	6
Local charities	2
Local substance misuse practitioners	2
Local substance misuse staff	5 female
Local transport provider	1 male
Total	**37**

Table 0.3: Respondents involved in county lines

Respondents involved in county lines	Number of respondents
London USG affiliates and active CL operatives	6 male, 1 female
London ex-USG affiliates and ex-CL operatives	4 male, 1 female
Active drug runner/dealer in CL supply networks	7
Active local home-county gang members and CL managers	2
Active male drug users	12
Active female drug users	2
Parent of active drug user	1
Total	**36**

of activities/behaviours was used as prompts for discussion (Gilbert, 2008; Harding, 2012a).

Undertaking gang research into illegal drug use or CL networks is 'high risk' (Aldridge et al, 2008) and always highlights ethical considerations

Table 0.4: Focus groups

Type of focus group	Number of participants
Local councillors' forum	22
Local youth services manager/staff	4
Local community safety partnership group	5
Youth Council Schools Focus Group 1	9
Youth Council Schools Focus Group 2	10
Youth Council Schools Focus Group 3	12
Youth Council Schools conference group	85
Total	**147**

for the 'dignity, rights, safety and well-being' of participants (Stuart et al, 2002: 3). The research was conducted following the ethical guidance of The British Sociological Association Statement of Ethical Practice; The Code of Ethics for Researchers in the Field of Criminology by the British Society of Criminology; the Ethical Guidelines of the Social Research Association (2003); the Research Ethics Guidebook: a resource for social scientists at www.ethicsguidebook.ac.uk and the ESRC Ethical Guidelines. This study was granted Ethical approval from the University of West London (March, 2018).

To minimise harm or distress to researcher/participants all possible impacts were considered and monitored (Gilbert, 2008). Transcription was undertaken by the author for all USG and ex-USG interviews. Stakeholder interviews were largely transcribed by a professional agency under strict contractual terms of confidentiality. Transcribed interviews were allocated a unique reference number.

Site visits, participant observation and ride-alongs

Participant observation (Stephens et al, 1998; DeWalt and DeWalt, 2002) was undertaken to inform and contextualise data and formulate new lines of inquiry. Webb and colleagues (1996) talk of 'unobtrusive measures' to collect data by walking around the area, waiting at bus stops and so on. Field visits were logged to monitor activities and observe changes (Gilbert, 2008). Twenty-five site visits were conducted over several months. Each involved travel to and from the area, sometimes by car and sometimes by public transport. I visited local working men's cafes, barbershops, drug misuse and drop-in centres, food banks, job centres and bus stations. I spoke with local heroin users begging on the street and with bored youth playing basketball on rundown local estates. During each visit I was able to observe the arrival of county lines dealers, many of whom were known to the police or had been pointed out to me. I would observe local users emerge from bedsits or flat shares to engage briefly with them and purchase drugs. On a couple of occasions I witnessed the urgency of public space drug use, including one man who, having just bought heroin, utilised the local phone box as a 'safe' injecting space.

These many local observations and interactions provided a more nuanced understanding of the complex social world of open and closed drug markets and how they are tolerated or otherwise by the wider community.

Following personal support from the Chief Superintendent, the local constabulary kindly agreed extensive access to officers alongside 16 hours of ride-alongs in police patrol vehicles. This provided unique opportunities to observe local areas, street dynamics and street populations, permitting observations of various routine interactions with CL participants, providing first-hand observation of policing drug distribution networks. Interactions with street-gang affiliates, CL operatives and drug users were observed providing opportunities for one-to-one engagement. I was given open access to policing activities, interactions with users and criminals, conversations, tactics, drug raids, investigative methods and detailed insight into previous and ongoing criminal activities. Lengthy conversations with stakeholders from all agencies revealed many frustrations with organisational policy, frustrations with partners and clients, and wider social or political comments regarding the lack of funds or the futility of the work. Other conversations focussed on the personal or team pride taken in having a success with an individual or an intervention.

While researching street populations, local users, drug runners, and local gang-affiliated young people, it was likely I was viewed differently after stepping out of a police car. Consequently I surmise some responses were self-censored, adapted, truncated or refused. However, without the ride-alongs, access to such diverse CL participants would not be possible or safe. Once credentials were established respondents were candid as to their feelings about the police, including local policing and police tactics. Local gang-affiliated youth or county lines crews were more cautious, however local users were often very candid indeed, with expansive interactions lasting from 20 minutes to an hour each. Often I would sit in their flat, bedsit or room, on a box, stool or on the edge of their bed while they recounted their life on drugs and the impact of county lines upon them, their habit and their environment.

A list of respondents interviewed in this study are presented in Tables 0.5 and 0.6.

Table 0.5: Breakdown of respondents involved in county lines

TAG	Gender	Age	Ethnicity	Details
USG 01	Female	28	African-Caribbean	Ex-CL manager
USG 02	Male	22	African-Caribbean	Ex-CL manager
USG 03	Male	23	African-Caribbean	Ex-CL manager
USG 04	Female	18	White	Ex-gang affiliate
USG 05	Male	30	African	Ex-CL manager
USG 06	Male	30	African	Ex-CL manager
USG 07	Male	20	African-Caribbean	Current CL operative
USG 08	Male	21	White	Current CL operative
USG 09	Male	20	African-Caribbean	Current CL operative
USG 10	Male	24	African-Caribbean	Current CL operative
USG 11	Male	19	African-Caribbean	Current CL operative
USG 12	Male	21	African-Caribbean	Current CL operative
Runner 01	Male	22	Eastern European	CL operative/local gang member
Runner 02	Male	18	African-Caribbean	Runner/dealer
Runner 03	Male	18	African-Caribbean	Runner/dealer
Runner 04	Male	17	Mixed parentage	Runner/dealer
Runner 05	Male	16	African-Caribbean	Runner/dealer
Runner 06	Male	23	Mixed parentage	CL operative/local gang member
Runner 07	Male	20	White	Runner/dealer
Runner 08	Male	19	African-Caribbean	Runner/dealer
Runner 09	Male	21	African-Caribbean	Runner/dealer
User 01	Male	30s	White	Heroin/crack user. Been cuckoo'd.
User 02	Male	50s	White	Heroin/crack user. Been cuckoo'd.
User 03	Female	40s	White	Heroin/crack user. Been cuckoo'd.
User 04	Male	30s	White	Methadone user. Been cuckoo'd.
User 05	Male	50s	White	Heroin/crack user. Been cuckoo'd.
User 06	Male	20s	White	Ex-heroin user now on Methadone
User 07	Male	70s	White	Parent of heroin user
User 08	Female	40s	White	Heroin/crack user. Been cuckoo'd.
User 09	Male	70s	White	Heroin/crack user. Been cuckoo'd.
User 10	Male	40s	White	Heroin/crack user
User 11	Male	30s	White	Heroin/crack user
User 12	Male	20s	White	Heroin/crack user-dealer

Table 0.6: Breakdown of stakeholders

TAG	Gender	Ethnicity	Details
Police 1	Male	White	Chief Superintendent
Police 2	Male	White	Detective Constable
Police 3	Male	White	Detective Inspector
Police 4	Male	White	Sergeant
Police 5	Male	White	Inspector
Police 6	Male	White	Detective Sergeant
Police 7	Male	White	Inspector
Police 8	Male	White	Detective Constable
Police 9	Male	White	Inspector
Police 10	Male	White	PC
Police 11	Male	White	PC
Police 12	Male	White	PC
Police 13	Male	White	PC
Police 14	Male	White	PC
Police 15	Male	White	PC
Police 16	Male	White	PC
Police 17	Male	White	PC
Police 18	Male	White	Sergeant
Stakeholder 01	Male	White	LA Youth Services staff
Stakeholder 02	Female	White	LA Community Safety
Stakeholder 03	Male	White	LA Community Safety
Stakeholder 04	Female	White	LA Youth Services staff
Stakeholder 05	Male	White	LA YOT staff
Stakeholder 06	Female	White	LA YOT staff
Stakeholder 07	Male	White	Gang consultant
Stakeholder 08	Male	White	Charity worker
Stakeholder 09	Male	White	Charity worker
Stakeholder 10	Female	White	School staff
Stakeholder 11	Male	White	Substance misuse worker
Stakeholder 12	Female	African-Caribbean	Substance misuse worker
Stakeholder 13	Female	White	Substance misuse worker
Stakeholder 14	Female	White	Substance misuse worker
Stakeholder 15	Female	White	Substance misuse worker
Stakeholder 16	Female	White	Substance misuse worker

Negotiating access

Researching London-based USGs required a third-party gang consultant to secure access to deeply embedded active USG members. Subsequent interviews took place after many months of relationship and trust building with the consultant, including regular meetings; his observation of my research style and techniques; my riding out with his local known gang members 'to see if I could handle it'. Only after passing such 'tests' did he permit access to a very hidden and hard-to-reach cohort of active USG members all engaged in CLs and with reputations for violence. Simultaneously, a reciprocal assessment was undertaken by me to ensure this research study and my approach was correctly communicated to potential respondents. Some potential respondents did not satisfy either myself or the consultant. Others failed to show up or were arrested immediately prior to interview. Snowballing techniques were used. A finder's fee was paid to the consultant. Lastly ex-USG affiliates were accessed via Youth Workers and charities supporting gang-affiliated young people. London fieldwork was conducted March 2018–June 2019. Home Counties fieldwork was conducted June 2018–March 2019.

Anonymity and terminology

During research I used an investigative field-title of 'Surviving illegal drugs and violence' to provide an easier entry point and facilitate spontaneous responses. This also reduced any potential stigmatising of the study area or participants as gang-affected. Research terminology was carefully moderated.

In writing up research findings, all commentary is anonymised so individuals cannot be identified, with respondents grouped into broad categories, for example gang specialist; police and so on.

Terminology regarding county lines drug supply

Throughout the book certain terminology is used to denote roles/status of CL participants:

- CL manager – manages county line drug supply networks at a senior level. They frequently established the line, managing and operating at senior levels. Some undertake operative roles working for other lines.

- CL operative – probably working at mid-level. The exact hierarchical position cannot be fully determined and may change slightly depending upon situation.
- CL runner/dealer – lower-level workers packaging, then delivering, drugs to end-users.

Thematic analysis

Once transcribed, data was thematically analysed (Rubin and Rubin, 2005; Braun and Clarke, 2006) – an approach adopted as theoretically flexible permitting data-set identification, categorisation, sub-division and grouping into themes/patterns. The data corpus generated data grouped by cohorts, for example drug users; the police; runner/ dealers. Thematic analysis then presented opportunities for cross-reading to locate repeated patterns of meaning and latent themes (Ryan and Bernard, 2000). Interviews were analysed for both surface-level semantic statements and latent meanings thus the analytic process aimed for a deeper interpretations, underlying assumptions and ideologies. Themes were reviewed, refined and tested. Complex themes such as CL Models, grinding and cuckooing were identified. While there remain some areas of overlap the data sets and themes are legitimate and coherently established. Every attempt was made to ensure data interpretations are consistent with the interpretive framework.

Research limitations

This extensive study was conducted in London and the south-east of England using respondents each with a different role or connection to CL networks, that is, users, dealers, USGs, CL managers, police (strategic and front-line), local practitioners, partnership agencies and finally local people. HM Government (2011: 13) list the enormous range of agencies involved in working with a gang member and his/her family, and it was not possible to interview each one. There was thus a limitation of practicality and officer availability. Access to USGs, drug dealing crews, and drug users was mostly non-randomised as determined by working with small selective groups each involved in distinctive activity. Such sampling strategies are subject to criticism for possible lack of representation and replicability, but commendation (Maher, 1997) for revealing insights from often hard-to-reach marginalised and inaccessible populations. The results, while supported by triangulation, may not be reflective of experiences of similar participants elsewhere in the UK, meaning that personal and common narratives derived from analysis here might also differ.

Presser (2009), and Sandberg (2010), caution that in qualitative research the respondent's veracity remains unverifiable. Thus it is not possible to make claims regarding validity, or otherwise, of any claims and narratives presented. Sandberg (2010), however, argues such narratives deepen our understandings of cultural norms, roles and processes, highlighting nuances of identity, interpretive differences in values and the inter-relationships of the actors involved.

I was also aware that participant observation, while offering insight into the 'backstage culture' (de Munck and Sobo, 1998: 43) of drug users and people being cuckoo'd, also brings limitations of gendered interpretations, selective bias, possible deception and subjective representation (DeWalt and DeWalt, 2002). While further research with drug users and CL crews would have been ideal, there are obvious compromises between safety and practicality in such dynamic and fast-changing situations.

Fieldwork relationships centre upon establishing trust between researcher/respondent. As far as possible this trust was established. Research placement and role was keenly acknowledged and with each interview I was able to identify my role, status and purpose generating honesty about intent and a meaningful discourse. Reflexivity throughout the study was paramount and helped situate the researcher within complex sets of fieldwork relationships. At noted by Attia and Edge (2017), reflexivity in this sense meant an ongoing mutual-shaping between researcher and the research. Reflexive field notes provided further insights into the research process (Kawulich, 2005), helping to shape understandings (for a useful insight into research practice in drug using environments see Parkin, 2013).

Throughout this research I have sought to articulate the social field of county lines networks and those participating from all sides. The opportunity arose to 'give voice' to voices seldom articulated, or heard. It is recognised that this process is also selective and in reality 'involves carving out unacknowledged pieces of narrative evidence that we select, edit, and deploy to border our arguments' (Fine, 2002: 218). While acknowledging this limitation, the quotations bring life to the arguments and humanise them through articulation of the lived experiences of the respondents. In such ways we broaden our understandings.

1

A Changed Landscape?

Definitions and scene setting

Over the past several years the evolution of UK drug markets has gathered national attention from the government, media and public. The recent Review of Drugs by Dame Carol Black (Black, 2020) tells us the illicit drugs market in the UK is worth £9.4 billion a year. This has centred upon the emerging development and expansion of drug distribution and supply networks from urban centres to provincial towns – in a process known as 'running county lines'.

While drug supply to small towns and cities is now new, the supply mechanisms and markets have altered significantly over recent years, such that it has impacted greatly not only upon the host towns, but also upon the young people involved – both as victims and offenders.

The shifts in drug distribution and supply networks from urban centres to provincial towns (from here on referred to as county lines (CLs)), have been facilitated by advances in technology, that is, mobile phones. Technological advance has profoundly altered transactional practice for ordering, supplying and distributing illegal drugs. This is achieved by establishing a database of active drug users (customers), loading this database onto a mobile phone as a customer database or network (a deal line), then undertaking regular distribution to this established network using a series of adaptive business models. Supply normally involves heroin and crack cocaine Black (2020). Hay and colleagues (2019) estimate there were 313,971 users of opiates and/or crack cocaine aged 15–64 in England in 2016/17. The National Drug Treatment Monitoring systems (NDTMS) estimated 279,793 were in contact with structured treatment in 2016/17. Over half (52 per cent) presented for problematic use of opiates. Of these, 43 per cent also presented for the use of crack cocaine. In the UK, an opiate user has an average age of 39, with three quarters of opiate users aged over 35. See Black (2020) for the most recent analysis of market trends.

Coupled with the development and expansion of drug distribution and supply networks has been the evolution of the urban street gang (USG) as prime movers in this profitable business. In many ways it is the convergence of evolved drug markets with evolved street gangs and technological change (including social media) which has recently altered the landscape of criminal activity in the UK. Moreover it is the convergence of these three elements which has created the conditions for increased interpersonal violence which we are now witnessing.

This book will focus on county lines drug supply networks (county lines) as a series of business models and explore the reasons for its emergence, how it works and how it has expanded, providing details of its internal mechanics. This book will also articulate the voices of those involved in county lines from all perspectives: the runner/dealers, the CL manager, the user community, the local police and local practitioners tasked with tackling county lines and addressing their impact.

Such is the advance and rapid development of county lines drug supply networks that it has been declared a 'national threat' (National Crime Agency (NCA), 2019a): 'The supply of Class A drugs through the county lines business model is a significant, national threat' NCA (2019a), and led to the establishment of a national County Lines Coordination Centre at the cost of over £3m.

Before going deeper, it is useful to get some definitions out of the way: County lines is defined by Her Majesty's Inspectorate of Constabulary, Fire and Rescue Services (HMICFRS) as:

> Criminal networks or gangs which use a dedicated mobile phone line (or 'deal line') to distribute drugs, typically from an urban area to a smaller town or rural setting. They often exploit vulnerable adults and children to traffic, store and deal drugs, and will use violence, weapons and coercion. (HMICFRS, 2019a)

The NCA define a typical county lines scenario as having the following components:

- A group (not necessarily affiliated as a gang) establishes a network between an urban hub and county location, into which drugs (primarily heroin and crack cocaine) are supplied.

- A branded mobile phone line is established in the market, to which orders are placed by introduced customers. The line will commonly (but not exclusively) be controlled by a third party, remote from the market.
- The group exploits young or vulnerable persons, to achieve the storage and/or supply of drugs, movement of cash proceeds and to secure the use of dwellings (commonly referred to as cuckooing).
- The group or individuals exploited by them regularly travel between the urban hub and the county market, to replenish stock and deliver cash.
- The group is inclined to use intimidation, violence and weapons, including knives, corrosives and firearms. (NCA, 2017b: 2).

A more simplified definition states: 'county lines, or "going country" means groups or gangs using young people or vulnerable adults to carry and sell drugs from borough to borough, and across county boundaries. It is a tactic used by groups or gangs to facilitate the selling of drugs in an area outside of the area they live, reducing their risk of detection' (Safer London Foundation, 2016).

Not all county lines are run or organised by street gangs; some are run by small drug dealing crews, some by extended family networks based upon kinship ties, others by independents (Briggs, 2012; Coliandris, 2015; Windle and Briggs, 2015a, 2015b). However, while they are not the exclusive organisers or purveyors of CLs, USGs have become inextricably linked to it. Experienced and skilled in drug supply these street-oriented youth groups have actively expanded drug supply (see Hay et al 2019), importing and exporting illegal drugs from large cities to provincial markets to meet demand (Hudek, 2018; Pepin, 2018). Central to this is their ability to find an endless stream of young people keen to make money and to act as runner/dealers. Organisers and county line managers are highly risk-averse and so use this steady stream of young people to supply and distribute the drugs, thereby mitigating their own risks.

Urban street gangs

Urban street gangs (USGs) are street-oriented youth groups involved in criminality and violence and who may, over time, evolve into organised crime groups (OCGs). Street gangs tend to be less organised than OCGs and more concerned with perpetuating a threat of violence or harm across a geographical area related to the gang's main activities (see HMICFRS, 2019c).

Urban street gangs are defined by the Centre for Social Justice as:

> A relatively durable, predominantly street-based group of young people who (1) see themselves (and are seen by others) as a discernible group, (2) engage in a range of criminal activity and violence, (3) identify with or lay claim over territory, (4) have some form of identifying structural feature, and (5) are in conflict with other, similar, gangs. (2009: 21)

It is this definition which is used within this study when referring to USGs.

Violence and criminality is, however, only one output of USGs' formation. An alternative definition might draw attention to hidden formative aspects central to their formation, for example a self-formed association of neighbourhood peers (Smithson et al, 2013) whose manifest actions (individual, collective, expressive or instrumental) demonstrate group-bonding and common purpose through criminal activity. These manifest actions create opportunities for more latent functions including generating street capital, respect, status, and peer approval.

The NCA note that USGs are heavily involved and central to CL networks, but also note the absence of commonly used policing terminology across the country (NCA, 2015). Thus definitions can vary slightly and some county lines groups are described as OCGs, Dangerous Dealer Networks or even transient drug dealers. By 2016 the NCA noted that street gangs from London were encountered in 85 per cent of areas reporting county lines (NCA, 2016). State authorities acknowledged the link between USGs and drug dealing through the creation of Gang Injunctions (HM Government, 2016a). These however have had limited take up and effectiveness.

Working on the premise of risk mitigation for the senior members of the USG distribution networks, county lines networks are heavily associated with criminal exploitation and child sexual exploitation (Beckett et al, 2013; Firmin, 2010, 2011, 2018; Pitts, 2013). This in turn is associated with high levels of physical violence, trafficking (OHCHR, 2000), modern-day slavery, organised criminal networks and weapons. Child criminal exploitation (CCE) is defined as:

> ...where an individual or group takes advantage of an imbalance of power to coerce, control, manipulate or deceive a child or young person under the age of 18 into any criminal activity (a) in exchange for something the victim needs or wants, and/or (b) for the financial or other advantage of the

perpetrator or facilitator and/or (c) through violence or the threat of violence. The victim may have been criminally exploited even if the activity appears consensual. CCE does not always involve physical contact; it can also occur through the use of technology. (HM Government, 2018)

Emerging perspectives of UK drug markets

Jock Young's *The Drugtakers: The Social Meaning of Drug Use* (1971) opened the modern period of academic drug misuse scholarship. This was followed much later, however, with a series of scholarly works focussed mainly on heroin use and heroin markets. These included an examination of drugs and violence (Goldstein 1985); an evocation of 'the New Heroin Users' (Pearson 1987b) and the conditions of social deprivation experienced by heroin users (1987a); links between heroin use and acquisitive crime (Parker and Newcombe, 1987; Parker et al, 1988; Stewart, 1987); an examination of UK drug markets (Dorn et al, 1992; Dorn and South 1990); and policing local retail drug markets (Maher and Dixon, 1999).

From the turn of the century, academic scholarship expanded with areas of specialism emerging, notably: international markets and the UK (Hough and Natarajan, 2000; Ruggiero 2010); the links between drugs, crime and social exclusion (Seddon 2000, 2006; Shiner, 2013); market segmentation (Pearson and Hobbs, 2001) and interconnectivity (Pearson and Hobbs, 2001); differentiated UK drug markets (May and Hough, 2004; May et al, 2005; Matrix Knowledge Group, 2007): traditional family firms operating at the lower end of criminal networks (Hobbs, 2001; Pearson and Hobbs, 2001); Middle Market Drug Distribution (Pearson and Hobbs, 2001; May et al, 2008); drug supply from metropolitan cities to smaller towns (Bennett and Holloway, 2004; 2009); prevalence trends (Black, 2020; Drugwise, 2017; Newcombe 2007); market hierarchies (Murji, 2007); localised drug dealing (May and Duffy, 2007; Coomber et al, 2014; Coomber and Pyle, 2015); distribution networks (McSweeney et al, 2008); social supply among users (Coomber, 2004; Coomber and Turnbull, 2007; Potter and Taylor, 2013), pusher myths (Coomber, 2006) and user-dealers (Potter, 2009).

In the second decade of the 21st century scholarship advanced these issues, focussing on: stigmatisation (Lloyd, 2010); links to poverty (Dunlap et al, 2010); public health (Stevens, 2011); social supply (Coomber et al, 2015; Moyle et al, 2013; Potter and Taylor, 2013; Taylor and Potter, 2013); the emergence of crack cocaine use, (Briggs, 2010; 2012); independent operators (Briggs, 2012; Coliandris, 2015; Windle and

Briggs, 2015a, 2015b; Hales and Hobbs 2010); the constrained choices of user-dealers and users who deal drugs to help finance their habits (Coomber and Moyle, 2014); the violence associated with drug markets, (Coomber, 2015). More recently, scholars have revisited heroin use in the UK including the moral economy (Wakeman, 2015); drug using environments (Parkin, 2013) and the role and history of heroin in the UK (Seddon, 2006) and drug policy (Shiner, 2013). Even Bourdieusian persepctives on drug use and dealing have begun to inform the academe (Moyle and Coomber, 2016; Parkin, 2013).

During this time, the evolution of USGs became a dominant oeuvre in UK criminology through the work of Aldridge and Medina (2010); Densley (2014); Harding (2012a, 2012b, 2014); and Pitts (2008). Each noted the link between USGs and drug distribution networks. Not all criminologists working on USGs shared the same perspective. Unburdened by field research, Hallsworth (2013: 21) not only fails to identify out of town drug dealing but outrightly rejects the 'evocation of the urban street gang as significant players in the drugs economy', stating that we should treat this possibility with scepticism.

UK drug and gang scholars increasingly identified the emergence of county lines drug networks in a series of key works, each influential in advancing our understanding of this phenomena, notably: migrating dealers and moving out of town to buy/sell drugs (Coomber and Moyle, 2017; Densley, 2013; Hallworth, 2016; Harding, 2014; Harding and Cracknell, 2016; Johnson, 2015; Johnson et al, 2013; Toy, 2008; Windle and Briggs, 2015b). Recent changes in the organisation of UK drug markets were researched (Andell and Pitts, 2017; Coomber, 2015) alongside exposition of a changing drug market landscape and the challenges for stakeholders and researchers in identifying this (Disley and Liddle, 2016), not least due to differing presentation and non-homogenous drug markets (Black, 2020; Coomber, 2015).

The impact of social media on gangs and drug supply were noted (Densley, 2014; Storrod and Densley, 2017) and amid the expansion of drug supply (Hay et al, 2019; Black 2020), it was found that face to face and personalised transactions are still favoured for heroin and crack cocaine dealing (Coomber, 2015; Coomber and Moyle, 2014). More recently work has centered on the increased business motives of USGs in terms of drug supply networks (Andell and Pitts, 2018); the entrepreneurial search for profits (Andell, 2019; Whittaker et al, 2019); business branding (Spicer, 2018) and increasing professionalisation (McLean et al, 2020).

Recent scholarship has now surfaced important elements relating to county lines drug distribution networks which hitherto remained hidden, namely: localised impacts upon host towns (Andell and Pitts, 2018); the exploitation of young people (Andell and Pitts, 2018; Firmin, 2018; Pepin, 2018; Robinson et al, 2019; Windle and Briggs, 2015a, 2015b; Whittaker et al, 2019); cuckooing (Coomber and Moyle, 2017; Spicer, 2018; Spicer et al, 2019); the contested notion of 'vulnerability' and victim/perpetrator roles within county lines (McLean et al, 2020; Moyle, 2019; Robinson et al, 2019; Spicer et al, 2019; Windle et al, 2020) and the identification that some young people enjoy working CLs; the acknowledgment that USGs operate in the middle market for heroin and crack cocaine in a process that shades into organised criminal networks (OCN) (Andell and Pitts, 2017).

Beyond the specifics of county lines, recent scholarship has raised issues regarding the alteration of UK drug markets, raising issues such as the co-option and/or elimination of competing distribution systems (Andell and Pitts, 2018); the existence of hierarchical relations in which street gang Elders are now the middle-level managers in markets for heroin and crack cocaine (Andell and Pitts, 2018); and evidence of an 'occupational culture' for county lines (Andell and Pitts, 2018) and development of entrepreneurial traits (Hesketh and Robinson, 2019).

Scottish criminologists and gang scholars are also now re-examining the Scottish drugs distribution network and its relationship with CLs (Densley et al, 2018a; Densley et al, 2018b; McLean, 2017; McLean et al, 2018a; McLean et al, 2020; 2018b; Harding et al, 2018).

Aside from the work of academics, the emergence of CLs were picked up by law enforcement, and voluntary and public sector stakeholders from around 2010 onwards, though informal identification of CLs does predate this. The practice of 'going country' or 'going OT' (out there) began to be more formally recognised during research undertaken for the government programme Ending Gang and Youth Violence (EGYV) (2012–2015) (Home Office, 2012; 2013a; 2013b; 2014). The policing districts registered for this programme began to report increasing numbers of arrests of young people from London and other metro-cites in local provincial towns (BBC News, 2014). The recent emergence of this phenomena is illustrated by the fact that the Metropolitan Police Service (MPS) Drugs Strategy 2010–2013 (MPS, 2010), titled 'Confident, Safe and Secure', makes no mention at all of county lines.

In 2016, with the switch in Home Office programmes from EGYV to Ending Gang Violence and Exploitation (EGVE) (Home Office, 2016a), it was clear that county lines had been identified as a significant component of gang activity, with child exploitation taking a pre-eminent role. This was further identified in an independent review by Harding and Cracknell (2016), which noted that authorities who participated in the first round of EGYV in 2012 were already mapping and recording escalating county lines activity (2016: 3), further noting that, 'Those who had included analysis of gang-related exploitation noted a shift towards County Lines activity and a higher rate of CSE/exploitation disclosures' (2016: 20).

Reports from both EGYV and EGVE programme sites across England and Wales (see Disley and Liddle, 2016) also noted the challenge of identifying and interpreting this changed landscape commenting that many council CEOs were reluctant to acknowledge any emergent issues or that USGs might be gaining a toehold in their communities. While at times the subject of criticism, the government EGYV/EGVE programmes were nonetheless central to improving understanding, mapping and strategising in regards to CL networks, notably the emergent issues of missing children (Missing People, 2016, 2017), criminal and sexual exploitation (Berelowitz et al, 2013; Firmin, 2010, 2011, 2018; Pitts 2013; Turner et al, 2019).

Local assessments and practitioner reports have also helped widen our knowledge, often focussing on specific issues such as missing children or CCE. While this attention is much welcomed, overall, our research-informed knowledge base seriously lags behind contemporary developments. At this early stage of building understanding and mapping the issue, many reports and academic papers have also perhaps engaged with more reportage than deeper analysis. It is therefore hoped this study will offer a deeper analysis, advance our knowledge and if possible reaffirm the findings of other academic work.

Flux and turbulence: shifts in social fields

It is helpful to consider the emergence of county lines drug supply networks within the context of criminological theory and determine how theoretical perspectives have explanatory value by offering insight and understanding, and presenting interpretive frameworks that move us towards public policy solutions.

Two of the most insightful perspectives into street gangs and youth violence to have emerged over recent years are social field analysis (Bourdieu, 1984; Fligstein and McAdam, 2012); and street capital theory (Harding, 2014; Sandberg and Pederson, 2011). It is these interpretive frameworks that are employed here and which underpin the methodological approach undertaken in this research study and again analytically within the book. Utilising the conceptual framework of social field analysis, the emergence of county line drug supply networks, or drug dealing crews, can be viewed as an evolutionary process arising from the wider gang social field.

Field theory established the concept of social actors building relationships to produce, reproduce and then transform their own social field using individual and collective strategic actions (Bourdieu, 1990; Bourdieu and Wacquant, 1992).

Bourdieu (1984; 1985) established the concept of a social field (a domain or market) within which social interactions are shaped by rank and position within the hierarchy. Social fields are structured by a hierarchy, with all hierarchical positions being related. Indeed, all social fields overlap and are interrelated such that movements or changes in one results in movements and changes in others: like pebbles being dropped into a pool, there will be multiple ripples occurring simultaneously.

In broad terms, a social field or domain could be abstract and widely conceived such as the art world, academia or a professional body (the civil service, for example); or operate more visibly or locally such as a corporate organisation, police force or local authority council. Within each field, social actors strive to overcome unequal allocations of resources and find their way to success. Turner (1974: 135) describes a social field as 'an ensemble of relationships between actors antagonistically oriented to the same prizes or values'. Those within the same field share values, rules and a common purpose determined by a shared 'habitus' (Bourdieu, 1984) – early socialisation of social conditions that, over time, have been internalised into a series of mental and bodily dispositions that then govern our actions (Harding, 2014).

Bourdieu (1984; 1985) conceives fields as an 'arena of competition' within which strategic actors or players (employees or participants) struggle for different forms of capital, for example, economic, social, cultural, religious. Struggle is experienced as a daily jostle for position, power and dominance, a higher place in the hierarchy, more pay, or even just for the opportunity to inch past their peers. In this way, one advances up the hierarchy, or at least repositions oneself within the hierarchy, to a position of greater influence and advantage. But within a social field all positions are interrelated and interdependent; repositioning within a social field can mean movements upwards, downwards and sideways (for example, a Cabinet re-shuffle or a boardroom coup).

Fligstein and McAdam (2012) conceptualised this in relation to corporate structures and, building on the work of Bourdieu, acknowledged that for any social field to emerge there must first be a 'settlement' among the actors involved that includes: a shared understanding of what is happening and the stakes involved; a set of recognisable actors with different status and power; a shared understanding of the rules governing the field; a broad interpretive frame that creates meaning and sense of the social field.

Bourdieu also identified that each social field has its own internal logic, or doxa (the value of the game), and illusio (a belief or acceptance the game is worth playing). Importantly, all actions assume a logic and importance pertinent only to that social field, and events outside the field operate outside the logic – for example, respect issues within a gang setting.

In *The Street Casino* I adapted Bourdieu's concept of social field and applied it to the urban street gang, identifying that this domain operated as a 'dangerous arena of social conflict and competition' (2014: 54). I theorised that the USG operates as a social field within which there is an internal struggle for power and dominance to achieve scarce resources, namely economic capital and street capital.

As noted by Swartz (1997: 124), 'field struggle pits those in dominant positions against those in subordinate position'. Thus the internal gang hierarchy pitches actors against each other in pursuit of dominance and access to resources. As in any social field, the interactions are based upon relative location within the field hierarchy. To advance within the gang social field, actors employ 'investment strategies' to achieve goals. These strategies vary depending upon one's hierarchical position. They include: conservation strategies – pursued by dominant actors who strive for stability; succession strategies – pursued by new entrants seeking dominant positions; subversion strategies – pursued by those with little to gain from dominant groups. I called this structuration with the urban street gang 'the street casino'.

Within any social field this constant movement of positions up and down is referred to by Fligstein and McAdam (2012: 12) as 'jockeying' and 'turbulence'. They also note the possibility of the onset of 'contention' and strife within a field when incumbents are challenged for their position or threatened by challengers or new opportunities. Social fields can usually manage or accommodate this dynamic, as actors within each field jockey for position. However, when the social field becomes crowded or overcrowded, vertical advance up the hierarchy becomes more difficult to achieve.

I argue that within the social field of the USG the increase in gang affiliates (both younger and older) has created a much more crowded social field. Upwards movements are thus made increasingly difficult or thwarted as the number of actors within the social field generates increased competition. In fact, downwards or sideways movements are now much more likely, stifling one's personal trajectory and diminishing one's horizons. Ripples from the many strategic actions occurring within the social field will spread out simultaneously, colliding and doubling up, overlapping and being subsumed. The intensity and speed of this rippling, I have termed 'flux'.

For years, territorial gang life in the UK evolved relatively slowly and for many was indistinguishable from subcultural or tribal groupings once so vibrantly dominant in 20th-century Britain. For many academics, a fixation on subcultural groupings and an inability to accept 'shift happens' (Densley et al, 2020) obscured our understandings of gang evolution. This view was much championed by Simon Hallsworth (2013) and his junior co-authors, who strenuously denied the existence of UK USGs until as late as 2015.

While the social fields of USGs are in a constant internalised dynamic state of flux, it is clear this flux has dramatically increased of late in the UK, resulting in ever-greater field turbulence. This now occurs both within and along the boundaries of the gang social field, upsetting the 'settlement' and ushering in new challengers to challenge the incumbents and the dominant conservatism of the existing gang Elders. Social media has impacted upon the internal field dynamics and unfolding time spans. Arguments are now quickened, stimulated and enhanced by social media, which acts as a social accelerant, speeding up issues and telescopically collapsing acceptable timeframes. Within each gang social field, there is constant pressure to act, adapt, adjust and change. *The Street Casino* (2014) sets out how this process works within the social field of the street gang.

It is important to also now consider how field flux has impacted and reverberated with other social fields to create the conditions of increasing interpersonal violence across the UK.

The social field of the drug dealing crew (youth involved in dealing illegal drugs and who generally claim no true affiliation to USGs) has also witnessed significant market evolution and dramatic change thanks again to the advent of IT and social media. In turn, the social field of the drug using community has also altered. The interplay between these social fields has witnessed multiple forms of turbulence of late, creating further additional flux. Key contributing factors affecting or causing flux within these three social fields include the emergence of many new players/ actors in each social field. In many areas this includes new arrivals (many from migrant families) (Perri 6, 1997) seeking new hierarchical positions in USGs or in drug dealing crews. They may bring new rules and upset the settlement within their social field. Greater numbers of gang-involved youth increase the competition within USGs. USG members have become younger at one end of the spectrum and older at the other end as they fail to 'mature out', with USGs becoming more 'adhesive' overall. This greatly adds to the overall numbers now competing against each other within the social field of the gang, making competition fiercer and more vicious.

With new players in the Game, USG rules now change more quickly than before. This leads to an onset of contention within, and across, the USG social fields, that is, more contentious episodes with a clash of rulebooks and perceived primacy. This in turn disrupts the overall field landscape and creates greater turbulence. A fuller exposition of the USG is covered in the following chapter.

Add to this the emergence of new drug dealing crews, not all affiliated to USGs. In Bourdiouesian terms, this equates to the emergence of a plethora of subfields. Their field rules differ slightly from those of the USG, operating with a greater focus on contractual and transactional relationships. This again creates tensions and disruption of 'the settlement'. New 'stars' with fresh ideas can rise quickly to the top of the social field or generate violence in their determination to push others out of their way as they climb to the top.

Add into this mix greater contact with the user community (traditionally only interfaced via older middle-aged drug dealers). Now younger gang-affiliated boys are having far greater interaction with the social field of the user community than ever before. Previously selling weed on the estate, they are now moving more widely and selling different drugs to a different clientele. The traditional middleman has been cut out and street gang/drug user interactions have increased. This too has created additional tension between these two social fields, which in turn has created greater upset and turbulence among user communities. The advent of county lines distribution networks has seen attempts by USGs to control both dealing crews or the user communities with new mechanisms of control appearing as de facto, or imposed, rule changes.

The social field of the user community are also now developing new hierarchies in response to this field turbulence. With these three social fields now ever more closely intertwined, there is now also greater movement of actors/players from one social field to another, creating possibilities for promotion and acceleration alongside rapid positional movement up, down or sideways.

In this way, flux within one social field has impacted quickly and profoundly upon the others. One outcome of all this is greater violence among all players/actors across all these social fields. Increasingly, this is now played out in public view.

In summary, street-oriented communities are changing and adapting to a new evolved criminal landscape. We have been slow to realise this and to act upon it, and slow to research the impact of technology and social media upon the criminal activities of street-oriented communities. The changes now identifiable within street-oriented communities are also rippling upwards towards organised crime. Here the interface between the social field of USGs and the social field of organised crime networks is blurring, but also expanding with new opportunities. This interface is overdue for research that might map these new relationships. These evolutionary changes in the social field are now felt and witnessed by many ordinary members of the public, but the reason for this evolution and the exact nature of these changes has not been well understood or well-articulated.

County lines as a business enterprise

Essential to the success of county lines is its conception and formulation as a business enterprise in which business principles are followed and adopted even if unwittingly. It is important to conceptualise the CL phenomenon as something which is situated within the criminal world but also within the world of entrepreneurship and business. Framing county lines from a business perspective helps to reveal the internal motivations and dynamics operating within county lines.

Adoption of business principles exemplifies a re-orientation of drug supply towards end-users and customer. This embraces concepts of market definition, market research, product placement, product branding, brand management, customer value and satisfaction, digital and social media marketing, product marketing, and pricing. This means keener development of customer relationships management. The principle route to satisfying customer needs is via marketing.

Marketing is defined as 'engaging customers and managing profitable customer relationships' (Kotler and Armstrong, 2018), so by engaging with customers, building strong brand values and customer relationships, CL operatives create customer value, then value (profits) in return.

Successful CL operatives now focus on the marketing mix – the set of tools including product, price, place and promotion – used to produce responses in the target market. Widely understood as the 'Four Ps of Marketing', these variables can be increased, decreased or 'mixed' to ensure profit maximisation (see Figure 1.1). In CL networks, Product is both heroin and crack cocaine; Price equals the money paid by customers to obtain this product; Place includes the various activities which go into making the product available to customers; Promotion relates to the activities which communicate the merits of the product then persuade customers to purchase it.

The four 'Ps' concept prioritises the seller whereas buyer perspectives might translate this into the four 'As' which then operates as a tactical toolkit for positioning within target markets.

Kotler and Armstrong suggest that 'Acceptability' relates to the extent products meet customer expectations; Affordability – the extent to which customers will pay for the product; Accessibility – the extent to which customers can readily acquire the product; and Awareness – the extent to which customers know about product features, are persuaded to try it, then repurchase it. Clearly when the product is illicit drugs pre-existing relationships between customer and product drives demand. Product and product quality can differ significantly between county lines, and savvy customers will shift their loyalty to address their values and needs of the four 'As'.

Further elements of business operations relate to how products are marketed to customers, including real-time marketing and engaging customers in the moment (deemed critical to the success of county lines). Mobile marketing – using smartphones as a digital marketing platform –

Figure 1.1: The four Ps and As of the marketing mix

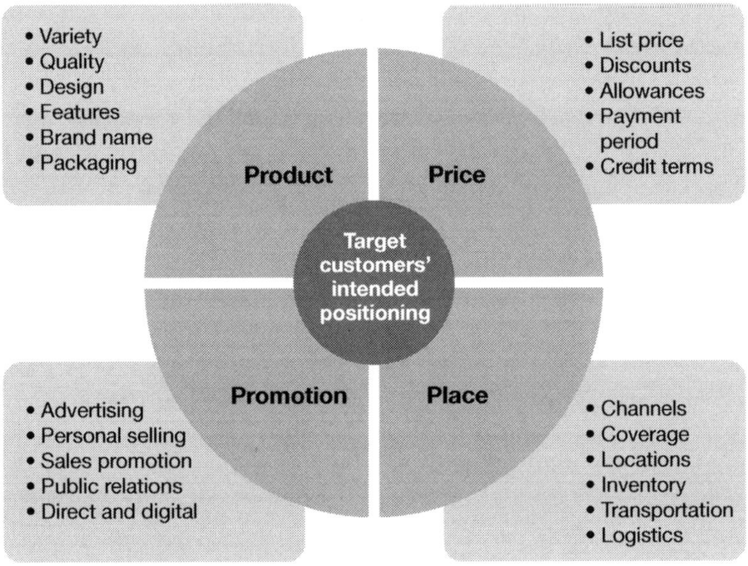

- Variety
- Quality
- Design
- Features
- Brand name
- Packaging

Product

- List price
- Discounts
- Allowances
- Payment period
- Credit terms

Price

Target customers' intended positioning

Promotion

- Advertising
- Personal selling
- Sales promotion
- Public relations
- Direct and digital

Place

- Channels
- Coverage
- Locations
- Inventory
- Transportation
- Logistics

The four Ps into the four As:

Seller's perspective	Buyer's perspective
Four Ps	**Four As**
Product	Acceptability
Price	Affordability
Place	Accessibility
Promotion	Awareness

Source: Kotler and Armstrong (2018: 78–9)

has been extremely profitable and is now ubiquitous. In normal business marketing a key centrality is the ability to digitally link brands to important moments in their customers' lives. Again with heroin and crack cocaine it is this pre-established history which underpins and drives demand. Clever marketing will, however, build the brand and, if reinforced by a quality product, will evoke memories of a quality experience.

Competition in this business is also now much more than simple competition between rival competitors: it is now competition within the entire value delivery network (suppliers, distributors seeking to improve the performance of the whole system of customer value) (see Kotler and Armstrong, 2018: 73).

Customer relationship management

A defining element of county lines drug supply networks is use of technology to effect change in drug markets. Rapid development of mobile/digital technology and hand-held devices has enabled development of more sophisticated systems for managing personal relationships, interactions and customer purchasing journeys. In this way the CL operates as a direct interaction mechanism with multiple clients offering a bespoke 24-hour dial-a-dealer service.

This form of customer relationship management (CRM) enables direct customer communication and dialogue via technology. IT processes enable CL operatives to place customers at the heart of both strategy and operations to enhance customer value. This in turn drives profitability and success, allowing CRM to help create solutions to customer needs. Central to this is personalisation – achieved once more intimate end-user details are acquired, that is, needs, preferences, interests, social situations, using environments, contact frequency, spend, purchasing history.

Central to any effective CRM strategy is the acquisition, retention and utility of information. Thus circulation of information within this system is key. Information (data) is shared extensively and can be traded by users to runner/dealers in return for drugs or gifts.

Key elements crucial to this side of business include:

Prospecting (finding/identification of potential customers)

Here CL managers must utilise skills in determining positioning and location of potential customers: the premium source for this is referrals. Current customers are asked to refer others. Prospecting is also done by hanging around outside benefit agencies, pharmacies, substance misuse agencies and so on. Lastly cold-calling can be used.

In drug supply the normal selling process, while still transactional, is often truncated due to the captive markets. However, for new customers the normal sales pattern of approach, presentation, handling objections/questions, then closing, is often undertaken. Repeat customers can ignore this process and simply make fast purchases by only stating their desired purchase.

Customer knowledge

Knowledge of the customer base, buyer behaviour and consumer is central to any effective CL business strategy. It is here that CL operatives and USGs really do excel. Years of practice in meeting this market and working this customer base have honed skills and knowledge. Dealing crews are cognoscente of factors influencing consumer behaviour, for example cultural factors, social factors, personal (age, occupation/lifestyle) and psychological (motivation, perception, beliefs). Fine tuning of market variations as determined by regional variations are fed back by CL operatives into gang information systems, leading to adjustments.

Moreover CL operatives will rely on word of mouth to impact buyer behaviour. Such recommendations have a powerful influence on purchasing habits far in excess of simple advertising (see Kotler and Armstrong, 2018). This involves a form of buzz marketing whereby opinion leaders are cultivated to spread knowledge of a new product to wider communities.

Building customer relationships

Central to successful CRM for CL operatives is the need to move from the early established transactional model to a more customer-focussed relationship marketing model. This requires building loyalty.

O'Malley (1998) notes that varying levels of loyalty exist when building marketing relationships as shown in Table 1.1.

An effective strategy for CL operatives is to move customers higher up the 'Loyalty Ladder' (Christopher et al, 1991) to build in brand commitment. They suggest that customers begin as 'prospects' before becoming customers, then supporters and finally advocates for the brand, see Figure 1.2.

Table 1.1: Varying levels of consumer loyalty

Type of loyalty displayed	Characteristics
No loyalty	Not loyal to any brand or location and can be random consumers
Spurious loyalty	Demonstrating temporary/promiscuous loyalty. Easily influenced by promotional offers so easily influenced to brand-switch.
Latent loyalty	Customer retains a highly favourable attitude towards brand which is not always demonstrated in purchasing. Easily affected by inconvenient locations/peer influence.
Sustainable loyalty	High repeat purchasing by customer on a long-term basis

Source: O'Malley (1998: 50)

Figure 1.2: The relationship ladder of customer loyalty

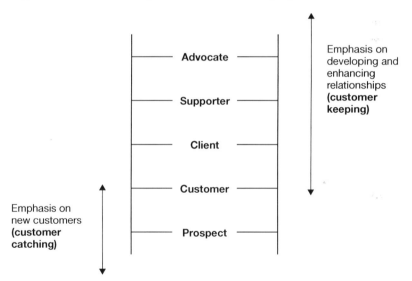

Source: Christopher et al, 1991

Building branding is a useful way to build customer loyalty and add value to customer purchases by utilising a name, sign, symbol or design signifying the products or services which differentiate them from others. Customers can attach meaning to brands and build relationships as it conveys messages regarding quality and consistency. The brand identity encapsulated in the logo is the position which CL operatives believe they hold in the mind of their consumer. Brand recognition can be achieved quickly which in turn builds into customer loyalty.

Direct and digital marketing strategies are now commonplace among CL operatives. This involves carefully targeted communications to individual customers, who are 'ad literate' to illicit an immediate response and build an enduring relationship. It offers a low, cost-efficient, speedy alternative to reach markets, often with special promotions or time-limited offers. This offers CL operatives greater flexibility for price adjustments offering a form of personal engagement. Personalised interaction can build relationships permitting dualistic interactions whereby sellers answer customers' questions. This furthers the concept of a personalised-selling approach. Such approaches are appealing to many drug users as it helps normalise transactional arrangements, making them feel less threatened. Direct marketing permits real-time marketing where special offers can match important moments/events in customers' lives: again building customer engagement and personalised relationships.

Pricing strategies heavily influence customers, customer relationships and retention. Strategies might change as products pass through different stages of its lifecycle. Different strategies are adopted depending upon the market stage, type, location:

- Market-penetration pricing – the most common starting price for a new CL, that is, setting a low initial price to penetrate new markets quickly, attract new buyers and build market share.
- Pricing bundles – allows products to be sold together.
- Discount pricing – offering straight price reductions for limited time periods is also popular. Other quantity discounts are offered for those who buy larger amounts of product, and functional discount (trade discounts) are offered to those in the distribution chain who store/ keep records.
- Psychological pricing – used for short-term selling to build customer perceptions that higher-priced products equal higher quality – though with heroin and crack cocaine, pricing is frequently determined by overall market rates (often referred to as the reference price).
- Promotional pricing, that is, pricing the product below its market value to increase short-run sales is common. For CL operatives running multiple lines geographical pricing adjustments might be made. They will keep eyes on competitor pricing, making adjustments favouring their own brand and sales.

It is possible that evolving CLs will shift the type of consumer product from convenience products (low price, widespread distribution) to different types of purchasing such as less frequent purchasing or speciality purchasing which brings benefits of higher pricing and exclusive distribution.

Customer satisfaction includes utilising varied techniques by runner/dealers seeking to maximise customer satisfaction, for example a follow-up conversation to ensure customer satisfaction with products. Over time this builds mutually profitable relationships.

Building competitive advantage involves analysing the competitors to assess their strengths, weaknesses and market share. To achieve success here they must first identify their competitors. This is not always easy and intelligence is used to benchmark competitors and test reactions. Customer value analysis is undertaken whereby CL operatives determine the benefits most valued by end-users. A key route to success is locating uncontested market spaces. This element motivates CL managers to seek out the new undeveloped markets.

Competitive advantage is currently the overarching aim of those involved in county lines driving all forms of innovation in quest for profit.

In Chapter 2 I move on to describe in more detail the emergence of county lines, including the push/pull factors evident in their emergence. I shall suggest different evolutionary models of county lines networks, each operating differently across the UK at different times which results in a colourful but kaleidoscopic presentation of county lines.

2

Emergence and Change

This chapter will consider why and then how county lines drug supply networks began to emerge in provincial towns across the UK. It also sets out several pre-conditions (variables) which, once ripened, led to the creation of county lines drug supply networks as we now know them.

Theory of change: creating the conditions for emergent county lines

It is acknowledged that the supply of Class A drugs from urban centres to provincial/rural towns has been taking place over many years and long before the current rash of headlines citing county lines. This traditional model (or Pre-County Lines model) is illustrated in Table 2.2.

Notwithstanding this traditional model, the emergence of county lines, as we currently understand them, has its origin in a series of push/pull factors. It is useful to analyse them to illustrate how cumulatively they have created the conditions leading to county lines. More specifically how these conditions present as a challenge/problem to which working county lines is deemed the effective solution. These conditions now establish themselves in London (and other metropolitan centres) acting as push factors, while the conditions operating in host locations act as pull factors. Table 2.1 illustrates visually how these factors are grouped. Each factor acts as a variable which may/may not occur in certain metropolitan locations. In London each variable is readily identifiable and subjected to analysis and research permitting a degree of verification.

These push/pull factors operate as a series of event variables occurring over time (with time also an extant variable).

Evolution of London urban street gangs (USGs)

As heralded by the most recent and informative key UK academic works on urban street gangs, *Reluctant Gangsters* (Pitts, 2008), *How Gangs Work* (Densley, 2013) and *The Street Casino* (Harding, 2014), UK street gangs have been rapidly evolving, with the number of USGs increasing and the volume of gang-active participants similarly increasing. Gang-affiliates have become younger (Harding, 2014) with USGs increasingly focussed on instrumental rather than expressive crime (Whittaker et al, 2019). In Bourdieusian (1984; 1986) terms, this signifies a change in the settlement of the social field of USGs. In fact, multiple changes have occurred, leading to significant alterations within this social field. It is important to consider these changes, illustrating how they interrelate and affect this agenda. This synopsis is offered:

There has been a noticeable deepening of the Pool of Availability (see Chapter 3). Ten years of economic and fiscal austerity have impacted heavily and profoundly upon the most marginal UK neighbourhoods, exacerbating poverty and deprivation (Sibley, 1995). In turn, this has widened social inequality, increasing the numbers of children and young people living in poverty (Pitts, 2008, 2010; Wacquant, 2008). Such young people then in turn top up the Pool of Availability and become the next potential recruits for urban street gangs.

Within this increasingly crowded Pool of Availability, youth with limited education, skills or prospects struggle to visualise a way out of their perceived predicament. Others recognise that survival will now be paramount and they begin to orientate their lives towards a survivalist mode. Hustling to survive (Fields and Walters, 1985) becomes second nature to some young people, especially those in marginalised communities. Those with social skills or criminal networks thrive the most. Within these communities, habitus (Bourdieu, 1985) acts to both restrict and constrain what is possible for those living there. Through a combination of habitus and poverty, the social trajectories of many are now moderated and their life horizons are shortened. Austerity again diminishes this further by restricting social mobility and employment opportunities (Davis, 2006).

As austerity bites harder and hustling becomes normative (Brown, 1965) and necessary, opportunities offered by the USG become evermore appealing. More young people gravitate towards the USG as a potential route to survive (Hagedorn, 2007; Moule et al, 2013). Entering the gang for many is only a small step. As more affiliate to the USG, it becomes more recognisable in these communities, more widely acknowledged then more visible. Increased USG visibility and increased presence serves to increase its normativity within certain deprived communities (Thrasher, 1927). In these deeply deprived communities and areas USGs become ubiquitous and familiar to young people (Deuchar, 2013). Young people, including their family members, now elect to affiliate; often local families benefit financially from such affiliations. These financial benefits are acknowledged by some while the increasingly attendant violence repulses others. USGs now become more prevalent in these marginalised neighbourhoods (Vigil, 2002). Awareness and knowledge of them becomes commonplace.

For young people surviving in these marginalised neighbourhoods, entering the street gang now becomes an expected (normative) trajectory rather than an abnormal or aberrant one. Propinquity to gang rules/ gang logic makes it familiar and easily comprehended as a disciplinary code, offering structuration to many young lives. Gang rules and logic in turn becomes a known vocabulary among the local youth, acting as a default grammar against which all actions are measured and tested (Anderson, 1999).

Gang rules/gang logic (Bourdieu, 1990) now begin to widen out, embracing ever-younger, ever-wider groups of wannabees, associates, affiliates and extended family members. The extension/widening of the USG now offers multi-variant roles which all must be filled. A widening Pool of Availability will help this. Increased role differentiation now occurs in the USG generating expanded opportunities and new hierarchical positions, for example Tinnies aged 12–14, or those with social media and music production skills. This leads to age-group expansion within the gang social field and numbers increase. The gang social field now becomes more adhesive, generating ever-greater traction, which becomes much more difficult to step away from (Harding, 2014). Older adult members (24 and over) and affiliates now get stuck in the USG and find desistence difficult. As always, the benefits (mostly economic) of criminal activity often find their way into the informal economy, which then further sustains this process of adherence, making it difficult to walk away.

Austerity reduces the pathways out of USGs, ensuring a deepening and greater embeddedness of those already immersed in its social field. As social mobility decreases, austerity cuts now sharpen the very edges of ordinary life. Survival mode kicks in not just for young people but for most living in deprived communities, and hustling (Fields and Walters, 1985) becomes more widely acceptable as a default position (Krisberg, 1974). Some young people now openly engage in criminal activity in order to bring something to the family table.

Over time, an extended social field (Fligstein and McAdam, 2012) now exists for the USG – this includes younger affiliates who are younger, at one end of the spectrum, and with Olders/Elders no longer maturing out (Laub and Sampson, 1993), at the other end. In consequence, the USG social field now becomes more crowded than before, meaning it is more difficult to achieve distinction (Bourdieu, 1984; Harding, 2014). Achieving status and hierarchical advancement within the USG is now more challenging and certainly much more competitive.

As greater social competition now exists within the USGs, it becomes harder to stand out and get noticed. Crucially, creation and retention of street capital becomes harder. More competition brings greater opportunities for street capital deflation. It becomes an imperative to build and maintain street capital through the one effective mechanism that is now left open to all – the employment of ultraviolence (Burgess, 1962).

Employment of ultra-violence as a strategic action generates a considerable increase in interpersonal violence, not just within the USG but also across wider neighbourhoods. Adoption of ultraviolence then creates violent landscapes of fear for all those in the social field of the USG (Harding, 2014). Ultimately it alters the normative social values of what is a credible action within the social field (for example the throwing of acid), creating a myriad of unsafe spaces through which gang-affiliated young people and non-gang-affiliated young people must navigate. Both gang-affiliated and non-gang-affiliated youth want out of this violent landscape. For many, drug dealing becomes the key route to exiting (Dunlap et al, 2010) as austerity shuts down other possible exit routes (with the perennial exceptions of music and sport).

Increased numbers of young people now within the gang social field means more people are now actively trying to utilise drug dealing as a strategic action to achieve personal advancement. However, this too creates a newly crowded marketplace, and opportunities become restricted. Neighbourhood marketplaces for localised drug dealing have now become increasingly constricted due to ongoing turf/postcode wars (Kintrea et al, 2011; Tita et al, 2005; Whittaker et al, 2019) thus increasing the potential for multiple violent localised outcomes. The key challenge for those within the USG now shifts to questions of how to advance within this highly competitive social field and still make enough money to exit the social field (Decker and Lauritsen, 2002), that is, how to identify, action and maximise any 'strategic competitive advantage'. This requires testing out the most effective competitive strategy. This in turn leads to a flurry of personal (and gang) strategies to generate a strategic competitive advantage. This in turn generates unforeseen outcomes and further normative and extreme violence. This in turn ripples through the social field, destabilising 'the settlement' while increasing turbulence and generating yet more flux.

Strategic competitive advantage within local drugs markets

In line with street gang evolution, local drug supply markets in metro-cities has recently altered with adaptations and characteristics now presenting as follows:

Most, if not all, USG affiliates operate in small-time supply of cannabis within social circles in their own community (Coomber and Moyle 2014).

Drug dealing operates as an entry point into instrumental criminal activity for USG affiliates (Harding, 2014).

As the local USG evolves (accelerated/sharpened by austerity) more young people enter the drug supply market – acting independently, in duos, small crews (Desroches, 2007), larger crews under the auspices and direction of USGs.

Increased drug dealing activity in some communities brings greater competition (McLean et al, 2020). This can bring additional violence (Moore, 1990; Reuter, 2009; Pyrooz et al, 2016). Drug dealing for some Youngers is hampered by postcode wars preventing movement across rival territory, restricting dealing and shortening profit margins. However, postcode violence repels customers, decreasing profitability, leading to mini-saturation of highly localised markets and severely limiting potential drug dealing revenues.

Mobile phones have by now created new opportunities for networking and mobile contact. Alongside other developments this shifts drug supply towards closed market structures reliant upon IT, (May and Duffy, 2007; Pitts, 2008; Briggs, 2012). This significantly impacts upon local USG distribution networks as it favours more mobile Olders and those with licences.

To achieve strategic competitive advantage USG affiliates and drug dealing crews must now maximise profits by utilising increased mobility to ensure they now take drugs to the customer (facilitated by Blackberrys and mobile phones). BMX and push-bikes become habitual delivery methods for rapid delivery of drugs to end-users. This offers a clearly defined role for Younger runner/dealers who can now finally again secure a useful functional role within localised drug supply, beyond simply supplying weed.

Aspirant dealers quickly recognise that strategic competitive advantage can be gleaned by switching from BMX bikes to mopeds/scooters to deliver drugs. This permits faster delivery, delivery of greater quantities to further locations, thus permitting Youngers to deliver without the need for a car/licence, opening up multiple opportunities. Thus drug supply now begins to move actively beyond the confines of localised gang turf or estate boundaries. Drug supply is now possible to much wider regional networks and expanded customer bases. Expanded reach and expanded customer base ensure profits quickly rise and more young people employ the strategy of drug delivery via moped, further increasing profits.

Some young people (including independents) quickly recognise multiple opportunities offered by mopeds to engage in divergent side-line activities of acquisitive crime, for example moped-enabled robbery. Others thrive on the adrenaline (Presdee, 2000) and excitement (Katz, 1988) of the police chase and become more deeply immersed in 'Bike Life'.

Utilising mobile phones and mopeds means drug supply can now move from the Formalisation to the Professionalisation model, embracing door-to-door deliveries. Strategic competitive advantage is now achieved by getting the best drugs to the customer in the fastest time – coined as 24-hour Dial-a-Dealer (Harding, 2016). Some moped crews become targeted for robbery and acid attacks to take them 'out of the Game'. It becomes acceptable to 'Kill the Competition' (Daly, 2016).

The emergent 'gig economy' offers a structural model for new drug delivery and supply markets with increased mobility, choice, availability and reach.

USGs and drug crews can now deal actively across wide swathes of London at all times. Postcode issues which inhibited market expansion are now increasingly irrelevant to Olders while some (less mobile, home-based) Youngers still cleave to vigilant control of turf (see Whittaker et al, 2019).

As perceived territorial boundaries now recede (but not completely), some open drug markets start to reappear, for example Tower Hamlets. Increased quantity/frequency of supply now means use of cars for larger/more frequent drops with grouped deliveries for safety. Guns might now be present for risk management.

London markets quickly become saturated due to the volumes now actively involved in drug supply, facilitated by new methods of mobile delivery/ordering; multiple avenues of purchase and supply. Rivalry now leads to violence (Pyrooz et al, 2016) leaving entrepreneurs to question how to increase profits in a crowded marketplace.

The solution to this challenge is simply to expand beyond saturated markets. This involves entering the hitherto very limited, often independently run, modest supply lines operating to areas outside London; sourcing those as potentially new markets; exploiting them and building them up to maximise profits – via regional drug supply networks. Now known as county lines this offers increased Strategic Competitive Advantage to USGs and drug dealing crews. The aspirations of local and gang-affiliated youth now turn towards running their own county line and generating profits.

Overtime the street gangs have evolved, as have the drug markets and supply networks, creating a new landscape for young people. Shift has happened and we are struggling to comprehend these changes (Densley, Deuchar and Harding, 2020).

Local pull factors

In addition to push factor variables (propellant) driving CL networks out of London and metro-cities, several pull factors (receptors) also act as gravitational pulls into host locations. Each variable acts as accelerant to CL evolution – but also feeds their initial establishment and formation. These local Host Variable Factors (see Table 2.1) include domestic drug markets; changing local demographics – new arrivals; housing re-settlement from London; prison re-settlement; local gang evolution; and social change arising from IT and social media.

Table 2.1: Push/pull factors for emergent county lines

Propellant push factors	Social change factors	Receptor – local pull factors
• Gang evolution and gang social field changes • Increased competition • Saturation of local drug markets	• Gang evolution • Social change – IT and social media • The gig economy • Austerity	• Domestic drug market • Changing local demographics – new arrivals • Housing moves from London • Prison resettlement

Domestic drug markets

It is common fallacy held by many that county lines drug supply involves simply pushing illegal drugs onto unsuspecting 'country-folk' in rural or seaside idylls. In reality each provincial town hosts its own domestic drug market, though often hidden from view. It is this domestic market which is tapped into and which acts as the initial pull factor for emergent county lines. Even moderate numbers of heroin or methadone users will require a substantial supply of drugs. Usage will also increase when supply increases. Such is the congregation of users in some areas (notably deprived seaside towns) that they acquire a reputation as a locale for certain user groups:

> 'We used to call [town name] the "brown town" cos of the heroin – with strong links to Lewisham. This has been running for 25 years. Many of our clients are actively involved. It was

very noticeable. This area does pills; this area does heroin; this area does coke. It's all different areas. Young people tell us they have cuckooed others in supported accommodation – they call them "nitty". They look down on them.' (Stakeholder 15)

Stakeholders in the study acknowledged very high levels of deprivation matched by very high numbers of local users with substance misuse problems, especially heroin addiction, but increasingly also crack cocaine and methadone:

'I think you've got a level of need, there's more vulnerable people. I think the cuckooing is a new thing, certainly for this area, the amount going on, that's relatively new. But you've got a level of deprivation, so people are more vulnerable.' (Stakeholder 11)

One stakeholder acknowledged that supply to the local domestic market had been taking place for many years but with some alterations:

'Ten years ago, you'd still have local networks with London networks running to it. Sometimes you'd have [stuff] coming up from the coast. So, at [Name] at one point, they had a lot of pills and stuff coming in, I think they were Russian, coming up from the coast rather than from down in London. But that's a local thing. More like really, really strong benzodiazepines – a high risk of overdosing on them.' (Stakeholder 11)

County lines as a business model simply seeks out these domestic drug markets and hones in on them, finding inventive ways to ensure the product reaches the end-user as efficiently as possible so as to maximise returns.

Operating from the key metro centres, each receptor will play out at different speeds over different time intervals, each interacting with other different variables – each unfolding in ways bespoke to their location, strongly influenced by variant push (propellant) factors from urban areas.

The outcome, as we know, is the emergence of county lines in surrounding provincial towns – each new market emerging in different ways, at different rates, and at time intervals. It is this time variant which permits a single parent gang to operate numerous CLs at the same time, as each location is at a different stage of development. The variant progress of push/pull factors in different towns then offers multiple potential opportunities for those wishing to set up county lines.

Evolutionary models of county line drug supply networks

The Home Office Ending Gang and Youth Violence (EGYV) programme and the EGYV review (Harding and Cracknell, 2016) made clear that different UK towns are at different developmental stages regarding emergent county lines. In fact it is difficult to identify two locations with exactly similar presentation of county lines given the complex interplay of variables across different time periods.

One result is that local police, local stakeholders/practitioners and local politicians cannot agree on what they are seeing. Nor indeed can national policy makers agree on what the national benchmark position should be. The waterline is not clearly established thus move above or below this is hard to determine. Stakeholders view the problems differently leaving consensus absent or out of reach.

To overcome this empirical challenge and policy confusion there is a need to clearly establish the different evolutionary stages of county lines in a series of explanatory models which evoke the visible characteristics evident at each stage. This then brings one of the first key outputs of this study, a Typology of the Evolutionary Models of County Lines.

This typology offers an opportunity for policy makers and stakeholders to more clearly identify the roles, structures, actors and dynamics operating at each level. It also offers opportunities to identify a theory of change or evolution of county lines models indicating a progression or spectrum from the #1 model to a #4 model. Presently four clear stages, or models, are identifiable arising from data analysis in this study. They are presented here as a unique contribution to the literature. These stages, illustrated in Table 2.2, include:

- Pre–County Lines – traditional drug supply model;
- County Lines #1 – commuting model;
- County Lines #2 – satellite model;
- County Lines #3 – market consolidation and expansion model;
- County Lines #4 – market and product diversification model.

It is not possible to state with certainty that this evolutionary model or spectrum applies to all county line regional networks in UK cities. However, it certainly appears to be the evolutionary model at work in London and the Home Counties. Other models may exist.

Kaleidoscopic presentation of county lines

As emergence of CL networks is determinant upon variable propellant and receptor factors it stands to reason this is not equally distributed across the UK. The presence or otherwise of variables determines that each town is at a different evolutionary stage. Essentially each has different pull factors operating at different levels of amplification and strength of pull. Additional factors such as distance from major urban centres and national road and rail transport links similarly operate as push/pull factors. Critically each has different county lines models operating at different positions of the evolutionary spectrum. Towns may skip a stage or remain stuck within one stage before advancing along the spectrum. Progression rates vary as will levels of facilitation/resistance driving by the action/inaction of policing and stakeholder interventions. Different progression means we may look in vain for immediate commonalities against such a kaleidoscopic presentation.

Despite having over 2,500 (NCA, 2019a) operational county lines, the national landscape of county lines across the UK is highly variant with regional constabularies and local partners all reporting different things. The lack of any typology of county lines models means that they struggle to perceive the same thing or accurately determine where they sit on the evolutionary spectrum.

I shall now consider each model in turn (see Table 2.2).

Pre-County Lines: traditional drug supply model

A Pre-County Lines model is characterised by local drugs for local people. Supply was usually provided by a local Mr Big, stereotypically a 'Fat Sam' character, a working-class, middle-aged, white man with a large extended family who were well known to the police and local courts. These local 'crime families' would travel monthly or bi-weekly to wholesalers in urban centres to collect drugs which Mr Big and his family would then distribute locally through criminal networks, either known heroin users or through door security networks which they managed:

> 'Yes. Yes, we've had people who, years ago, would fit that criteria, and have moved on, and don't do that now. But yes, they would fit that criteria where they'd be getting a large supply and then distribute it. I'm not certain how many people … because, when we were in south-east London, a lot of people would go up to [borough] and score up there. So, they'd be travelling to school.' (Stakeholder 11)

'Otherwise it was very much initially local users driving up to London – through the outskirts of SE London and meeting up with a London supplier bringing the stuff back and then serving up from their home address. Never made any more out of it. Basically supplied themselves and perhaps a couple of friends from where they were living. That's how they did their business.' (Police 09)

This traditional supply model into rural, provincial, market or coastal towns in England often followed the same proven method of supply and delivery. This model was reactive and sedentary with no need for customer service as clients sought out the distributor. Local distribution was uncompetitive and rested solely with one or two crime families. Occasionally users would also travel out to score in larger metropolitan centres such as London. It was noted, however, that most users simply do not have financial capital to travel out of the area to score their drugs:

'Some would. Obviously, they'd have to be mobile, and stuff like that, but yes, some of them would travel out. I don't think that happens here, because I don't think the … the nearest one would be [town], or further down the coast, and I don't think those places are larger. So, I don't think people are travelling out, to go and score, they're travelling out to bring stuff in, yes.' (Stakeholder 11)

The stasis or continuation of this model depends upon multiple local factors but it is evident that this model has been undergoing change for some time.

Impacted by changing technology, mobile phones, internet and social media alongside increased mobility this 'traditional model' was ripe for change. London USGs were all to ready to cut out 'the middle man', and having established network links to wholesale supply, take the drugs directly to the customer.

County Lines #1: commuting model (formalisation)

As drug supply moves towards this first CL model the emphasis is on selecting an area and getting a foothold in the market. This is described by Coomber as 'commuting' (Coomber and Moyle, 2017).

The stage characteristically includes a gradual move away from the status quo or traditional Pre-County Lines model to the commuting model. This cuts out the 'middle man' and eradicates any mediation. USG members now surveille a town to establish market potential and viability – often done by trusted mid-level USG members. Prior network contacts may exist between USG dealers and the host town meaning host pull factors are quickly assessed. Here initial runner/dealers are often USG members including Olders/Elders keen to demonstrate and utilise street capital by making fast initial determinations of shared habitus and market potential. Once assessed work passes quickly to runner/dealers, usually Youngers keen to earn their stripes by generation street capital. Ethnicity of these runner/dealers mirrors the parent USG, thus runner/dealers are often Black, Asian and minority ethnic (BAME). This generates risks which must be mitigated:

> 'That early model then graduated slowly to us stopping Caribbean nominals who were illegal immigrants who'd come over on students visas, incredibly naive and really stupid and would wander round in towns which at the time had almost no indigenous Afro-Caribbean population. They'd wander around the prostitutes. It was like shooting fish in a barrel. They weren't clued up at all. They weren't street wise.' (Police 09)

Runner/dealers will usually commute from the parent gang (for example London) by road or rail and may 'holiday' over in the host town for a night or weekend, before returning. Day-tripping is also common, as noted by Coomber and Moyle (2017):

> 'When I was in Intelligence here between about 2010 [and] 2013, we used to have young kids pulled off the train station by officers who would stop them and say, "What are you doing here? Have you got drugs on you?" These young kids were pulling huge amounts of drugs out of their pockets – just school kids. One had a father [who] was in a very significant role in a city financial institution, so you saw a lot of that.' (Police 06)

In this stage CL can be, and indeed are, viewed by many local dealers/users, as a formalisation of existing drug dealing activity. It presents as a modest change or even an opportunity for competition or better-quality products. Often market formalisation offers opportunities to more clearly define local market functions. Roles might stay the same, or modify only slightly, however, roles, players and supply networks come into sharper focus now. Local police might notice activity:

> 'County lines I think is for some a shift in something more formal.' (Stakeholder 01)

The overarching governing intention central to CL managers differs and evolves at each stage of the evolutionary model; expressed in Table 2.2 as strategic outcome. These strategic outcomes take time to be realised and recognised, so present as 'lagged timeframes' often only fully in place after CL managers have commenced the next evolutionary stage of the spectrum. Local resistance often determines how possible it is to progress to the next model. Such assessments are made by local CL Managers in consultation with the parent gang in London and are likely to include adjustments, adaptations, testing market boundaries and police operations.

The characteristics of each stage are not definitive indicators but generalised perceptions reflecting what is perceived by stakeholders and users, and reported by USGs and CL operatives at each stage. They are not mutually exclusive and may overlap. As this is a dynamic process in constant flux it is unlikely that they are sequentially arranged or must all be in situ prior to progress to the next stage. They are thus presented as indicative, visible, recognisable signs of each stage.

County Lines #2: Satellite Hub model (professionalisation)

Transition or progression between models will occur over weeks, months or even years.

The Stage Two Model sees evolution of the business model to one more centred on the host location. The local traditional drug supply network has been formalised and market clarity achieved. Networks, users, products and so on have all been identified, clarified, sourced and set in place. Levels of resistance have been assessed and tested by CL operatives. The next logical strategic objective is to build the lines to make them more profitable – Professionalisation. Recent work by Hesketh and Robinson (2019) and by McLean et al (2020) have similarly identified professionalisation in their studies of county lines in the north of England. This is achieved via creation of a locally situated dealing or business Satellite Hub. Early adoption of this model utilised local rental properties or Bed & Breakfast accommodation. Risk mitigation means such visible public spaces are eschewed. Valuable profit margins are now secured by

Table 2.2: Evolving spectrum of county lines drug supply

Model name and type	Pre-County Lines Traditional drug supply model	County Lines #1 Commuting model	
Dominant strategic outcome	STATUS QUO		FORMALISATION
Key characteristics of model	• Regular but variable supply to key local distributors • Role of local criminal families/businessmen/ independent dealers • Local distributor travels up to London (or vice versa) or receives package to be distributed locally via local trusted networks • Limited network/high level of police knowledge	• USG members commute to target/host town • Young black men used as runner/dealers • Travel from metropolitan centres to provincial market towns; seaside towns; prison towns • Building lines and customer base/some supply to local networks	
End user/target	• Addicted daytime heroin users/students/speed users/recreational cocaine/ cannabis users	• Addicted daytime users of heroin and crack cocaine	
Key products	Speed Cannabis Heroin Cocaine	Heroin Crack cocaine	
Evolutionary direction			

moving into non-rental properties. Thus favoured accommodation is one belonging to a vulnerable user which has been taken over to ensure drug supply is managed and controlled locally. This process, known as cuckooing, offers benefits of reaching a wider user group (that is, those wishing constant drugs supply out of normal hours). To respond to this the local Hub is available 24/7. Managing this model means an elevated level of professionalism is required:

'Yes, it's been professionalised.' (Police 09)

County Lines #2 Satellite model	County Lines #3 Market consolidation and expansion model	County Lines #4 Market and product diversification model
PROFESSIONALISATION		**DIVERSIFICATION**
• Establishment of a local dealing Hub • Cuckooing addresses used for local Hub • 24-hour dealing in host town • Use of younger children as runner/dealers • Child exploitation and control increases • Violent interface with local networks/gangs • Improved customer service	• Extensive dealing from satellite/Hub • Local users become user-dealers • Cuckooing adapted/plus other Hub locations used • Creation of multiple lines • Consolidation of lines • Tighter control of user-dealers • Original local networks taken over • Hubs now run mini-lines to more rural locations	• Market expansion into new areas in the same location and in new locations • Franchising • Consolidation of key branded lines with fewer county lines networks • Diversification into new products • Increased links into organised crime
• Anytime addicted users of heroin and crack cocaine/sex workers	• Anytime addicted users of heroin and crack cocaine/sex workers • Emergence into recreational users	• Anytime addicted users of heroin and crack cocaine • Recreational and casual users in the night-time economy/party crowd • New users of new products
Heroin Crack cocaine	Heroin Crack cocaine Cocaine MDMA	Heroin Crack cocaine Cocaine MDMA Steroids Fentanyl Xanax Spice

Greater professionalism means business is no longer casual and must be managed seriously. Increased profit signifies more to lose and risk mitigation becomes an over-riding management concern. County lines build recognition and reputation through branding, while inventive marketing techniques serve to increase sales, customer loyalty and ultimately, revenue.

Twenty-four-hour drug supply requires greater product quantity, supplied and distributed with greater frequency with dealing now 'round-the-clock'. Neither activity is attractive to USG members now seeking to stand back and manage operations allowing Youngers to bear the burden of this strenuous activity. USG members who previously 'went OT' (out of town) are now experienced in line operation and let others do the hard grind.

Increased demand means increased product quantity arriving into the area. Increased transportation and supply means increased risk of arrest. Olders now stay with the parent gang in London and no longer commute – unless to collect profits. Some Olders stay in the Hub overseeing wrapping and bagging and supervising runner/dealers. Young BAME men can no longer be used to operate so openly or frequently in this model so other operatives must be sourced. Here younger children, both male and female, are sourced as runner/dealers. Many are recruited or groomed for this activity, and child exploitation increases to maintain a steady supply of active runner/dealers. Increasingly inventive and adaptive control measures are now enacted to manage and control them.

A local Satellite Hub means the creation of a local Hub management and delivery structure. A local management structure will mean stronger communication lines and intelligence returning to the parent gang HQ, including: monitoring of police movements, user demand, rival movements and so on, generating much more useful intelligence than before, this information is then used by CL managers to adapt local tactics more rapidly. Previously intel was slow, unreliable or inaccurate, now with CL operatives on site daily, intel is improved dramatically. Improved information flows and market pulse become indicators of greater professionalisation. Police movements are regularly reported upline so management can make regular minor business adaptations.

Local tensions begin to appear among young gang-affiliated men in host towns who now understand the market is changing fast and they stand to lose out. Local tensions surface in terms of public affray and police response.

County Lines #3: market consolidation and expansion model (marketisation)

At Stage Three the business model has further evolved to one ensuring investments in time, money and staff now pay off. These investments have generated profits and now the goal is to consolidate profits, extend opportunities and retain market share. By now the market is becoming busier and USG members and CL operatives are aware of potential profits, so some CL operatives now start out on their own. Increased competition now exists in the local host market and rivalries can surface.

Dealing from the local host Satellite Hub intensifies and more properties become cuckooed as dealing Hubs. As police and social services are increasingly alert to cuckooing, other properties such as caravans and Airbnb properties are sought out as risk mitigation, largely to avoid rival dealers but also increasing vigilance from police and authorities. To further mitigate risk and meet increased demand for both 24/7 lines and multiple lines, new runner/dealers must be found. Utilising child exploitation from London is becoming less viable as a business method and local users are now more attractive as runner/dealers. Utilising locals as user-dealers opens up hidden markets niches while cutting costs and increasing profits. Profit maximisation can therefore be achieved in this model. User-dealers are, however, a fickle bunch to employ or manage so must be tightly controlled. This model brings increased violence towards the user-dealers.

The Stage #3 model now starts to have serious impacts upon local User Communities. Local drug users who previously only used drugs, or dealt socially to friends (Coomber and Moyle, 2014; Potter, 2009; Taylor and Potter, 2013) or as dealers apprentices (Moyle and Coomber, 2015) are now 'professionalised' to work in the drug supply market. This represents a significant change in the delicate balance of user community creating distrust and upset. The homeostasis of this community is then ruptured. User-dealers can be used, targeted, coerced, exploited, convinced, recruited into high-volume dealing, signifying a shift in the number of local people who are actively criminally engaged. It also signifies a shift in volumes of people now linking into street gangs. Vulnerable users who even a few years ago would be trying to source their next hit are now dragooned and employed into a new management structure whereby they are tightly and violently controlled to sell drugs for street gangs. Most, or many, are unprepared for this interface with the USG.

Local traditional networks are by now taken over or overtaken by opportunities to merge with CL operations. Some CLs begin moving into supplying recreational drugs (for example cocaine, ketamine, MDMA) for the night-time economy. Local supply to pop-up brothels (Sanghani, 2018) and sex workers in now more firmly established. New links or business arrangements are then established to ensure these new markets are understood, identified and supplied.

The strategic objective in this model now moves from professionalisation to market and product diversification offering a full product range to a wider market of end-users. CL managers now seek consolidation of their lines, to buy out rivals or engage in hostile takeovers. Consolidated lines bring benefits of tighter control over supply and transportation routes, maximising profit margins. They also offer opportunities for USG members and CL operatives to move up-rank and run lines as a franchise or subsidiary while still working for the same parent gang.

Some local Satellite Hubs are now so profitable they act as sub-regional distribution Hubs operating mini county lines out to more rural locations, extending the reach into smaller rural villages.

User-dealers

The use of user-dealers was noted by Coomber, 2006; Potter, 2009; Coomber and Moyle, 2014; Moyle and Coomber, 2015.

Several issues arise by switching delivery methods from runner/dealers to local user-dealers. Diminished trust between CL operatives and user-dealers means smaller product volumes are supplied to user-dealers. Many user-dealers are previously known to the police so are candidates for stop-and-search. If arrested losses are limited due to smaller quantities which they can claim as personal use.

Smaller quantities, however, mean user-dealers must reload constantly, so walking trips are multiplied. Increased visibility generates public attention and alarm. Policing opportunities also exist at this stage provided local surveillance teams are aware. Multiple reloading trips mean routines become habitualised increasing risk of arrest and robbery. As robbery also occurs via techniques of creating debt bondage and as forms of management control, user-dealers are at greater risk. Increased local footfall of drug users leads to greater public visibility and attention. The public can now feel the area is unsafe leading to increased police attention. Increased visibility can attract rival competition into the area, followed by increased robbery and yet further users.

Thus utilising user-dealers has many downsides. If not tightly managed this strategy becomes a crime generator in its own right. Tight control is needed to keep this model effective, however, for various reasons local crime is often generated. Use of user-dealers further creates more suspicion and paranoia among the user community. Previously mutually supportive of each other, trust now evaporates (Fukuyama, 1995) and grassing escalates (Yates, 2006). User-dealers also know all the local users and how they live which further increases vulnerability of some users. In this way the homeostasis or equilibrium of the user community is further ruptured. Utilising user-dealers generates multiple risks for all concerned suggesting a partial answer as to why violence is increasing in parts of the UK.

County Lines #4: market and product diversification model

Stage Four represents a well-developed and advanced CL model operating for some time in a local area. It has fully established branded lines working effectively and professionally and is now ready to further diversify its market coverage, reach, product offering and range. Within this new arrangement role differentiation can now occur which might mean new roles for user-dealers. Specialisation is now possible and permissible. This occurs firstly in terms of expansion within the local market and its surroundings. Multiple lines are now owned by one USG or crew and operated within, or to and from, the same location. Line consolidation starts to see all lines into a specific town held by the same USG. Rivals have been bought out, pushed out or co-opted. Previous forays into recreational drugs and the night-time economy are now actively pursued and developed bringing cooperation/rivalry from other suppliers, for example Travelling Community and Eastern Europeans.

This acts as a potential new market generating further profit margins and fresh distribution networks. This offers links into traditional family-run supply chains. Local dealers, local peer-groups or gang-affiliates again become attractive as they retain access into night-time economy networks.

Cuckooed properties might now be used by several different CL networks intermittently allowing some users to operate a 'hotel-like' semi-permanent 'guesting' service to several dealers. This generates modest income or regular drug supply and potentially elevates them above others in their user community. Other CL managers seek to mitigate risks by diversifying accommodation arrangements or using mobile homes, caravans and university accommodation as Hub locations.

Product diversification also offers opportunities for expansion including supply of new products, for example Zanax, Fentanyl, Spice and steroids (Black, 2020; Home Office, 2016b). The CL operatives running CLs at Stage #4 are now earning large volumes of money and increasingly dictating supply terms to organised criminal networks upline.

County Lines #5: the future

It is not possible to accurately determine the next stage without further research though some logical assumptions are possible. Locally we may see increased mobile serving-up from cars and fresh innovative ways of supplying markets.

More certain is the fact that CL operatives will, by Stage #4, be making considerable amounts of money. This will require them to increase and improve business links to organised criminal networks. It is possible that USG affiliates who have risen up through CLs, building and running their own branded network of lines and developing as business entrepreneurs in their own right, will have their own view of how international drug supply should work, (for example, length of supply chains, costs and risks involved, production location and so on). Future development is likely to involve upline changes via stronger links to organised crime. This might include greater ethnic diversification of those holding the purse strings at the top; greater diversification of those involved in organised criminal networks; new routes of international importation, for example from Brazil to Portugal; from the EU via Belfast into the UK; new local delivery models and business diversification into human trafficking, money laundering and fraud.

Respondent awareness of county lines

While respondents focussed on different visible elements, each characteristic that they identified is easily aligned with an aspect of county lines, for example:

Evolution

> 'It's amazing how organic these organisations are, how they've evolved and developed from … this wasn't a problem for me 20 years ago, at all. Just to see that evolution, Wow!' (Police 04)

> 'There has been a noticeable change. Some of our young people are scared. Now it [is] more severe and more coordinated'. (Stakeholder 04)

Age and ethnicity

> 'Yeah. It's a lot younger lately to save like 15 or 14. Yep, it's predominantly young black males. A lot of [them] coming from Croydon.' (Police 13)

> 'Predominantly it's young black guys that we're seeing. That's the dealers. We had a spate of young Asians then that fizzled out. Then it was young girls. Somalian for a while, cos they

look different, distinctive. Then we had a Liverpudlian white dude. There was a lot of Liverpudlian connections at one point. Then the two Brummie lads. See, [town] is a money-earner, so there's a lot of business here for them so everyone tries their luck. Even some of the local drug users have come into a bit of money through inheritance and have tried to set themselves up in business. They've got the contacts and know the users. A couple of people have tried that, haven't they?' (Police 13)

Missing children

'I know we had a period of lots of.... A few people we were working with regularly disappearing and they would have matters in being arrested, all around the outskirts of London, Suffolk, Surrey.' (Stakeholder 06)

Increasing sophistication

'Much more prominent is the use of local users to do the running for the drugs networks, and they're generally adults. Potentially I think what's happening is I think these gangs are becoming aware of the ... you know, I mean everywhere you look it's about county line offending and they can't not be aware of the press that it's receiving. I think they're starting to understand if you use children to deal your drugs and your core, it's going to aggravate your sentence, it's going to make it more likely that the police are going to look at you, and all these sorts of issues. So I think potentially we are seeing a little bit of a shift away from the use of children, certainly in what I've seen locally. I'm not saying it's not going to happen, but I have seen much more common is the use of adult users from the town at the moment.' (Police 06)

Ethnicity of CL operatives

Street gangs originate in areas of poverty and deprivation (Thrasher, 1927; Wacquant, 2008; Pitts, 2008). In the UK such areas are characterised by communities on low incomes living in poor-quality and overcrowded social housing estates (Pitts, 2008). Over the last half-century in the UK these poor communities have become increasingly diverse and now include different BAME communities (www.gov.uk/government/

collections/households-below-average-income-hbai--2; Kenway and Palmer, 2007; Hernandez et al, 2018). In London poorer communities are widely recognised as being Black African, Black Caribbean or Asian in ethnicity (Pitts, 2008).

Street gangs originate from, then represent, the communities from which they hail. Consequently where communities are composed of ethnic minority communities, the street gangs will reflect this and are also composed of minority ethnic youth. Thus, presently in London and the south-east, many gang-affiliated young people will be people of colour. Elsewhere in the UK diversity may not be so pronounced, for example in Birmingham and parts of Manchester, deprived areas are more ethnically mixed (white, black or Asian). In Scotland and parts of the north of England the deprived areas remain largely ethnically white.

For London USGs running CL operations to the Home Counties one immediate problem for CL managers is how to send BAME runner/dealers into provincial towns which are mostly homogenously ethnically white.

One BAME USG member commented:

> 'I stuck out like a sore thumb but walking around the town centre I felt comfortable. I had all these girls looking at you. White girls trying to talk to you. It's different. They like you, so it's a bit weird.' (USG 06)

When asked if her ethnicity ever attracted police attention, one BAME female CL operative responded:

> 'Well, it did because they were surveilling to catch the boy when he got arrested. When we were in [County name] they were all white. Here [County name], different, completely different, black, white, loads of Scottish. Loads of Scottish in this county. There was a big Scottish man who made a crack pipe out of Johnson's Baby Lotion! Me, I'm obviously ethnic, the Turkish boy I was with, the black boy I was with, we stood out. We talk different as well. We dress different.' (USG 01)

Responses from local police to the emergence of BAME youth in their local area differ across areas, however, one black CL manager interpreted police surveillance as racist:

> 'The police have come a couple of time. I don't want to seem racist but they are racist bitches. We're two black youths in a

heavily white area, predominantly white area and we're in a very nice car and we're driving around so people just didn't like that, I don't know why, they just didn't like that and they'll call the police. The police would come and bother us but by the time they come to us we've already hidden the drugs so the police never find anything ever.' (USG 03)

In this study area considerable data supported the evidence that the ethnic composition of the area had changed over the past 20 years. Notable was the emergence of Slovaks, Romanians, Roma, and Albanians in particular. These new arrivals were thought to be 'network poor' and at times vulnerable to criminal exploitation. Local police found their sudden arrival a challenge and felt under-prepared for policing these new communities:

'We had no one who spoke the languages of the newcomers. No way of cracking those communities. No informants, cos they don't trust the police, or their police are corrupt or involved in criminal gangs. They hated the police and were terrified of all the agencies and social services who could take their kids off them. So all of a sudden we had all this criminality – nobody would talk to us. We couldn't talk to them. We are so ill-equipped. It's so resource intensive. Imagine the resources required on a Slovak/Romanian drug supply with a lack of knowledge of their culture, their language. Trying to do surveillance on people who don't speak our language. Nobody locally who can penetrate their gangs, cos they are insular communities who don't talk to us.' (Police 09)

Police and stakeholders noticed that some of the Eastern European youth were now affiliating with local domestic gangs or were being used by CL operatives as runner/dealers. This was thought to be partly a reflection of ethnic groups within the local communities but also acknowledging that some members of these new communities were also drug users. It was acknowledged that for Eastern Europeans heroin is smoked rather than injected. This then can create a whole new market opening.

In this study it appeared that potential for gang-affiliation arose mostly due to shared habitus and lived experience growing up in poverty and deprivation:

'I think with some of the Eastern Europeans, they have moved here for a better life and I think they maybe see their parents (if they're working) working in agency work, earning not a great deal and then there's the offer of a better life really, although it is not through legitimate means. They can get the money, it is on their doorstep. Quite often, they have not got a great deal of supervision, so they're easily kind of hanging around, they're integrated in the groups anyway. They're seen as adult earlier, definitely. There are pockets of deprivation sometimes you go to and it is horrible. Like the different conditions.... So, I think the boys that come out of those areas will be the ones that get engaged.' (Stakeholder 05)

Stakeholders acknowledged that while London street gangs could at times be more exclusively ethnically grouped (as a reflection of dense ethnic groupings in some communities), in the more ethnically diverse study area 'that definitely is not played out here' (Stakeholder 05).

The issue of Eastern Europeans affiliating to the local gangs or becoming runner/dealers was widely recognised:

'We have noticed that quite a lot of the Eastern European community are attracted to gangs, they have jumped on that.... So, whilst it has been predominantly black young boys that have brought it down and occupied the upper echelons of whatever structure we have, Eastern Europeans have ... jumped on that, gravitated towards it and become part of it? We have had lots of robberies and gang-type of behaviours and gang language; from the Eastern Europeans. Well, I think like you say, the deprivation and poverty and identity.' (Stakeholder 06)

'Well, [our local street gang] is a real ethnic mix, isn't it? You have got black British. See, the boys who came down from London came with the gang thing. So, you had London black kids, black kids from other parts of the country, white kids, Roma ones and Eastern European ones, all in one kind.... So, the [gang name] little phenomena is a truly multi-cultural group.... It is inclusive. It is probably one of the most inclusive forums in [district] for young people. All you have got to do is stick a knife in someone.' (Stakeholder 05)

Rehoming from London: moving families into the host district

A further issue which is simultaneously both push/pull is rehoming families from London in the study area. Widely acknowledged as a 'hot potato' by all police and stakeholders many viewed it as a major contributory factor to the development of both county lines and also domestic or local street gang emergence.

In addition to looked-after children and Sent Away Children (see Chapter 5) many provincial towns are required to host families being relocated from London. This includes where London local authorities have purchased cheaper provincial housing to relocate and house their overspill or families in crisis such as those on Osman (threat to life) warnings, gang exit programmes or fleeing domestic violence.

Included within relocated families are vulnerable young people who may have previous exposure to gang culture or gang-affiliation:

> 'A lot of the time, we can understand why their families have moved down here. Early on, the courts in London used to bail people outside of the M25. That practice has stopped, we haven't had that for years now. I think that is really good, but yes, it is a drift out of London. These kids have often come from areas where gangs and violence has been more established. They come with that kind of in them, and then it gets acted out here. Often they're traumatised, I think, like the guy I wrote the report on, he was shot within a week or two of arriving, his mum had OD'd, had referrals to major children services as soon as he arrived. It is kind of like, well, he is here, and he is not involved in a gang down here, so what are we meant to do with him? I think that these very damaged young people; we ought to be planning and anticipating how we deal with them because they are going to move around the country.' (Stakeholder 05)

Several police and stakeholder respondents commented that this had led to a change in local youth present, leading to increased gang-affiliation, increased violence and anti-social behaviour and increased sophistication of gang presentation. Many also noted that youth relocated from London either set up county lines themselves or acted as networks links back to CL operatives in London:

'But north and south London boroughs have moved gang members out to us. Sometimes the YOT are informed before they arrive and they are aware and we'll discuss them in the High Risk panel meetings and sometimes find out about them after they are already here. And it isn't just gang members. It's young looked-after children that are vulnerable to CSE. Then they effectively just slip between the cracks. No one is supervising them in London any more cos as far as they are concerned, they've moved them out to us. We assume they are coming out every day then going back to London to do whatever it is they are doing. Then they come back to us and sleep on us. And nobody is really supervising this. So nobody has put any conditions on them. So it doesn't achieve anything, except for London it's out of sight, out of mind.' (Police 07)

In addition certain ex offenders must be resettled in the area:

'Cos the prison is here ... if he comes out of prison homeless then we are responsible for having him cos he's a juvenile. So they are not allowed to say "we are not housing you". So they need to find him somewhere even if it's emergency accommodation.' (Police 07)

For some stakeholder and police respondents this all added to this perception of the area as a net importer of crime, gang and drug issues which might be termed the Sponge Effect. Essentially local authorities and agencies feel the area continually sucks in criminal elements and never fully dries out, leaving them constantly on the back foot in 'firefighting mode'.

Others, however, cited local deprivation as the key driver and were keen not to view incomers pejoratively:

'And there are issues in young people here that contribute to that behaviour. But it is not a matter of those young people infecting us.' (Stakeholder 06)

Some respondents wished to comment that relocations have led to social and community change:

'We have lots of young people being relocated here from London. Since [the] 1980s it is now a different area. Back then it was no[t] multi-cultural and ethnics all stood out. It was a real local community with a thriving High Street. Now people are relocated into this area. This is the stem of the issue. Previously some of them were also in prison. Culturally the area has changed and there are more people on benefits and more poverty. Areas are now deprived and visibly so. [Town] High Street is now deprived – no market – it's dead and skanky. Relocations take place as they are maybe on Orders and not allowed back to London.' (Stakeholder 15)

Respondents noted with some annoyance that London agencies and local authorities are very poor in informing the host authorities that young people or families are moving down:

'I think we're often the first to know and sometimes you get shoddy practices from some authorities and it may just be down to an individual practitioner, like got a case, thank God they're out of Hackney. So, I think there is a sense that people are like farming out their problems.' (Stakeholder 05)

'And then sometimes when potentially other services are notified, it is up to them whether they take any notice of that notification.' (Stakeholder 06)

One stakeholder with considerable experience in this topic lamented the failure of agencies to act appropriately or responsibly towards the families or young person being relocated, or towards the host authority:

'There were instances of London agencies actually bringing people down and leaving them on the doorstep of the council and saying "declare yourself as homeless". What you're finding with children's homes is staff getting placement of young people where information has been omitted from the risk assessment, sanitised, so they get the young person on behalf of the out-of-area placement and then suddenly find out that young person is grooming their kids. Then go back to the placing authority who said "oh, yes, they are, sorry, we didn't put that in the…" So what you do create is systems that because of the pressures on agencies create the raising of risk thresholds, create sanitisation of, on occasion, sanitisation of reports which proliferate the gang seed by those placements and impacting on more.

'When you talk to children's home managers, what is at stake is if you admit to a child being gang affected, then that means an increase in the fees you have to pay to reduce the risk around that kid of grooming others. So if it's omitted and then you place, you're not paying as much for that service. The funding is not there to mitigate those risks. When agencies have had their resources cut back substantially and when your resources are cut back substantially, the only way that frontline staff can manage the risk is to up risk thresholds, write stuff in a certain way that maybe offloads the risk somewhere else.' (Stakeholder 07)

Local stakeholders acknowledge the difficulties of rehoming issues and the potential for increased violence in the host authority:

'I think we have got to be ready to recognise that these people are coming and ready to respond, that some of the people that now we get transferred here come with more propensity for violence than we see because of the gang-associated issued and require more support. I think it is a learning curve [we are] still going through.' (Stakeholder 05)

Local police are also aware of rehoming issues with the potential for increased violence which may arise from this practice:

'More and more what you get down here is rehomed gang members or gangs from down here. They're gonna get so big it's only a matter of time before they are stepping on each other's toes. That's when the problem will start especially if it's around drugs business cos everyone wants to be profitable and earn money.' (Police 10)

Local police refer to an intelligence gap in terms of being notified about young people being rehomed from London into the host town. As one police officer noted:

'The intelligence gap between the rehoming in the area is massive, for example we stopped a lad for a search – some of the people are really stupid – because he was serving up. And he gave his address when they searched him. So when the police went through the door there was loads of crack/heroin on the table. So he got arrested straight away. He was on bail for murder for a gang feud where he'd stabbed someone. We had no idea he was living here. He's been rehomed down here, right in the busy patch. He obviously thought it's busy here. Someone said here's a load of drugs, go and sell it.

'And we don't know about these people that are being rehomed down here. We've got a massive [Housing Association name] place down here and they rehome quite a lot of gang members. Considering there is gang activity already down here. They meet up with their friends. We had another chap from Rochester [town] who was rehomed down here and we went round there and I found two mispers from London in there. So recent intel suggests he's been dealing drugs down here. He's been rehomed. That's one that we know about, but he's been rehomed down here…' (Police 10)

Continuation of gang-affiliation and involvement in drugs supply is also noted by one officer in relation to young people moved out of London:

'It's ridiculous we've got two brothers who are ridiculously involved in county lines. So to move 'em to get away from county lines they moved them to [town]! The exact same problem there though! They get nicked every week for carrying drugs and knives. They are always involved in county lines drugs supply. Their parents don't want them living at home any more. They are 16–17. So they've rehoused 'em. They've been in sheltered accommodation in [town]. It makes no sense. It'll not be too long before they go missing or something or are arrested in [district]. They are clearly attracted to the lifestyle. Dad said they moved from London to get away from gangs cos their kids were getting involved. They wanted to give their kids a better life. But the boys are clearly attracted to this and continued, so the whole family moved down. They are a black family. The older brother aged 18 worked full time. So do the parents. They've had enough. The kids won't change what they were getting up to so the parents kicked them out.' (Police 16)

In Chapter 3 I consider who seeks to join a county lines dealing crew, where they come from and what it means to 'go country' before considering different types of dealing and how CL operatives travel to their dealing locations.

3

Getting Started:
'Put Me On, Bruv'

The Pool of Availability

Loïc Wacquant in his foreword to *Urban Outcasts* (2008: 1) talks of neoliberalist policies producing 'stigmatised neighbourhoods situated at the very bottom of the hierarchical system of places that constitute the metropolis'. Characterised by 'urban marginality', he refers to 'lawless zones', 'problem estates', 'urban hellholes' and 'no-go areas' found in inner-city and peripheral urban environments. Charting the post-industrialisation degradation and disintegration of working-class territories in Western European cities he notes a process of 'advanced marginality' arising from stigmatised territories, the withdrawal of the social state and fragmentation of wage labour (2008: 236–8). In such places community bonds disintegrate and collective efficacy withers away to be replaced by 'social fragmentation and symbolic splintering' (2008: 244) and symbolic derangement (2008: 245). Wacquant focuses heavily on the role of the state in the sustained production of advanced marginality citing the overarching structure of neoliberalism. These 'tainted' urban spaces or 'neighbourhoods of relegation' (2008: 239) become subject to over-policing, experimental policing and 'special measures' which further marginalise 'defamed' communities.

The changes articulated by Wacquant in *Urban Outcasts* are also trailed by Norbert Elias in *The Civilising Process* (1994); Jock Young in *The Exclusive Society* (1999); Slavoj Žižek (2009) in *First as Tragedy Then as Farce*; Mike Davis in *Planet of Slums* (2006); and John Hagedorn in *A World of Gangs* (2008). Disengagement by executive authorities and marginalisation of residualised, vulnerable communities are commonly cited as contributory factors for the gestation of street gangs who evolve to fill the vacuums. John Pitts in his book *Reluctant Gangsters* (2008) locates these arguments in a UK context citing neighbourhood transformation in the 1980s/1990s as being formative in creating the circumstances in which youth street gangs might thrive. Pitts argues that deindustrialisation, income polarisation, structural youth unemployment, a rolling back of the state and economic marginalisation have become increasingly concentrated in areas of disadvantage. Scottish scholarship, notably Deuchar (2009), and also Fraser (2015) in his study of youthful peer groups, similarly identify issues of deindustrialisation, social deprivation, disenfranchisement by educational failure, unemployment and poverty as key reasons for street gang affiliation. These areas in the UK (at least in central and southern England) are increasingly inhabited by BAME communities. Racism, inequality and over-policing further consolidate suspicion and frustration supporting narratives of embedded social injustices. Among such narratives, argues Short (1997), shared common social values can be usurped by 'alternative cognitive landscapes' in which young people validate the urban street gang as the embodiment of rage and logical validation of survival.

It is the discarded youth of such communities that constitute the Pool of Availability.

The Pool of Availability comprises young people who have grown up in such communities, and through a combination of habitus, social field and social environment are now readily available and even conditioned to step into the street gang. Where street gangs become the logical answer to the prevailing conditions, the youth who affiliate to gangs do so as 'rational agents' joining 'rational organisations' (Densley, 2013: 3).

For young people raised in areas of multiple marginality their early socialisation, habitus and deterministic sense of social fate constitutes early graduation from the School of Hard Knocks and the University of Life. Earlier academics similarly identified such schema in gang-affiliated, or gang-attracted, youth. Miller (1958) noted the ever-present notion of fate 'as a focal concern of lower class culture'. For many, a realisation they can do little to effect change ensures limited future planning. Others focus purely on economic or psychological subsistence and survival. This author has re-articulated this as a Survivalist Credo for Life:

The Survivalist Credo
The World is Unfair! Hard work won't get you out of this Dump! Hustle, move fast – to avoid getting stuck here. Authority set the rules – but then they break them. Authority interferes – so don't trust them – don't invite them in – don't tell them anything (grass). Defend your

patch and get your punch in first. Take the man down if he comes for you. Set your own rules to get power. Avoid powerlessness – it means victimhood. Above all – when you find a friend who's good and true:
Fuck him, before he fucks you!

Such a credo is utilised, rehearsed and embodied to legitimise entry into 'the Game' and simultaneously to neutralise objections or criticisms (Sykes and Matza, 1957).

Propinquity = one small step

While the Pool of Availability creates different entry points into the Game, it largely comprises youth from multiply deprived neighbourhoods whose poverty and marginality presents them as ideal candidates for street gangs (Hope, 1994; Pitts, 2008; Wacquant, 1992; 2008). In such communities 'hustling' becomes a normalised and culturally accepted practice (Polsky, 1967) or cultural adaptation to the 'endless pressure' of poverty. Krisberg (1974: 122) talks of 'ghetto-hustlers' who have 'developed social-psychological mechanisms which seemed to them appropriate to the task of personal survival'.

Concepts of strain theory (Merton, 1938), differential association (Sutherland, 1947) and family entanglement with criminality, makes street gangs an ever-possible, ever-present part of life. When family and friends demonstrate daily involvement in criminal activity, entry into a street gang becomes 'one small step' and often one which appears logical and realistic. For a fuller exposition of UK street gangs please consider Densley, 2013; 2014; Densley et al, 2018a; Fraser, 2015; Harding, 2014; Pitts, 2008, and more recently McLean, 2019; Whittaker et al, 2019).

Deepening and widening the Pool of Availability

While the Pool of Availability largely relates to poor kids in poor areas with previous exposure to gangs, this has of late begun to change due to two key factors. Austerity has deepened the Pool of Availability, while making the street gang more adhesive. Simultaneously social media has widened the orbit of the street gang. The end result of both influences being a deeper and wider Pool. This essentially means more potential candidates for street gangs and increased competition for those already in the Game.

Austerity confines and constricts social conditions thereby influencing overall numbers in the Pool of Availability. By sharpening the edges of poverty and deepening deprivation it curtails opportunities, often raising them beyond reach. In this way trajectories of personal advancement are now re-calibrated leaving dreams eroded or shelved. The rising water of vulnerability covers the lowest levels first and survival mode kicks in. Where 'racialised poverty' (Wacquant, 2008: 201) exists, communities of colour have heightened vulnerability. Increased vulnerability brings prospects of victimhood and further status deflation. Deflation must be countered by generating respect and boosting reputation. This in turn moves from being a desire to an imperative. Declining opportunities, limited skills and poor-quality, inner-city education all conspire to nullify career employment as a potential pathway out of these estates for many young people. For some, the street gang offers the best, the most obvious, or most immediately available, route to build respect and reputation – and thus to reduce impending vulnerability.

Social media and its relationship to street gang and gang dynamics is an emerging area of scholarship (Harding, 2015; Irwin-Rogers and Pinkney, 2017; Storrod and Densley, 2017).

The presence of street gangs on social media permits USGs to represent their brand, either individually or grouped via rap, grime and drill music videos. These visual representations now reach more widely into non-gang-affiliated audiences attracting interest from youth seeking greater interaction or proximity to USGs. Such platforms are highly influential to ordinary youth with no previous gang connections but who now find the visual/musical representations attractive or seductive. Longer-term engagement can bring closer USG affiliation, susceptibility or suggestibility (Harding, 2016). Termed 'Gang Fans', many are unaware they play roles of spectator, audience, bystander, or enthusiast in unfolding online dramas.

In such ways the Game comes into view for those previously distant or far removed from it. As the street gang orbit and social field expands its rules becomes recognisable, quotable, attributable, understood. Gang cultural mores become conversation topics in ways not possible when gang-affiliation meant living on gang turf. What was once distant is now attractive and adjacent. Given propinquity to the Game, entry requires only one small step...

The Game

For those within its orbit, the Game is now everywhere with new affiliates from new areas. Ability to recognise its presence, even when hidden from others, suggests an awareness and preparedness to participate. Survivors and hustlers are already pre-schooled in its rules and tropes which by now are recognisable; easy to do; familiar; obvious. Illegal activities are reframed as 'just bending the rules'. Candidates for entry into the Game talk of betting on a 'fast life' with fast returns, tax-free profits. Others have already identified that 'drugs work can provide all the skill I need to get by and I can learn fast' (USG 07). For some youth, joining a gang is a logical small step…

Another dealer/manager described his entry into the Game thus:

> 'We all wanted to make money, so I started selling weed. I had a close friend, we grew up together and got babysat by his older brother and aunties at the family house. I started selling weed, he was selling coke. I don't know if coke was making much, but I could see he had money and was doing good for himself so I jumped on selling sniff as well.' (USG 06. This respondent went on to operate two major county lines.)

For this young woman entry into the Game was via her (now) ex-partner:

> 'So, my ex-partner who got me involved in all of this stuff, his whole life has been criminality. His mum is in and out of prison, his dad too. That kind of thing. I believe everybody who is in that Game, if you're high-ranking, you're serious and you're about that kind of life, it's because you've **been** that kind of life. So, your mum does it, your dad does it, they do it, they don't care. You're giving them a bit of money. Everyone's making – except the little ones.' (USG 01. This respondent went on to be an operative in a major county line.)

Case study: one small step – USG 02

'Basically, where can I start … I was young, my mum she was on drugs, crack to be specific. My dad wasn't there, he was never around me. He's Jamaican, so was always in Jamaica. I was mainly on my own growing up. Me and Mum never had a good relationship so I had to look for guidance really. So, where do you look for guidance? There were people around my area showing me stuff, showing me how to survive, showing me how to do certain things and do things properly and before I even knew it, the crazy thing about it is I found that the same people that were teaching these are part of the gang members but these are older, they are teaching me a few things.

'There's a thing, I never got into it, it was that thing where "I'm just going to jump in with you and we're going to start doing this". At the time it was people from that area would see me, this is how crazy it is, people would see the way I'm living, the way my lifestyle is because they could see that in my area I was living the hardest one out of all of them, out of everyone, my mum was on crack, it was a thing where no one would dare, I was always [at] crack houses, I was always in different places. I was always sleeping around. Mum left me with so many different people at a young age. That's the thing, I was lost basically. I didn't know what my purpose was, I didn't know what I was doing, I didn't know what was happening so when I got into this, I wouldn't call it a gang I would more like call it a family, back then you're calling me a family, you say that's "your people" so they are there to show you love, they show the way, they show you what to do. They showed me how to survive really. They weren't showing me things that will matter, do you understand?

'I was young, 14, very young, maybe even younger. I had to grow up very fast from a young age. When I was in this gang I was making money which means I was eating, means I wasn't going to school with holes in my trainers any more, ripped clothes. The only time I got to eat was when I went to school. There was no more of that. Things were changing and I was eating more, I could buy stuff I liked, food, clothes, and I could help my mum out. If Mum needed money I could say "take that". Sometimes I would say to her, "Take this £20, I found it", I used to have to drop these notes and say "I found it outside, take this." So, it changed a lot because when I gave that money to my mum it meant a lot because it altered her, I could see the smile on her face. She could eat now. Everyone can eat now. I never thought being in a gang was negative. It wasn't the right thing to do. It wasn't a bad thing. I never thought that. I thought I was making money and my family was eating. For me it was more about weed. Selling weed. I wasn't a kingpin with the weed but I had enough and it got me my meals, at morning and night time.

'I saw this activity taking place around me all the time. Every day, in my neighbourhood. Right in front of my face someone would be getting robbed, somebody having a fight, someone would get stabbed, like it was nothing. Someone running off, everyone scattering and then a body just dying right in front of me. And the worst thing about it is you walk past it because it's an everyday situation. That's what people do. It's an everyday situation. So, these things are just happening constantly because this is how life is. I saw this where I lived, mostly in my area. I got kicked out of school – I'm 18 now – got kicked out when I was maybe 14/15. In my first year, I'd just finished primary school, went to Year 7, wasn't there a month max and I was gone because I was bringing negative energy from the streets into school.

'At the time it wasn't gangs … more of like a group of people making money. If you want to … call it a gang … but at that time you're not calling it a gang, it's a group of brothers making money, let's make money together. So, that's your goal. For me back in the day gangs were built, you have to build a gang, the gang had a leader, for me this was more like a group of brothers that are about to make money and they want to help me make it because they can see I'm struggling as a kid. And me personally I don't really like to be hand fed, you know, I had to do it myself.'

This respondent went on to be an independent dealer and individualist.

Case study: entering the Game – USG 01

'I went to an All Girls' Catholic School run by nuns, lovely … supposed to be lovely. I'm obviously mixed heritage. Being brought up, I didn't see colour, I didn't see anyone as different, never have, never will, but by secondary school I was noticing a big divide. There really was and we're only talking about 2003 or something so it's not like Apartheid times but it was really, really, it was there. So, I had friends but it was really segregated. So, you had the black girls, the Caribbean girls, the Hispanic girls, the white girls and the Chinese girls who liked cartoons and things like that. So, the first two years in Year 7 and 8 were fine, I had friends, it wasn't that bad, people would make their little racial comments and stuff but it wasn't that bad. When it came to Year 9 I was told you need to pick sides, this was by the African group of girls: "What side are you on? If you are black you need to cut your hair and you need to get contacts because black people don't have green eyes. And if you're white you don't talk to us". So, I'm the kind of person "you're not telling me what to do, so bye bye". I thought it was a joke at first but it wasn't and the bullying that followed was just absolutely astronomical. It was physical, mental. I was so vulnerable because I was so alone because you had the white girls in the other groups who still wanted to be my friend and they didn't see the issue with colour, but were told by the African girls that if you accept me and were friends with me then we're going to make your life hell as well.

'So, nobody wanted to talk to me because they were scared. So, I was by myself. I was isolated. I'd go into school, register, hop over the wall or wouldn't go in at all. I'm talking ages ago but back then there was no communication between my parents and the school. So, I'd say goodbye from my mum and dad because I'm from this nuclear family like Mum, Dad, brothers, sisters, cat, all of that. "See you later, bye bye". Professionals my family, both my parents, they thought I was going to school but I wasn't. I started smoking a lot of weed. Tried little bits of cocaine, stuff like that. Extremely vulnerable, extremely depressed, self-harming, suicidal. The school was aware of what was going on but they did nothing. I was 14. They did nothing. So, obviously I needed places to go during the day, so I started hanging out with different people and it went from there.

'I was smoking a lot of weed. Then one day the dealer from my area wasn't about so he gave me the number of his cousin, a boy in [Area]."Go and meet him, he'll give you a draw or whatever". So, I went to meet him. He was 21 and I was 14 and from that very first moment he was obsessed with me. I thought it was love, him buying me things, taking me out, he used to say, "No, you're going to school, I'll collect you so everyone can see you're with me", that type of thing. He was my knight in shining armour. He started a sexual relationship. I was very young. He meant everything to me. I thought he was so special. And it was a great relationship; I thought at the time, I thought it was lovely to begin with.

'I was so young, so naive; I thought he sold a bit of weed, that was it. His phone would ring and now I know what he was doing. I had no idea what he was doing or what he was involved with. I knew he had been to prison before but didn't quite know what about. It didn't bother me to ask, I didn't care. But then things started going a little bit sour. He wasn't seeing me as much. Two hundred messages a day, then it was like one message every other day. Obviously I was still having trouble at school and I wanted him back so he was like, "It's business problems" and I would say, "What can I do to help you? What can I do?" He said, "I don't want you to be involved" and then he started asking me to do little things for him. So, "Would you drop this round the corner?", it was weed, "Yeah, no problem". £20 worth weed, yeah, I'll do that. Then one day he asked me to take this bag. It was a Fitness First bag I remember that, the funny details you remember, it was a Fitness First bag, big black sack, take it on the train, get on the train at Stratford and take it to somewhere called [Town] and at this point I didn't have a clue where [Town] was.

'I know it very well now, he could have been sending me to Scotland or Australia. No idea. But I went. He said, "You'll be back tomorrow. You're going to stay in a hotel. You're going to meet a friend up there". I knew the friend I was going to meet, I knew this boy through him already. "You're going to stay in a hotel, come back tomorrow, everything will be sorted", something like that. Obviously I was excited because I hadn't been seeing him a lot. So, he dropped me off, it was a Thursday. I changed out of my uniform. He dropped me off at [name]. He took my phone. He said, "Your parents are going to be freaking out because you're not going to be going home overnight so just be in touch with me and my friend", so I got on the train. It was like half an hour into the journey that I thought, "What's in this bag?" That shows how young I was because I honestly didn't think "what's in this bag?" I thought it's probably loads of weed. I didn't know.

'I looked in the bag and there was a firearm, like a gun, ammunition and bricks of something. I didn't know what they were at the time. I didn't have a clue. I knew they were bad. Didn't know. Wouldn't be able to differentiate. It was obviously crack cocaine/heroin but obviously I'm seeing this gun, I didn't know people could have guns. I've seen guns in films. I was 14. I had no idea. I was just horrified. I had no phone. I didn't know where I was going. I knew someone was meeting me at the other end. I thought, "Right, you're obviously dealing with somebody who is involved in something you had no idea about, you are going to go back to him, tell him you haven't done what he has asked you to do, hand him back a gun [and say,] 'Here you go, here's a gun, sorry I've upset you, have a gun or are you just going to get it over and done with type thing?'" So I said, "Just get it over and done with. You're going to be in a hotel". I went in the hotel. I got up there, I met this boy, he was really nice to me up until this point. I was taken to a crackhouse, trap house, bando –

'I was a missing child for two weeks that first time. The police were looking for me. It was really bad. My friend told my mum the boy's road name, and obviously my mum told the police that I might be with this boy. They put his name into the Gangs Matrix – No. 3 or something like that, horrified, literally. So, he'd been in prison for possession of firearms, intent to supply before and only got out four months before I met him in the summer. So, I started seeing him in October. We were up there. We were in/out of different squats, different crackhouses, offering 24-hour service/delivery. So, I know now it's changed but back then we were bringing it to wherever they were at whatever time. Now, there's normally meeting points and they're only going, they'll deal to certain areas like Costcutter or like I've heard they use the benefits office or the bench, there are specific points they will go to but we were going wherever anybody was, come rain, come shine. All throughout the night. At first I didn't have any vehicle, I was 14. We got a pushbike a couple of days into it which made things a bit better. So, crack cocaine and heroin.

'We had to obviously store them internally, so vaginally, anally, that was the worst thing ever for me because drug users know that's where you've got the drugs, so if they want to rob you they're pulling down your trousers and putting their hands in places they shouldn't. That happened in the first week. If you're held with a dirty needle you can have whatever you like but the first time I was robbed obviously I thought he's still my boyfriend, he does still love me and I hadn't seen him since I went up the very first time but I was in contact with him because I given a little track phone. I thought he'll understand.

'Him and his friend came up and beat me senseless. I had a broken rib because I got robbed and I lost them their money. It wasn't my fault. Occupational hazard, it happens. But they weren't hearing any of that, so from that point onwards that's when I knew there is no love in this, there is no care in this, this is what it is type thing. And what I was involved with and the fact that he let his friend palm me as well … so obviously where we were staying at first, because it was an established line, drugs line, but it was in its early days so this was before we got into people's houses and stuff and we started cuckooing, which is what it is now called, so going into people['s] houses. The first one was two drug users, there was, like chalets, like little caravan type things so we would pay them in drugs to cook the drugs, bag up, weigh up, all that kind of stuff.'

This respondent went on to be an active county lines dealer.

Going country…

From weed to powder

At some point young runner/dealers who were actively selling weed on their estate for months, or even years, decide they want to move on to a county line. Some are approached by Olders or peers:

> 'Moving up to cocaine, honestly, if you know the right people, the right connections stuff like that you can get, you just have to know the right connections. You don't say I'm ready to sh[o]ot this stuff now, It will happen more casually. If they drop on you they drop on you, if they don't they don't. Me personally I never dealt with that.' (USG 06)

Once the decision is taken, or offer made, success pivots upon dedication to the market:

> 'You can go any way, you can go brown, you can go white, you can go coke, you can go weed, as long as you're dedicated to what you do and make your own money, you'll get your money.' (USG 07)

Again trust is central to this next stage:

> 'Yeah, they have to trust you, but you're part of the team so once you're part of the team they trust you but I do understand the person has to trust you himself. When you're part of the team you're part of the team. Regardless.' (USG 02)

An early decision is what to call your line:

> 'I can't remember, was it [Street Name], there was another name as well and I remember the Cats used to call me [Street Name], it was funny. Using moving names. You could use Mitch – or other weird names. It just depends what you want them to call you – Reggie even – whatever, it's just something. You just make it up, you can be a different person. It's crazy.' (USG 06)

Deciding to join/manage/own a county line

County lines networks offer several potential business models presenting opportunities to work with others or for oneself (see Figure 3.1) including:

- Lower level – joining an existing line;
- Management Entry level –
  a) establishing a whole new line;
  b) establishing a new spin-off line;
  c) buying an existing line;
- Become an independent trapper.

Entry points are determinant by which business model is operational (see Chapter 2) and the staffing role desired/required. Roles are linked to different models or working methods, including managing a line/crew; working as a runner/dealer; becoming an independent trapper. Each role represents different hierarchical status (as acknowledged by others) which determines how you are verbally addressed, directed, managed, tasked, treated or abused. It also determines opportunities or restrictions including widening/contraction of opportunities; introductions to/ removal from networks and supply chains; provision of/exclusion from intelligence and information.

Point of entry into CL is heavily linked to experiential exposure to drug dealing, USGs, criminal activity, one's habitus, age, family connections, networks (Sutherland, 1947) local influence, wider personal networks, timing, opportunity and skill. Gender and agency are additional individualistic determinant factors each determining points of entry (Deuchar et al, 2018). While habitus (Bourdieu, 1985; 1990), and street socialisation has already created a ready-made Pool of Availability, it also shapes readiness and skill level to enter this particular part of the Game. Thus point of entry reflects both habitus and skill level in the Street Casino (Harding, 2014).

Over time, a shift in any variable factor might lead some to vary roles, or switch lines or models. Occasionally shifts are imposed. However, with greater skill, experience and agency, positions and roles will alter or experienced runner/dealers seek to establish their own lines or strike out as independent dealers (indie-trappers).

Taking the above pre-conditions, situational and individual elements into account the young person is presented with options – join CLs as staff, that is, a runner/dealer; enter at a management level managing others; become an indie-trapper. Management roles offer the widest set of opportunities (see Figure 3.1). Timing plays a key role as not all options may be currently available.

Figure 3.1: Options for setting up a county line

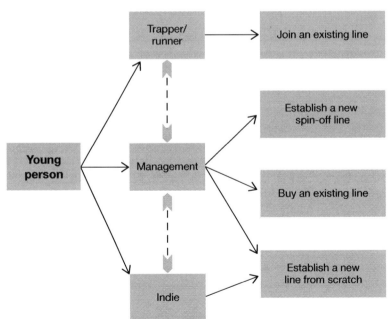

Pre-requisites for joining a crew

County lines has brought adaptations of street terminology with the term 'crew' often favoured above 'gang'. Indicative of smaller more agile business teams, active in supply, it is often widely used recognising that hidden highly-structured parent gangs might spawn several crews. Drug dealing crew members might, or might not be, affiliated to a USG:

> 'Most young people do not recognise the Gang as "the Gang" – thus they don't recognise what they are getting into. Gang is [an] old-fashioned term for some. Crew is preferred. Every single one of us knew each other, they were picked out specifically and there was a leader on top and everything, but he would not class himself as leader. He wouldn't refer to it as gang because he himself wouldn't class as leader, he just wanted to make money. That's what I'm saying. Yeah, he's the top boy, he's the source. Without him no one could have made money.' (USG 02)

Processes for joining crews appear fairly straightforward (hence its appeal); mostly informal; based on links to local networks, friendships and family. However, latent processes are detectable via informal, hidden individual assessment involving USG Elders/Olders/CL managers adjudicating on suitable candidacy. This assessment of street capital bears resemblance to credit score checks by financial companies with key criteria including:

- availability pool
- attitude to making money
- aspiration to advance
- aptitude and ability – street capital
- authenticity
- allegiance and assurance (trust)
- adrenaline

Any youth seeking to be 'put on' a crew will be known to them. Assessments include peer-group opinions and peer nominations means quick co-opting. Others simply offer their services. Candidacy assessments occur informally over months as Olders spot those 'with potential'. Junior runner/dealers (considered disposable cannon fodder) have this recruitment process condensed into quick assessments. For some this process might be unrecognisable. Where those 'vouched for' gain entry, that is, where a known street-name confers credit, the new candidate will owe a favour to the street-name who introduced him.

Availability pool and free time

The fact a candidate is being considered to 'jump in', or 'put on the line', is validation they originate from the right Pool of Availability and deemed 'appropriate', surfeit with intent and ample free time. Those with 'real jobs' are expected to surrender it to 'go cunch'.

Attitude to making money

Central to any effective team is the bonding attitude towards hustling to make money. This includes opportunities to bond over shared deprived backgrounds, domestic or personal privations and 'making do'. By age 14/15 most street-oriented youth have made money selling weed and are ready to move up to the next level of shotting white or brown.

> 'Moving up to cocaine, honestly, if you know the right people, the right connections stuff like that you can get, you just have to know the right connections.' (USG 02)

Most young affiliates see no real difference between selling cannabis or selling crack, except cannabis is shared and smoked widely among the crew. Crack is not widely used by many CL operatives and is just another product to sell, albeit involving different customers, supply and distribution routes. Group or team work becomes more common, though many still continue to sell their cannabis when possible:

> 'Yeah, everyone make[s] money on your own or together, either way, but when the time comes, if they would beef us, for example, if there was a problem with another area he had to shove us back. You would make money together or you don't but the plan is to make money together in this specific area because this is where we are, that's it, keep it locked down. Weed, cocaine, whatever makes money. Literally whatever makes money, do it. That was the motive. That was the way we thought back then.' (USG 02)

One youth revealed strong financial motivations underpinning his involvement in CL with comments resembling the sales talk of corporate sales professionals, echoing the *The Wolf of Wall Street* or *Glengarry Glen Ross*:

> 'Well, you get the money, innit? The money is pushing dem packs, pushing dem packs, you know, pushing packs, pushing packs. You gotta push dem packs. You get your money, do you know what I'm saying? Once you get your money back, you get your team, you get your empire, you get your respect, what everyone has dreamed of, you'll get just from simply pushing packs.' (USG 07)

Despite sidestepping the corporate WASP-ish world of work, the work ethic among CL operatives appears keenly understood and embraced, but also validated and reified.

Aspiration to advance

The current aspiration for many is no longer to defend territory or turf, but to run a county line:

> 'I just started from early still. Seeing the Older man do their thing, that's when I started. I was growing up just wanted to get my line started. It was mad cos everyone's doing the same thing, they're all just trying to get out, just got work and grants.' (USG 12)

> 'But a lot of boys aspire to that and they think if I have to work my way up it's perfectly fine but that's (1) if you survive and (2) if you don't get locked up.' (USG 01)

An aspiration to run CLs demonstrates a desire to be a Player in the Game. Young men actively generate street capital by boasting about how their different management style would increase profits. Future management planning becomes an expression of social trajectory, signalling intent to become more embedded in the Game, using CL as the route definer. Such actions become expressions of their authenticity in the Game and an active routine for many Youngers. Ability to realise these aspirations is monitored by others. The speed and ruthlessness by which some achieve their goal will determine what kind of Player they will be in the Game (Harding, 2014).

Aptitude and ability: street capital

Assessments of street capital are made routinely and continually – even pre-approach to join a CL. Being in the Pool of Availability itself designates a certain stock of street capital. Candidates are expected to maximise this:

> 'So, then I made a good profit on weed. My mum used to give me £2 a day, just £2 and that was transport as well but it was cheaper back then and I had school dinners but I used to take that £2 plus what I used to steal, put it together and then I'd be eating McDonald's, we'd be going to the cinema, doing different things. Going to meet girls. Having a good day. Bunking off school a lot. And with the fights – but making money on the side. I was only 14 in Year 10, one of the youngest in the year.' (USG 03)

Assessment of personal accounts of street capital will determine role allocation within CL networks which in turn confers hierarchical status by others in the Game. Such hierarchical positions, hitherto veiled, but with status confirmation comes validation and open designation. For some Youngers this is welcomed as their future route to climb is now mapped out.

Authenticity – be a real 'gansta'

One's authenticity in the Game can be evidenced by being a runner/dealer, or being known to be an active participant in CLs (see also Chapters 7 and 8).

> 'Trapping is everything now. It is the Game!' (USG 01)

Without experiencing CLs as a lived experience, a bona fide USG member has limited conversational contributions to make and will find themselves excluded. Lived experience (war stories) of trapping now defines Olders from Youngers, that is, those who missed out on this lived experience are now differentiated from those actively doing it. It is now an activity-defining feature separating Youngers from Olders/

Elders indicating a generational shift between Youngers and Older/Elders. Elders who have never been OT (out there) struggle to relate to/advise furthering views among Youngers that they are 'behind the curve' and 'out of touch' so must move aside and make space for those 'coming up'. Bourdieu acknowledges field strategy whereby incumbents are challenged by younger members seeking to succeed/subvert higher ranks and re-position themselves more advantageously in the hierarchy (Swartz, 1997: 124; Fligstein and McAdam, 2012: 13–21).

Allegiance and assurance (trust)

An essential consideration for acceptance as a CL operative – is trust. Within street gangs trust is a scare commodity (Harding, 2014; Densley, 2013). It is also a complex variable upon which people place different levels of importance. Loyalty given to others and to the line is equally valued. Acceptance into CL networks demonstrates trust which is thereon continually monitored:

> 'Once you're part of the team they trust you. But I do understand the person has to trust you himself. When you're part of the team, you're part of the team. Regardless. There are not really any rules that go with being part of the team, not really. No rules, no codes, but an understanding. For me, one [of] the things wasn't trust, it was so I don't get caught. You've got to keep your distance. In this game it's survival of the fittest. It was nothing to do with friendship. You had to know what you were doing. You had to make sure that when you go you go home to your mum, you go home to your mum, no one else, even though we had each other's back and all of that. We all had to have each other's back.' (USG 02)

By working together, loyalty is continually demonstrated and reinforced. CLs bring multiple opportunities to demonstrate loyalty to friends, brothers, the line and the crew. Acknowledged loyalty reduces personal risk, keeping operatives safe by removing/reducing suspicion and thus operates as a risk management strategy which must be maintained. Keeping loyal is also part of the Game demonstrating one is an authentic 'G'. The Game requires this constant demonstration, monitoring and testing which is not easily done 'On Road' as things get misconstrued. So a working arrangement (such as a CL) helps abstract things out of social circles into a cooperative businesslike environment where semi-professional codes apply. Thus expectations can be codified, aired and expressed as business or contractual arrangements. Expectations, hitherto unspoken, are laid out and openly expressed. Those demonstrating little loyalty develop reputations for untrustworthiness as:

'A flip flopper. Someone who changes sides? Yeah. He has no loyalties. He has no morals, zero. To anyone. To anything.' (USG 01)

Disloyalty is often cited as reason for demotion/exclusion from a line. When this occurs, the hierarchical status of the operative will determine if violence ensues, for example this operative took demotion as his opportunity to establish his own line:

'My partner, whatever, he got for whatever reason demoted down to that so when he got demoted and he was up with us he fell out with the [name] boys and he said, "Do you know what, I'm taking you," – me – "and we're starting our own line" so we started our own line in [name].' (USG 01)

For those in the Game, trust is expected as a reciprocal arrangement expressed and embodied in the term 'Bro'. In reality, trust is often situational and conditional. In CL drug networks, trust becomes conditional, expected, business-oriented and contractual – relational more than reciprocal. It is possible this change leads to mis-interpretations of actions and outcomes potentially sparking conflicts:

[Are there any rules that go with being part of the team?]

Not really. No rules, no codes, but an understanding. You stay loyal to each. Be right with each other. That's about it really. If you're not loyal then you will pay the consequences. If you're loyal then you get loyalty back. No one really decides if you are loyal or not. You have to be loyal or you don't be. No one really makes the decisions. It's a bond thing. It has to happen organically. It's a thing where you have to see it as this is your brother, this is who you're making money with so in that case don't you want to have a relationship where you two can make money together continuously and keep that going? If you do then they'll stay loyal to you. It's like that. It has to happen. If you don't want that to happen then you're not going to be loyal and if you're not going to be loyal then you have to pay the price.' (USG 02)

Trust, for some, then becomes part of the business relationship rather than friendship relationship. As one runner/dealer said, 'That's why. For example, I wouldn't invite any of them to my house.'

One CL manager who ran several lines was highly discerning about his allocation of trust:

> 'If you ask me I've never trusted anyone. I don't care how long I've known you. There's probably one, maybe two people out of all of us that I trusted. Anyone other than that, even from their mum's house and I break bread with them he's my brother. That's how I see it but these are people that I've actually known from the age of five so we were ... together through thick and thin. I'm my brother's keeper. So, this is how it is. But the rest of them ... I just know them through other people and it's been like six or seven years, and we've not really been through anything for me to actually say, "Do you know what, I trust this guy 100%". No. But it's all smiles and cries when you're on the road; you just have to play the game. That's all it is. Smiles and cries. Play it. You have to say the right things just like when you're coercing a kid, you say what you need to say, just like these guys here when they tell you, "Hey, go and do this, you'd be rolling" it's like "yeah, yeah" from my heart I don't want to fucking go. It's not my problem. I'm inheriting your shit but you know what, if it's going to keep the line together and we are all still getting money, let's fucking go.... Yeah, so let's fucking go. We go there. It turns out the people we're looking for aren't even fucking there. We come back and I'm like, "Fucking take us to McDonald's, you cunt."' (USG 06)

It is possible that some of the recent upswing in violence in England and Wales is as a result of changes in how trust is now viewed differently among USGs and CL crews. For some, the loyalty is to making money, profit and possibly to the line; less so to others from a territorial background or common turf. Thus old-school territorial commonalities and habitus (Bourdieu, 1984) cease to be the glue binding them together as it once was. Newer contractual relationships perhaps operate differently causing difficulties for some in terms of experience and through misaligned expectations?

Adrenaline

For some young people CLs offer paid employment and opportunity, certain amounts of freedom and excitement. While such views probably fade over time, Youngers talk avidly of 'the buzz', and the 'adrenaline rush' of making money, avoiding the police and setting up deals:

> 'I love busting packs and then spending the candy. I get a rush.' (USG 10)

In terms of motivation for joining a street gang or crew, one younger runner/dealer had his focus elsewhere:

> 'What we do is we link girls. It's all we're here for is to link girls. It's all about the pussy.' (Runner 03)

Joining a line

As options for joining a CL present, the obvious option is to set up with your peers:

> 'It's just everyone had an age group. You're either with your age group or you're not. I ended up doing some research in an area called [Area] which is just up the road, so I started a line there. I had a few close friends, there was probably about five of us.' (USG 06)

Family connections do not necessarily confirm acceptance onto existing lines simply because your brother or cousin already works that line. Often this is seen as 'too political':

> 'Was going on 16 and I remember I had had enough, I wanted to sell hard food in [London area] but the Olders had it already, and I was like, "Can't we sell in [London area]?" They were like, "No, you're not selling here. You sell for us or you fucking don't". It was a bit complicated because it's a bit political because my older brother, who is one year older and currently with them doing what he's doing. I couldn't have worked for them, No, no because my brother's with them, it's different. It's quite different. Yeah. So, it was a bit difficult to start a line, it was a bit hard, plus

I didn't have a strong team. Half the people I was with were half-hearted.' (USG 06)

This respondent decided he was better off establishing his own line (as shown in the 'Getting Started' case study) later running CLs nationwide:

Case Study: Getting started – USG 06

'I actually believed I wanted to be rich, to have nice stuff. I would look at homeless people when walking past with Mum and my brothers, everyone has got their own vision of how they saw stuff. I used to see homeless people and I used to think, "How did this person get to where he is?" It's scary. I never want to be like that. I saw a fast option to make money. I saw some of the older boys and I saw them wearing expensive stuff back then, you had good clothes, you had stuff which is, now you've got all this new stuff, Christian, Louis Vuitton and all of this sort of stuff. That wasn't in fashion back then. Back then it was Iceberg jeans.

'So, seeing Olders wear this sort of stuff, having the world of money and coming into the barbers showing and wearing a Q and he would pay the barber shop when he gets his hair cut. He would have that respect. He would walk in, cut the queue, get his hair cut, give the barber shop £100, turn around and look at us young ones and be like, "You all cutting your hair?" and we'd be like "yeah" and he'd give the barber shop guy £70 and say, "That's for them". A lot of people were like "thanks" and they would call him uncle in whatever language. Me, I would look at it thinking I could fucking do what he's doing. I could fucking get that. What makes him better than me? So, I just got some money together. I went through stages. I had to sell weed to get a certain amount. I had to sell coke to get a certain amount and I remember buying my first half of each of brandy and whisky and not knowing what to do and I'm in this area. There's two of us.

'Then we've got these other people trying to fight us so I had to get some muscle in, I had to call a couple of people to come join us. I don't want to share money, but you have to. I've got a couple of people in, we're a strong team. A friend's window got shotgunned off so now we have to do what we're doing and we just put the foundation down. We bought a couple of revolvers and just became different.

'Yeah, so I would give £10 to one of the adults, the Cats, and I'd tell him, "Go pick up a £10 shot from them or whatever and bring it back to us". Yeah. And then I would get a vulnerable or Cat that I trust, that I know, you can't trust a Cat but someone that I know has my best interests, if that makes sense, someone that's loyal, I would get her to taste the food and get her to taste our food and she would tell me if our food is shit. She was zero tolerance but knew her stuff. So, she told us "their food was better, their whisky is better" and said our brandy was about the same but their whisky is a lot better than yours. So, I went to the Olders and said, "Look, where can I get better food from?" so they gave me another guy who ended up being the same fucking guy that we get it off.

'To be honest, I did something a bit out of my ordinary because I didn't want to ask my older brother or his friends for anything, I didn't want to do that because when we started the line a lot of people we're telling us, "These guys are going to run you lot out" and all this other stuff. They didn't know what we had planned. And I didn't want people to come with stuff. And some people when they do help you out they try and get their foot in the door, I didn't want any of that. I remember going to [London borough] to a couple of friends and got a bit of white off them, I think it was two and a Q. I came back and gave ten shots away, testers to certain people, and still I'd take her advice and her opinion on the food. I gave it to a few other people, I had Scottish, I had a few guys and they tasted it and they said, "Fucking excellent, man". I don't know if they were over exaggerating but they said it was like a nine or a ten and I thought, "Do you know what, I can fucking live with that". I started doing deals: three for £25, six for £50s.

'We would go up to him once a week and re-up, bag up the food and started giving the shots out a bit more. It got to the point where Cats from [Area] were coming to us. It was different. Word gets around. People getting around, these guys heard our line was probably making about £200 at that time a day. It wasn't even 24 hours. We had it on from ten in the morning until ten at night, that was it. It wasn't a 24-hour line. It's been a long time but it just boosted up there so quick I couldn't believe it. I rang the kids on the block and said, "How Much? What's the count, what you got?" and I remember the kid, we left him with a G pack, 500 of each.

'When that was making money and it was good and it was established I ended up going to Lincolnshire, I was new to that town. I had a girl that I met in London and I was just talking to her, she was a very bubbly girl, she was drinking Pinot Grigio and I was in the bar in Soho talking to her. I asked her where she was from and she told me she was from Lincolnshire and I'm like, "How is Lincolnshire?" and she was telling me about the area and I was just like "wow, okay" and never thought nothing of it.

'Then I remembered I had some of the boys from that area, some would go into different places, people were going to Luton and people were going to different types of places in terms of counties, people going to Portsmouth, Bournemouth,

Southampton all them places so I thought to myself, I did a bit of research on Lincolnshire and I typed-in recent crimes there, I got a PDF telling me about a world of stuff that happened there in 2006 and it was just saying whatever. Then obviously typing in different things and I literally went there on a trip one day. Obviously to meet that girl, that girl was just a girl I met. I went there, drove around, we had a rental, we drove around the area, spotted a few Cats, spoke to them and said, "Who's selling here?" and they told me some people are selling here, it turns out the people that were selling there were locals, but their shit was shit.

'Yeah. I would call myself a weird name, I don't know, whatever I would call myself. Back then what did I used to call myself? I was there for a week and a half when I first moved there because I was starting the line and everything. I was about 20. Lincolnshire just blew up, it just blew proper. Started going crazy.'

The indie-trapper

County line operatives, often those with greater 'On Road' experience, higher levels of street capital, or greater confidence and personal agency, might prefer to become indie-trappers, preferring to deal individually or with loose affiliations to others. Having gained experience with other crews some now prefer to strike out independently having realised crew shotting or trapping is not for them:

> 'Yeah. There are different categories of shotting. You can shot for someone; you can shot for yourself, shot with a team.' (USG 02)

One fervently independent indie-trapper argued his 'On Road' personality moulded him:

> 'Mostly robbing, money, weed selling, sell weed so you can get a little bit of money. Robbing dealers, anyone that was making money. It didn't matter who it was. Whoever had money and that was living good, in luxury, they were the target. Over time you could say I was seen as an "Independent."' (USG 02)

An individualistic character and dislike of taking 'orders' led him to recognise and value his own agency, coupled with a view of his role as 'a job':

'They would say that you have got to do certain things to keep
your stripes but I was my own leader, I didn't have to do any of
that. I do what I do to make money, if it's not making money
then I didn't want to do it. I was a different breed to people
in the gang, a different breed because everyone was doing
something to prove something to someone. That's how it was.
I had the anger, the rage. Honestly it got to the point where
I realised that being with them was a job because, back then,
I was saying to myself I'm more dangerous than all of them,
if you want to be realistic. That was another reason that made
me want to leave because I was thinking bigger, but it wasn't
positive bigger, but I was thinking bigger. They showed me
that they were smooth fishes and I have to work with sharks.
That's what made me slide away from them as well.' (USG 02)

Deciding to group-up with others or act independently usually comes
after careful consideration:

'Me, personally, I would analyse it. I would check it. I'd see.
If I was going to do that sort of thing working with someone
in that specific game if you were working within someone
they could stab you in the back so there's a bit of a risk with
that one. They see you're making a bit too much money, get
a bit jealous. You can work for someone but if you're a funny
kind of person you don't really work for someone.' (USG 02)

Risks and advantages of being independent

Indie-trapping realises several advantages: fewer people to manage, no
second-guessing, checking or agreeing decisions, faster decisions, less
worry about trusting your workers:

'But also that's the best way to do it. Unless you've got a brother
and he's your blood or you've got a brother that you're close
with then fair enough but in that kind of game you want to
do that for yourself, keep that load to yourself.' (USG 02)

Some view indie-trappers as very adroit in drug dealing and more skilled
in the Game bringing a highly tuned, high-fidelity form of street capital
– an acknowledged fact in the Game leading to heightened expectations.
A tightly controlled and managed reputation sustains respect:

[How did you manage to survive being an independent?]

'To be honest? Being nice. Dead honest. The most respect I've got is because I'm a genuine nice person, but I can easily become a different person if I need to be and that's the side no one wanted to see because that's the side that no one can stop. In that gang thing I was saying to these people, you couldn't make a move to me because of that – I was an angry child. I would do something evil towards you if I knew I was threatened. I was just a very wild child. I'd flip out at teachers when they were asking questions I didn't like.' (USG 02)

Key advantages include increased profits and working conditions:

'You're not working for someone so any money you get is yours plus you can as fast as you want and as slow as you want.' (USG 02)

Risks exist for indie-trappers, however, the need for is reduced to trust in one's own judgement:

'You've got to be more aware because you're shotting to a person that could be undercover. It's more risky but because it's more risky that means more money.' (USG 02)

Dealers lacking enhanced street capital are unlikely to take this route. Assumptions indie-trappers were more at risk through lack of trust was challenged:

'If anything, being independent is safer because it's your operation. It's how you work it. It's how you do it. Like I said, if you have someone you don't have to worry about that person being obvious because when you work alone you know you're not going to be obvious so you just focus on yourself, it gets done quicker.' (USG 02)

A decision to become an indie-trapper rests more on family/peer connections, On Road duration, contacts, opportunities and personal drive, than upon age. Once established as an indie-brand it becomes difficult to re-brand:

'You can do, but if any street n****r … sorry. If you get smart drug dealers they would know you work on your own. Then they wouldn't let you in. So stay independent. Because when you think about it, it just comes down easily, stay safe, watch your back.' (USG 02)

Managing county lines

Purchasing an existing line

An alternative method to establishing a CL is simply to purchase an existing line, and buying a CL phone might offer faster routes to faster profits. Phones, or CL, can be sold/swapped for tens of thousands of pounds. This is the equivalent of a company selling on a database of buyers. Acquiring such a line ensures the line, or new owner, is up and operating instantaneously, without the need to create a new user database.

> 'So, there's a boy I know, he just sold his line, I don't know where his line even was but he was from Holloway though, he just sold his line for something like £150,000 cash.' (USG 01)

'Selling on' can bring risk if the phone is 'dirty', that is, being tracked by police, or comes with attached or inherited debt. Vendors might be aware, but *caveat emptor* applies leading to retribution and violent attacks conducted against the new, unsuspecting owners or their staff. New owners might then take action against the vendors selling a 'dirty line'. This scenario is recognised by the police:

> 'Yeah, that can happen. That is … more common is if somebody knows that they're going into jail they will instruct someone else they can trust to carry on that line while they're in jail.' (Police 02)

Setting up a new line

For some, a decision to set a new CL is influenced by strong inter-personal relationships. For this female respondent being pulled off one by her partner only meant he wished them to set up their own line:

> 'I never wanted to be part of them [the dealing crew] anyway, I just wanted him. I didn't want to be part of a gang. I was never a gang-banger, I was never a hood-rat girl, one of them

girls at all, I was just part of that line. So when he said, "We're coming, I'm pulling you out" I was like, "I've got him back and he's going to come to his senses". I still thought like that and at this point, at home, my parents, I was being in so much trouble they said literally, "We can't have it any more, you're either with us and we will look after you and protect you or you're out of the house" and of course I said, "I'm staying with him". So, I was staying with him which sounds awful, his mum had just got out of prison so we were staying at his mum's, bail release place or whatever hostel and then we just randomly, and I've been asked this so many times and I can only ever say the same answer, randomly how did you decide to go to [name] in [name] to start this new line, literally random. I said, "[name] is not that far away", and he said, "Let's have a look round there then". Ended up in [name]. So, us wandering into [name] was very risky but we didn't know – Now it is the [Gang Name], yeah. We didn't know who was there, we never came up against anything. We never did. I don't know if we weren't there long enough. We never came up against anything.' (USG 01)

Deciding where to establish the line requires management decisions regarding potential locations, risks and potential profits. In reality this varies considerably but usually involves planning. Others are influenced by geography, transport networks and pre-established networks. There is a recognition some areas 'belong' to certain London USGs, so CL operations often follow pre-established lines of influence:

'Hackney kind of have Essex, Enfield have Hertfordshire and so on. It's respected but not entirely. But people know that's their bit type thing.' (USG 01)

Prospecting (market reconnaissance)

Decisions on CL locations are highly influenced by the existence of domestic heroin markets, and conversations provide intelligence on volume of drug dealers/users, rival suppliers, market sophistication and product preference. Opportunities are assessed with offers of joint working with local connections, often sealing the deal. Once identified as a potential dealing locations operatives commence market reconnaissance – known as prospecting. This often involves female operatives visiting the scene and reporting back. Intelligence is assessed and sifted as to 'potential'. Prospecting can involve walking around the town looking for beggars, dealers, users, alcoholics, people on benefits, unemployed and so on, to produce intel on who is dealing; from where; at what market rate. A skilled CL operative can quickly assess the local situation:

> 'That was the way to make money. Go OT to try and make something happen. I only went once. It was only like going to get sources, finding connections, basically networking really. So, for example, if you live in East London you'd [get] to places like Essex. You either have a set-up already, like a place where you go to sleep or you find something but the main thing to go OT is to get that money. To have a way of making money so when you go back down you have the money ready. I've only been a couple of times, not a lot, because OT wasn't my thing.' (USG 02)

CL operatives retain pejorative terms for local customers:

> 'There's an Alchie and a Nitty – it's a way of establishing who you are targeting.' (Stakeholder 15)

A seasoned CL manager understands that local users will exchange details of other users for free drugs; a technique which opens the possibility of establishing a new line in a new area. Post-reconnaissance, this CL manager noted one provincial location was not ideal for his young black male runner/dealers:

> 'And just talking to them, yeah, because my theory was I would only have to meet four Cats in that whole area and them four would know every Cat. That's how the window opens. So, I started a line there. The line started making about £2,500 so it was making two grand something a day. This was a money-maker because the line only ran from nine to nine, not 24hrs, so it was completely different to the area. Different to borough based. Then what I did was I got a couple of kids, but I found it hard because the kids I was bringing from London they don't want to stay there for long, they felt out of place and stuff.' (USG 06)

Other engagement techniques are part direct-marketing, part street-based intervention:

'I would just walk past and give them a card and then when I get further down, look back and wave my hand to tell them to follow me then take him out of sight. I would give him a free shot right there and a little card, something I would have the number written down on'. (USG 06)

Managing a crew

The crew (team) constantly generates new ideas and new money-making opportunities, thus markets are maximised and amplified:

'Well, you'd ask one of the team if they had any drugs to sell, if they have any you take it off them, you sell it then Boom! If they don't you're going to have to find something. It's not a thing where someone drops it on you, you run away, you come back, you give them the money and then they give half the money. You have to make your own meal. Being in this team is already giving you the opportunity to do that because now you have other minds to come up with plans to think of ways.' (USG 02)

These arrangements and conversations occur naturally and bonded collaborations are established:

'But it happens naturally. It's not a thing where that's your position to that, it happens naturally. If you want to make money this is what you've got to do. If you don't go, go home.' (USG 02)

Crews can evolve from, merge or splinter from USGs. As USGs move from expressionist crime to instrumental crime robbery and drug dealing become central to their gang repertoire (Harding, 2014).

'In Hackney there was up to 50, 100 maybe more [in the crew]. A lot. Some are still around today. It was mostly Olders. That's why I say personally it was a gang but it was more of an organisation to make money, if that makes sense. We didn't really call ourselves a gang; we had problems with other areas, you know. Honestly, back then it was team, crew. Every one of us knew each other, they were picked out specifically and there was a leader on top and everything but he himself would not class him as leader, he just wanted to make money. That's what I'm saying. Yeah, he's the Top Boy, he's the source. Without him no one could have made money. They refer to him as the Plug, The source. It wasn't a thing where he was highly respect[ed] like "yes, boss". He's a general, there was real respect but it wasn't a thing within the team that was our general we take orders from him, he sends us out there, we do what he says, it wasn't like that. Yeah, everyone make money on your own but we are all here; everyone make money on your own, or together, either way but when the time comes, if they would beef us, for example, if there was a problem with another area he had to shove us back. He was older, way older than me. I don't know his age. I'd say in his late 20s. You would make money together or you don't, but the plan is to make money together in this specific area because this is where we are, that's it, keep it locked down. Weed, cocaine, whatever makes money. Literally whatever makes money do it. That was the motive.' (USG 02)

The size of the crew can vary:

'It can be how many you want. So, it depends on how many of the brothers in the team you know. If you know all of them you can call of them. If you know all 100 of them you can call all of them. If you know ten of them you can call ten of them.' (USG 02)

Training

Such is the experience now of running CLs some operatives benefit from a sideline in training others offering rewards of amplified street capital:

'Yeah. I got so good at it people used to send their Youngers to me, send their youth to me to get trained because I was that good at it. Sit them down, show them how to wrap up the drugs, how to tell if drugs are good without taking it; teach them how to serve a customer while concealing because a lot of people are "there you go", there could be a camera that could see everything. Yeah, you've got to do the sly pass. If it's a girl you might have to kiss her so it's passed by mouth.

Different things. Up to today I've never been caught for drugs. I haven't even had a warning for smoking weed.' (USG 03)

'So, a weed line anybody can do and it's just local boys, Youngers usually, doing their own shit on a local estate but a white line is the start of the next level up.' (USG 06)

Teamwork or brotherhood?

'Yeah, it was teamwork. It was proper good, good times back then. A lot of people, even in my workplace now, they ask me, "What do you miss the most?" I miss the brotherhood, that's the only thing I miss. I miss all of us being together as a group, going out to eat, simple stuff. Going raving, going to do this, that's what I miss. I don't miss the headache of bagging up and feeling that pressure when you get a phone call from the little young ones, "There's police around in the area and we're in the fucking house chopping up food", it's fucked up, man, I don't like that feeling but at the same time having that adrenaline made me enjoy what I do as well. I can't explain it. So it's different.' (USG 06)

Recruitment and grooming

Churn in CL operatives can be high due to numerous arrests and attrition. To overcome this there is a need to constantly have a supply of young people ready to join the line. Some lines have an informal waiting list of young people keen to be 'put on'. The usual process is for the CL managers/parent gang to constantly assess potential future candidates. This process is habitual and seamless. For a detailed examination of criminal and sexual exploitation, including grooming, please see Beckett et al (2013); Firmin (2018) and the Children's Society (2019). Concepts of child criminal exploitation (CCE) have recently emerged to help delineate how techniques of grooming, coercion and manipulation are used to entreat young people to act in ways which benefit the CL managers or USG (see Chapter 5).

The recruitment of young people as runner/dealers takes many forms. Central is the concept of making fast money:

'It's easy cos many just want to make money.' (Police 11)

For some young people generating a wage via a CL permits them to act as a de-facto breadwinner in homes where parents might be absent (emotionally or physically) or struggling to raise families. Young men view this 'assistance' as demonstrating masculinity or as doing masculinity (Messerschmidt, 1993) and 'coming of age':

'The young people that I work with in the Pupil Referral Unit, they were like, "Miss, we only come in on a Tuesday because you're coming. Every other day we run country". They said, "First week we are in [town] in [County], second week we're in [town], third week they have everything planned out". I said, "How did you get involved in all this kind of stuff?", just out of curiosity because these are really bolshy boys, they don't seem vulnerable. Well, they are but they are not your typical vulnerable. They said, "Someone snapped me and asked me if I wanted to make money". So they sent them a snap on Snapchat, "Do you want to make money?" and it evolves from there. I said, "Didn't you ever think it could have been the police maybe?" "Well, I took that risk and now I'm making money, now I've got trainers, now I can help my mum", and this is coming from 13- and 14-year-old boys. "Now I can help my mum". So common. And their parents know what they are doing. I never had anything to show from it at the beginning for a very, very long time but these boys are obviously getting a little bit more.' (USG 01)

Young people would not necessarily view this as grooming of any kind but simply being offered an opportunity. One local authority youth worker noted two different types of grooming in her area – classic, and exploitative:

'There is a lot of kind of, "Oh, I bumped into a guy on the high street, and he asked me to look after this". Or, "I bumped into a guy on the train and he said I could earn some money if I just looked after it", but then actually they're arrested with a number of wraps. So, it's like well, if they gave you "a" lump, how has it got into a number? Their stories don't match up, but it is along the lines of they were given something to then do something with. So, there is a few of that but it doesn't seem to be any kind of coordinated way really.

'We also used to get Suffolk boys in our court and our boys in Suffolk court, so there was clearly [a] line [that] had been set up between us and Suffolk. The twins that I have just been involved with – they are local boys and when they described what happened to them, they were describing a classic exploitation thing. Like one of them said he got given a bunch of gear and then the guy said, "There was more than that, you owe me. You have got to do me some work". So, I do think that there is getting the locals to do it, That is one incident. I have no real sense of size and scales.' (Stakeholder 06)

Local police are aware of myths circulating among CL operatives that younger boys cannot be searched by the police for drugs:

'I think there's a myth, cos they say, "You can't search me cos I'm only 14". Or, "You can't strip search me cos I'm only 15". Well, we can. We just need an "Appropriate Adult". That's probably one of the reasons why they're sending down so many young people as they think they can't be searched. We had a job out of here recently, he's just died. He was being cuckoo'd. We stopped him out in the street as he was about to serve up. He said he was being cuckoo'd and there was someone in his flat so we went in and it was a young lad, a gang member – he was only 16. He had a lot of gear on him and a massive sword down the back of his trousers. We could go through hundreds of jobs we've done though.' (Police 13)

Some young people acting as runner/dealers for CLs demonstrate considerable agency or myopic focus on making money:

'That's the other side to this – no vulnerability – but the chance to make some easy money. The learning around that – most guys don't realise that if you get caught serving up Class A – you're going to prison. More often they'll go to prison for that – even just bagging up.' (Police 13)

Local agencies would clearly identify people of this age as vulnerable. However, it seems apparent that young people do not have the capacity to risk assess their situation or CL involvement often dismissing risks through a sense of invincibility.

The endless stream of young recruits for county line work – both male and female – is recognised by the police, agencies and also the CL operatives. Often described as 'cannon fodder' by local agencies, these young people will be put to work as runner/dealers. Retention on the line is based upon success with more successful lines recruiting more. As one CL manager ruminated:

> 'The thing is they come and go as well. One will go, another one will be there, the turnover is pretty quick as you could put it, so I'd say at a time, for us in [name] we managed about six at a time.' (USG 01)

Getting staff to the customers

Travel logistics create headaches for CL managers, and one, two, or more runner/dealers require transport to location efficiently and effectively. Different options are available and selection depends upon: the need to avoid detection; the purpose of the trip, for example dropping off staff; collecting money; dropping off drugs; distance from London; total people travelling; time of day/night. Finally a further determinant is which county line model is operating.

In his analysis of CL dealers and non-CL dealers who had interactions with the police in north Essex, John Hallworth (2016: 41), found CL offenders travelled an average of 71 miles further (from their home to the place of police interaction) than non-CL offenders. The mean distance travelled by CL offenders was 79.84 miles; while the mean distance travelled by the non-CL offenders was 6.85 miles. Major product transportation, for example from Liverpool to Essex or Dover will naturally be further.

Public transport

Public transport is favoured by CL operatives as it is considered easier for runner/dealers to blend in with other travellers. Moreover underage runner/dealers might not drive or have a licence and the travel mode fits with chosen narratives, for example, 'I'm going to the seaside'/'I'm visiting my aunty in...' Expenditure receipts are producible for suspicious CL managers though some purchase tickets in advance to achieve discounts.

Trains

The NCA 2017 National Briefing Report (NCA, 2017a; 2017b) acknowledged that the full extent of use of railways was not fully understood, noting however that of the 29 police forces responding to their survey, 67 per cent reported use of rail. The 2018 NCA Intelligence Assessment (2019a) noted 40 per cent of transport linked to branded lines was by rail. Key national rail hubs were identified as key points of access to the network though smaller local or suburban stations are used as entry points. Some CL operatives are known to disembark trains before arrival to avoid police detection.

As the agency tasked with national policing of railways the British Transport Police (BTP) have a significant role to play in tackling CLs. In their 2018/19 Annual Report (2019: 6) BTP state they work alongside the NCA 'conducting both regular BTP specific and joint policing operations nationally across the network'. This includes intelligence gathering, intercepting and disrupting lines. In 2016 BTP launched Operation Defiant to address CLs with learning later brought into national policy.

Key challenges remain between BTP and other UK police constabularies, not least regarding intelligence gathering and information-sharing with multiple different forces and divisions. The fast-moving, fast-evolving nature of CLs is made more challenging due to a mixed regional picture arising from different CL models.

Buses

An alternative to more expensive rail travel is bus travel. Frequently used by those with less money, this provides a useful cloak for CL operatives:

> 'Yeah, I used to pay for National Express and stuff. I was a stingy cunt. I used to put them on the Megabus all the way there. It was funny. I used to drop them off at Victoria and just tell them to jump on that. I would give them an address to go to which is for vulnerable adults and they would work out of there.' (USG 06)

Private cars

Private cars are favoured by CL operatives as they offer defensible excuses, if the youth is found sleeping in the car (an occasional necessity if travelling and dealing). Cars will be used to serve up drugs directly from the car. Vehicles are thought to keep middle-ranking CL operatives more mobile and possibly protected from attack, while signifying acquired status.

Hire cars

Hire cars are an effective way of transporting staff, drugs and weapons to the dealing location with vehicle hiring usually undertaken by females, or adult drug users. Harding (2014) noted that young women can manufacture street capital and kudos among street gang peers by operationalising their networks and skill sets and conducting small-scale business activities which might not be an option for the young men or which are deemed too visible or risky. Girls who operate at the high end of the Social Skills Spectrum (p 227) are trusted to hire cars and present their personal details as they can operate as 'clean skins' with no prior offending history.

> 'Girls, their mums, aunts, whatever! Always a different car every week. Never a car of their own. I obviously wasn't driving at that time but the boys who would drive us up, the older lot, all their cars were hired cars. They were never their own cars. And obviously they weren't hired in their own names. They always had a different car every time you saw them.' (USG 01)

Due to the frequent need for car hire, a discrete network of under-the-counter hire arrangements operates from the metropolitan cities. Local family or local criminal networks are utilised to circumvent hiring from the high street car rental companies. Here local men hire out their cars on a fee-only basis for several days at a time:

> 'I would get someone to hire it either from Avis or more times I would just go to the Bengali Boys in East London, rent a Golf R32, a Golf R they call it now. I don't have to put a deposit down. It was a mutual understanding. I would just give the money for however many days.' (USG 06)

Such businesses are not operating as bona fide car rental services and only provide this personalised service for those within their collaborative criminal network or extended family. This also can be enacted via a personalised recommendation. In this way, paperwork is minimalised or paper trails obscured or deleted.

> 'They're doing their own kind of enterprise. It's like a rental company for themselves. The only difference is it's better than a rental company because they're not charging me £300/£400,

deposit. Yeah, knowwhatImean? Even though I would get my deposit back but it's just not ideal. Then when I get the car, I rent it for a few days. So, then I would rent it and I would pay however much for it, I have it for seven days and then after the seven days is finished I could just extend it for another seven days, just put the money in his account and he's good and I can continue. So, it's different.' (USG 06)

Taxis

On other occasions CL managers use taxis to collect product or revenue. App-based taxis are an emerging trend for transportation while local minicabs (at times linked to other forms of criminal activity) are favoured.

Risk mitigation regarding transport

Transport of product, revenue and runner/dealers carries inherent risk of identification from the authorities. Careful CL managers will identify these risks then mitigate/manage them effectively.

This can be done using female travel companions to deflect attention or project an image of an affectionate relationship by utilising a female travel companion. Child car seats and toys can be scattered on the back seat to give the impression of family car. As one young county lines manager recounted:

[Were you nervous?]

'Not really. Not when you've got a girl with you and you're going to give her a hefty amount to do it. It's good to take girls that actually love you. So, my theory was that a girl has to love you more than you love her because she would go to the ends of the earth for you, that's how it works, man. So, if she's plugging it, muling, taking it up there.' (USG 06)

At other times females will be tasked with transporting the product themselves and returning with revenue. Again as this presents inherent risk, on occasion a single cab trip offers the best risk mitigation:

'It got to the point that we just became comfortable where she's in the back of the cab and paying a cab driver about

£400 to take her to Lincolnshire and she's in the back, it could be [Addison Lee] whatever, she's actually just got the drugs in her bag, she's dressed as if she's just going raving but over there. There isn't anyone who is going to stop her. No one is going to stop an Addison Lee car. She will get there, she will meet the boys, the boys will take the drugs from her and she's catching that cab straight back and then the boys when they get the drugs they will go into the park or the field, it's like a nine bar of each so it's all bagged up in G packs, you've got two G packs and then you would have 20 packs of stuff, all in 20s.' (USG 06)

Risk mitigation also exists for private cars. The 2018 NCA Intelligence Assessment (2019) noted an emerging trend of cloned number plates – procured in attempts to confuse police Automatic Number Plate Recognition (ANPR) systems. CL operatives aware private cars are tracked will use adult drug users to drive to and from Hub locations. Females are often used and encouraged to fit child-seats in the rear to imply family use. Occasionally the product is dispatched separately in case the 'staff car' is stopped by police.

Risk mitigation for runner/dealers is a key consideration for CL managers who assess personal presentation and insist upon modifications:

'One of the boys the other day funnily enough he was wearing Converse and he's not a Converse type of guy and I said, "Oh my God, when did you get them?" and he was like, "My G told me that I need to blend in so I've got to look trendy init so he got me a Barber jacket and Converse", so they were obviously trying to make him look a different type of way, grow his hair out, and not have the fade and not do the … so on … so they are clocking on in little ways.' (USG 01)

One common risk mitigation is to send runner/dealers to locations in school uniform. This offers a clever presentational advantage which is intended to deflect attention from authorities while providing opportunities for blending in. It also grants opportunities for masking nervousness or shyness while offering an understanding purpose for being on the street.

'I changed out of mine beforehand, not on the train. No, before. When we were at his place. Before he dropped me at Stratford I got changed. He told me to get changed. But I must have been there in my uniform at one point, come to think of it. Definitely would have been.' (USG 01)

Arrival challenges

Arrival at a new location poses various challenges for CL operatives, some of whom are experiencing their first-ever trip outside London. These include: avoiding CCTV cameras; basic orientation; blending in; meeting principle contacts; locating dealing Hubs; finding accommodation. Often accommodation must be found quickly or girls are used to book rented accommodation (Harding, 2014):

'Even hiring out rooms and flats and you've obviously got to have payslips, and this, references from jobs. When we were in [name] some girl hired a little place for us in [name]. None of us could have done that at that point. It's always girls that do that kind of thing.' (USG 01)

Accommodation in rented flats, shared addresses, or cuckooed properties, takes time to organise. Arrival accommodation often means 'making do', for example sleeping on the floor, due to expediency, or unexpected police activity. Frequently operatives must ingratiate themselves with active users. One female runner/dealer reported her first-ever time 'going country' meant sleeping in a filthy abandoned house (bando) with no working facilities, but full of users injecting drugs:

[Do users lie on mattresses?]

'If there is mattresses on the floor ... but on old sofas, bin bags, sleeping bags and they don't pay you any attention because they're all nodding. They didn't scare me. I didn't want to sleep, well, you couldn't, but I never wanted to drift off and be unaware what was going on around me. But if I was to, I doubt anything would have happened because they were just all off their faces. Me personally, I never got robbed by anybody who we were around when we were staying in the kind of environment. Only people you were going outside to meet.' (USG 01)

Risk mitigation regarding arrival

Risk mitigation techniques involve avoiding rented accommodation or being tied into a specific property. This also brings additional advantages as noted by one CL manager:

> 'No, we were smart. Staying in the car, sleeping in the car. The reason being is because you can move. You're always concealed and you can move. If the police come to you, they appeared loads of times, I got stopped by police and if I had the drugs enough times, I can hide the drugs because I'm in a car. Whereas if I'm in a house, they have to kick off the door and that's it. So, a lot of people nowadays don't use houses, they use cars. If I needed to get back to the endz, back down to Hackney, back to North London I don't have to worry about transportation or worry about police on the train or anything, you're in a car. If you need to go and sell some drugs to someone up in the country I don't have to worry about it, you're in the car, go. I'll send you the postcode. Wherever that person is, go.' (USG 03)

Those using this method would simply find a car park for the evening. Drugs might be stashed near the vehicle in the shrubbery:

> 'Yeah, it's somewhere in the bush, because the first thing they are going to do is search you and search the car. They are not going to search by because they don't have any reason to. My story, if I say I'm here because I got kicked out by my girlfriend so we're just sleeping in the car, well, once you search the car, you search me, you find nothing you've got to believe my story, there is no other suspicious. I got away a lot, I'll be honest. There is a lot of times the police almost caught me but I got away.' (USG 03)

In Chapter 4 I shall consider how the actual processes of county lines drug supply networks work in reality. This set of dynamics is unpacked in detail in what CL operatives usually refer to as 'grinding'.

4

Grinding

The daily chore of wrapping drugs, bagging them, taking phone calls, delivering drugs to user, 27/7 from a local dealing Hub or trap house is referred to by the runner/dealers as 'grinding'.

Establishing a user database

Upon arrival in a new dealing location the first action is to immediately construct a user database – this will become the County Line phone line. The police commented upon familiar and proven techniques used by CL operatives to build their user database:

> 'On WhatsApp you send a voice message. They talk constantly about building up the round, build up the round, and that just means they come into an area, infiltrate the area and over two to three days, build up a customer database. They go down to [town] High Street at 11 am, sit outside the tunnels. You'll see them going to score drugs. You've only got to approach one of them, "Hello, mate, y'alright, where you getting your gear, blah, blah. What's your name? I sell a bit of gear. What's your number? What's your mate's name? How many mates you got who take kit?" In one conversation you've got six names and numbers of people in town that are addicts. In two or three days you can build up a round. You've only got to give them a couple of free samples that they know your gear is good and they'll spread, "Oh, there's a new fellow knocking about. He's knocking out some gear. His name's so-and-so."' (Police 02)

Product delivery

Product is supplied from parent gangs in London to CL destination, for example seaside town. Product delivery mechanisms depend upon the weight to be shifted. Product is shifted every few days by USG Olders in a car. Alternatively product is dispatched via CL Operatives using cars or public transport. Often transportation functions are considered the work of girls, young women and trusted 'soldiers'.

> 'She'll get there, meet the boys who take the drugs from her and she's catching that cab straight back. Then the boys they will go into the park or field, it's like a nine bar of each so it's all bagged up in G packs, you've got two G packs and then you would have 20 packs of stuff, all in 20s. A 20 being basically £200 for a small little cling film … (mini wraps), yeah, so you would have like five balls of 20 which is a G pack and another five of whatever and then there was just a lot of Food and they would hide a lot of it, they would get through the whole Food and then someone would go to them once every day and a half, go and collect however much it is, bring it back and then it was all right.' (USG 06)

Alternatively, smaller product batches are packaged and taken by runner/dealers alongside money-floats and weapons to commence distribution from a cuckooed property.

Taking the call

The key function of the locally established CL operatives is to ensure the product gets to the user.

Central to this is IT and mobile phones. To manage risk, the deal phone (which receives calls from users) is held back at the parent gang base. Orders are placed using the county line phone number. Orders are then relayed via another call to runner/dealers to specify then execute the deal. As noted by one operative:

> 'You know how it works where we would have a phone, the drug users would ring the line phone, who they've got, the gang's got back in London – make the order with them – they ring us and tell us where to go. We never had that line. We're never in contact with the drug users until we see them. Never

ever. We're not trusted for that. That's how all lines work. The workers on the line, the drug sellers, me, let's say, we're not in contact with them. We never have that line. No, no. So, they're sitting in their bed. Yeah, they might take turns because they don't want to stay up 24 hours even though they're not doing anything and they take the orders, and they make the meeting places, and they send you out to do it. So, they give instructions down the phone, "You're going to meet Dan, he wants three of both. Yeah, white, B, dark, light". So, that's how all lines work.' (USG 01)

Different models of this arrangement operate, however, and it is increasingly common for the local dealing Hub to hold the trapline or phone as this is closer to the marketplace (NCA, 2017b). Product distribution is highly risky.

Business is done using low-tech phones (a Burner phone) which is not trackable:

'A burner phone, one … just a little drugs phone with no internet – just call and text, so generally, they don't use iPhones – too much information to get them into trouble so they can sell it, so it auto-deletes all texts after they've been sent. They're not connected to the cloud so if you lost your iPhone you can get all your numbers back from the cloud … your contacts and photos. Well, the burner phone's not the same so we'll find lists everywhere. When we search people's houses they'll be handwritten on notepads, just name, phone number; name, phone number; name, phone number; name, phone number, so that if they lose their phone they've got a backup. They've got their 150, 100, 200 users on handwritten notes in their house. Then get their new phone from ASDA, £10, go back and sit there then add them all in again, so because that is everything to them, their most important asset is the list of names and numbers for their drug users is going to earn them the money.' (Police 02)

Collating all user data on a single CL phone clearly creates risk. Commonly this central database phone does not leave the parent gang or travel outside home-base, lest it be stolen, lost or confiscated. When this happens then problems occur:

'There is a wealth of intelligence where dealers are beaten up daily and robbed of drugs, cash and phones, and even if the person who's robbing the pone, all he wants, he wants that list, he wants to build up the customer list straight away. So if I nick your phone now and it's accessible and unlocked – burners generally don't have pin locks – I can just get all your list, all your contacts from your phone and put it into my phone. I've now got a hundred drug users that I can supply drugs to. Throw it in the bin, ditch, field, but I've now got myself a hundred users that I can send out texts to every really day and they can buy my drug instead of yours.' (Police 02)

Re-entering lost user data takes time:

'So, it's a procedure. Takes a long time. That is hard to do and it is a headache on your part.' (USG 06)

User/customer data can be exchanged and sold on for £30,000–£50,000 (NCA, 2017b). In business terms this parallels large multi-nationals trading customers account data:

Call centre techniques

An effective CL network must operate an effective phone system whereby demand (requests for drugs) are relayed to a central number operated by parent gangs. Operatives answering the phone alternate daily or weekly, thus users remain unaware to whom they are speaking. One police officer noted similarities to a call centre:

'You speak to users sometimes, you say, "Who are you getting your drugs from?", and they'll say, "Oh, Spider". I'll say, "Who is Spider?" "Oh, it's a different person every time". So the drugs franchise name is just like ASDA – every time you go into ASDA you are served by a different member of staff, and it's exactly the same with the drugs line. The name is X, they're buying it off a name but the person who actually hands them over the drugs would be a different person every time, it's like a call centre, exactly the same. It's very interesting, very challenging.' (Police 02)

Moving product quickly to end-users can prove challenging thus multiple techniques are used which vary depending on location, area size, operatives' ages. Older operatives might invest in hired cars; others use pushbikes.

■ **On foot**

> 'I started the line and I knew once they saw us it was going to kick off because we have to go out doing our promoting and whatever we were going to do. We were on foot, we didn't have a car, we were on foot, every day just walking up and down. Yeah. I got skinny, man, I became skinny. It's a good way to lose weight. So, I was doing all of that.' (USG 06)

■ **By bike/car**

> 'We started having our pushbikes. There was an older boy further down the line. He had a little car, he had a Punto but before that, that was the later stages of the [Name] Squad, you're walking or on a pushbike. They got them when we were up there. And I was never a tomboy anyway so me and the pushbike didn't get along. It's in all weathers and you're exhausted because you're not sitting at home bingeing on Netflix for 24 hours. It is constant. It's constant and some of the places aren't five minutes away, they're 15–30 minutes away.' (USG 01)

■ **Serving up by car**

On occasion, for example when a regular is out of action, runner/dealers 'serve up' from their car:

> 'This car owner is a vulnerable male. Two county lines boys have intimidated him and get him to drive them around. They sell from the back of the car. They are linked to the [Name] network. They'll drive down and deal from the car. They'll both sit in the back of the car and he'll be told to drive around.' (Police 16)

Risk management in distribution

Distribution carries significant risks and runner/dealers must consider: robbery by rival gangs and local users; time and energy levels; travel distances. These are exacerbated by lack of familiarity with new towns. As confidence grows delivery methods might alter. Risk re-assessments are constantly undertaken, for example repeat travel along the same route can draw attention.

> 'Most of the time we'd carry more than that drop. You're taking that risk and we were told not to do that but they didn't know that we were carrying more which is why if we were robbed we'd get into so much trouble because we were told not to do that. If it saved us going back we would take that risk. We would. In this small area of several streets there are probably about five addresses that continually get used to sell drugs. Just in this area alone. Largely cos it is so easily accessed from the arterial roads from London.' (USG 01)

Some runner/dealers compromise their activities by acting contrary to the advice of CL managers.

Plugging

After wrapping and bagging, drugs are passed to runner/dealers who must ensure their wraps are hidden and undetectable during transportation. Many are instructed by Olders to 'plug' the drugs (insertion into the anal cavity). Large quantities of drugs can be stored there. Plugging is a common mode of transporting drugs by both males and females:

> 'This other guy just with 200 shots up his arse, three years ago. He was with a girl, she just held the phone. He had 16 grand in the car. He was a big old boy. I chased him and we was quick. He had his own Taser with him which he threw in the river. He dropped the drugs and managed to get to the car.' (Police 10)

On occasion when Olders enforce sanctions against Youngers, the Older will stab or insert a knife into the anus to cut the rectum opening. This injury prevents further insertion of drugs into their rectum. This sanction is referred to as 'dinking' and is much feared.

Girls and young women hiding drugs in their vaginal cavity are often sexually assaulted by CL managers to locate their drugs. Several female runner/dealers referred to boys forcibly thrusting their hand down their pants and into their vaginas to locate concealed drugs noting this can happen suddenly, randomly and without any pre-cursor warning. More respected females are asked to decant their drugs.

Interview with a runner/dealer

Runner 09 is a 19-year-old British African-Caribbean male detained by police in the company of known users. He denied running/dealing but openly admitted using crack and heroin for a year before stopping. He has been arrested before and says he regularly comes down from East London claiming to stay with his 'aunty' upon arrival. Says the £300 found in his pocket was 'birthday money'. He has been down for three days, claiming to prefer it due to 'too many gangs in Stratford'. After protesting about the stop-search he agrees to a station-based strip-search. He claims he was buying a phone charger when stopped. Throughout engagement he phrased everything in the third person but regularly gave himself away as being heavily involved in CL but not really enjoying it.

Interviewer: So, what makes young lads go OT?

Runner 09:   It's probably because people are offering quite a lot of money 'n that and want young lads. Don't really have the opportunity 'n that, knowwhatI'msaying. Cos if you get excluded from school 'n that, you think 'oh no, what am I gonna do with my life?' No one will really want to work a nine-to-five, – knowwhatI'msaying. People can probably open at £500–£1,000 a week for working for them. You have to work for someone else and yeah.

Interviewer: Do they control you?

Runner 09:   They kinda control you, yeah. Some people start off by just buying people stuff innit, and like acting like their friend 'n that, buying them food, giving them money and this they like, yeah, it's all right 'n that. That's Food as in KFC 'n that, yeah. Or buying them new trainers and that. Then saying, 'We're going to be down here ... it's gonna be fun ... this 'n that ... we're gonna be making money'. So £500–£1,000 – Yeah, yeah, some people will pay that, yeah, yeah, some people will. But some people just like to mess about, people keep them down here and don't pay them a lot and then delay their payment, knowhwatI'msaying. It's risky, that's why I don't wanna be involved no more.

Interviewer: Can you leave if you want?

Runner 09: I think you can get out of it, well, it just depends who you're working for and how they take it. Some people, you would just be straightforward with them and say, 'I don't wanna do this no more', and they will allow it, yeah. Others might say, 'Can't you just stay down here for a week longer?', or something like that.

Interviewer: Would you go OT for a week?

Runner 09: I wouldn't be going OT for a week, no fam, no fam, mainly, it's boring.

Interviewer: Do you use as well as deal?

Runner 09: Boys who go OT mostly they don't use, no, no. The people who mainly use are like the big people, yeah, some of them would sniff 'n that. They wouldn't take crack or heroin.

Interviewer: If you pissed off the big guys, would they come after you?

Runner 09: Depends, if you were stealing from them, they probably would.

Interviewer: Could you put someone else on the line?

Runner 09: Yeah, or say, 'Do you wanna split it? All right, cool', or just drop you.

Interviewer: If you wanted to go back on as before, do you just ring up and say, 'Put me back on'?

Runner 09: Hmm, well, if they've already got someone who is already on, someone who is working better then probably your position will probably be gone.

Interviewer: So if they're a better worker than you, would they keep the other person and let you go?

Runner 09: Yeah, yeah.

Interviewer: I thought when you start working for somebody you had to keep working for them?

Runner 09: Nah, not necessarily.

Interviewer: Do they take a cut?

Runner 09:   Yeah, yeah, they get a bigger cut.

Interviewer: Do they agree it upfront?

Runner 09:   Nah, nah, they will just give you a set amount, like a day – a set amount, like they will pay you a day. They're not going to tell you how much they're gonna make. I get an allowance each day. It depends who you're working for, some people might just give you each week. Some people might just give you every day. It may be every three days.

Interviewer: If you are down here in a flat, how do they re-up?

Runner 09:   How do they do that? I'm not too sure about that … someone brings it down.

Interviewer: Do people carry weapons?

Runner 09:   Hmm, yeah. The drug users around here, they'll try and rob you. Well, some people who stay in a drug user's house 'n that, if you are not getting on with them, might just try and get their friends and group up on you when you're sleeping on the couch, Yeah. It's not happened to me, I'm mean, no, nah, nah, nah. But I heard it happen to someone. That's risky, Yeah, yeah. I heard one time that someone was asleep and when he woke up, there was a knife to his neck and all peoples around him 'n that.

Interviewer: When do you sleep?

Runner 09:   You just take naps. Then the phone goes and you have to be on it again, yeah. It means working a lot, more than if you were doing two shifts at KFC, yeah, hmm.

Interviewer: If they're always ringing your phone, that's a lot of work?

Runner 09:   Yeah, hmm. I was looking for an iPod charger so you can drop me here.

Police drop him off.

Phone batteries deplete quickly during distribution so runner/dealers must ensure they remain fully charged. Failing to do so brings problems upline. While being strip-searched the police offered further intel on the suspect:

> We know he's running with one of the East London gangs, we've arrested him previously. Yep, he's in too deep. There's no way, as far as we know you can just walk away. Once you are in that circle, it's very hard to get out. I'd be surprised if he had anything on him, after we drove past his mate went 'Old Bill' and he spun around again. So if he did have anything, it was dumped. We saw the messages on his phone which showed from him, 'Where are you? I've got cash now – where are you?' We looked at the phone, I guarantee it will come up as the [name] Line. (Police 13)

Runner 09 gets back in the car after the strip-search found nothing.

Interviewer: Are you carrying anything at the moment?

Runner 09:   No, nothing – no drugs, just my birthday [money].

Interviewer: How come you were here?

Runner 09:   Basically, to buy an iPhone charger and I went in the shop for a charger, and people were coming up to me for drugs and asking if I had anything.

Interviewer: Why were they coming up to you?

Runner 09:   I don't know, maybe cos of the way I look 'n that, thought I was dealing, yeah, cos of the way I look. The police keep pulling me in – that's harassment, innit? You saw that.

Interviewer: So, have you run OT before?

Runner 09:   No, but I've been asked to, I'm not gonna lie, but I decided not to do it. It's too risky, it's too bait. Obviously, if I was really into OT, you lot could've arrested me with a pack and I'd get five years, It's just too bait.

Interviewer: So, how do you know if it's too bait?

Runner 09:   Well, say if there's a person like me, you can come down from London, you get what I'm saying? I think it's better if you just grab someone more local 'n that so they blend in. Cos everyone around here, they all know each other. The police know everyone around here. So if they just saw an unfamiliar face, then they're gonna know it's a person from London, know what I'm saying?

Interviewer: But what if we asked to go OT to a different part, would you go then?

Runner 09: To a different part ... ah, but it's all the same through line, they all know each other, innit, these boys, everyone 'n that.

Trap house living

Living in the trap house, the dealing Hub, or cuckooed property presents a range of unfamiliar problems for runner/dealers, much heightened for those away from home for the first time. Difficulties include establishing control in this domestic setting; setting up spaces for bagging and packaging; demarcating living space between tenant/dealers; chaotic internal living arrangements; negotiating sleeping arrangements; separating business from domestic functions and ever-present security risks. A determination is undertaken to ascertain if dealing is achievable from the property and if other CL operatives can safely stay. Soon after arrival the grinding process commences.

Cutting and bagging

The principle operational element of CL is ensuring the product reaches the market. Runner/dealers must cut and bag drugs on an hourly basis to ensure product readiness for immediate dispatch. Requiring skill and practice, this generates street capital for some and anxiety for others:

'I'm awful at maths, numbers and figures. That is my downfall. So, when I learnt I had to start doing stuff like that I thought, "Oh my God, this is a recipe for disaster. This is going to bring you more problems than you're already in". That was short-lived because that takes time. You've got to be in a quiet environment, a clean environment, it can't be messy. You've got to be able to retrieve if things drop. But you are just told, I can't remember how much, you're given an amount, how much has to be in each rock and you measure it up, bag it up, plastic bag, burn it, done. Then fill it with the brick that you have, turns into the pebbles and stuff like that. Keep it separate obviously. You've got crack, you've got heroin. People buy both.' (USG 01)

Conversations during the bagging process generate opportunities for bonding and building trust. They also reflect the age and immaturity of participants:

'We'd talk about anything. Anything like "do you remember when we used to watch" like old TV programmes. Completely childish things that were completely nothing to do with what we were doing, I don't know, it was weird. We weren't like business, no, we were still kids. We were kids doing adult crazy things.' (USG 01)

If a CL manager is onsite during bagging he will initiate checks to ensure due diligence. This often becomes a flashpoint for accusations:

'The little soldier ... never trusted us. Which is a waste of time as well because we'd been checking and double-checking and then he's checking again to also make sure that we're not pocketing anything. The weight is going to add up to the profit which is going to add up, everything is accounted for.' (USG 01)

Learning on the job

Living away in a trap house 'grinding' every day ensures Youngers quickly enhance job skills:

'I can't say how much, I can just say how much the line was making so when we first started I remember the first two weeks I think we made about £30 to £40. It was hard. It took me a while to clock what I was doing wrong. What I'm weighing the shots at. What these guys are weighing the shots at. How good their food is. How good our food is, do you know what I mean?' (USG 06)

Boredom

An unreported aspect of trapping and CL is long periods of unrelenting boredom:

> 'It was boring. Actually doing it, it was, it really was. You're stuck in the house all day.' (USG 02)

Regular runner/dealers recognise this and some bring gaming machines or laptops with them:

> 'On this occasion, no. I'd bring little tablets, anything to keep myself busy but you just sit there, sometimes there's no action, there's no customers for hours and you're just sitting there watching rubbish TV. The weed helps, so it wasn't too bad, it was boring, it really was.' (USG 02)

Boredom, if not managed, creates conflict which impacts profit and generates violence/mistrust. For those staying away for lengthy periods, the parent gang or CL manager may favour or gift the boys. This positive sanction recognises hard work and might include a small bonus or a pair of trainers. Other incentives are 'gift girls' (see Chapter 5).

Operations management

Several different forms of operations management exist with prime objectives being to maximise profit and beat the competition.

Shift working

An advanced CL operation in a thriving market with heavy demand might require shift working for bagging production, call handling and delivery. Shifts include periods of eight or twelve hours and staff effectively 'clock on/off' at shift-end. Failure to arrive leads to pay being docked. This arrangement permits 24/7 operations which ensures greater market share via wider user appeal. Pressure, however, comes in maintaining regular supply to meet both demand and higher expectations.

Limited-hours distribution

Smaller lines or those operating in smaller more limited, provincial or rural markets might only offer a limited drug supply service. Here users are informed purchasing operates between certain business hours, for example 13.00–18.00:

> 'When we started our own thing in [area] we didn't do 24 hours. Phone was on at nine, phone went off at one. Even if the phone was on and we hadn't physically turned it off past one, 9am put the phone right back down again. Everybody knew that. Yeah, phone is on [from] nine to one. As soon as it['s] 9am the phone started. Nine to one. I wonder why one and not midnight?' (USG 01)

Domestic control

The business management side of CLs operates most effectively when the domestic dealing environment is carefully controlled and managed via techniques which ensure a smooth operation, manage expectations and reduce conflict. Techniques include:

■ **Providing a living allowance**
> 'They would give us a little change for the day, like £20 allowance so with that me and my friend would go halves and buy a little £10 worth of weed and then we got £15 for KC or whatever. It was a comfortable life. Especially for that age, eat takeaway every day, loads of money, the respect from the people in the area. It was very attractive.' (USG 01)

Variations or deductions to this allowance constitute domestic control enacted for minor infringements. Discount vouchers and perks are offered:

> 'You get your basic essentials paid for, credit for your phone, lunch, dinner, sometimes breakfast. A little £10 for weed. Yeah, they pay for your train ticket.' (USG 03)

■ **Visitor management**
Residency at a trap house can bring desire for company. Local regular, trusted users and other dealers might drop by to smoke weed and hang out, however, this must be carefully risk-assessed lest trouble arises:

'On one occasion people must have been up there with this little soldier guy who were his friends, not gang-affiliated but his friends, and then it was, "Why are you bringing people here?" And he got very badly beaten for doing that. Of course because "why are you bringing strangers", do you know what I mean? Dumb. He was an idiot. He was a snake.' (USG 01)

■ Remote mothering/surveillance

Social media and IT is used effectively by street gangs and CL operatives to monitor the movements and activities of other young people, particularly young runner/dealers. Wessells (2010: 142) describes how IT provides the ability to constantly track others, using GPS tracking, photo-imaging, location pinpointing and so on, in what is termed, 'remote mothering'. Storrod and Densley (2017: 688) note how such devices now present opportunities for 'remote mothering' – now widely utilised by USGs and CL crews to achieve compliance and control over dealers.

A CL manager exerting control over his runner/dealers might include GPS phone tracking or require staff to report hourly on sales. Others must report by text or WhatsApp when leaving premises or inviting visitors. CL operatives report they must upload photographic images via Snapchat or Periscope or live-stream ordering a pizza for verification. Those working CLs accept this control.

■ On-site supervision

Some CL operations use cooperative management with staff overseeing each other while retaining some autonomy. Other staff require direct line-management and supervision from Hub managers. Such roles are short-term, for example to kick-off a new line, establish working practices; facilitate tighter control on under-performing lines; focus attention on distrusted operatives (for example where profits decline or product goes missing). Runner/dealers describe this as micro-management and added pressure. Some Hub managers live onsite in the trap house while others seek more comfortable accommodation:

'The supervisor would come and stay over. They crash on the sofa or sometimes they'd get a little Premier Inn, sometimes they'd have that luxury. Lucky them.' (USG 01)

This elevates the Hub manager demonstrating rewards and this becomes a position of aspiration. One respondent claimed their presence created tension:

'Just kind of like "hurry up, man", that kind of thing. "Why are you taking so long?" "Have you got this?" "Have you got that?" Just overseeing how things were running really.' (USG 01)

'Hostage-taking'

This form of control refers to collation/retention of incriminating evidence against a young person, rather than physical retention. Referred to as 'online collateral' or 'hostage taking' (Gambetta, 2009) this includes screenshots, images photographs, unguarded comments, voice messages, compromising images or comments which are retained by CL operatives. The purpose being to ensure compliance and control through threats to distribute such collateral and cause embarrassment, exposure or potentially bring recriminations or violence. The increased transmission of sexually explicit texts and images further compromise many young people, especially girls. Such digital artefacts contribute to cyberbullying.

Cumulative effect

The cumulative effect of these living conditions is deleterious to those involved, many of whom are staying away from home for the first time. Physical and mental health can decline quickly, exemplified by poor nutrition, poor dental health, irregular eating of convenience foods:

'They gave you money to eat but not to sit down and go to Goucho's, chicken and chips, McDonald's. Not healthy. No. Awful. And you're not sleeping either. No sleep by itself is bad. No sleep plus you're not eating plus you're terrified, what it does to your body is awful and all these kids go missing all the time, you see them on social media "have you seen" they're all up country. Every single one of them.' (USG 01)

Clothes go unwashed as runner/dealers have no access to washing machines, nor the routines or experience to manage this function:

'Some of these boys are so deprived they get sent down here with a rucksack and nothing to live from, so their pants get filthy and they end up just wearing shorts, or Drill bottoms.' (Police 10)

'No, it was filthy. Stinking. And if you're a girl and it's that time of the month baby wipes can only do that much. It was awful. And this is how it still is now.' (USG 01)

In CLs, inexperience, loneliness, constant undercurrents of fear, threats of violence are accompanied by routine management. Witnessing traumatic violence and drug misuse is highly impacting. Such events underscore this in a world ungoverned by reasoning adults or normal society. Such a realisation compounds isolation and fear, reinforcing the need to develop street capital quickly in order to deal with this. Similarly this strengthens the control of Olders, Elders and CL managers who appear to operate in this world without fear or empathy but with swagger and expertise. As one reflective CL manager noted:

'I was so young and so naive and what you witness and what you see … have you ever seen someone use drugs intravenously before? And take out the needle and their arteries, you can't unsee those things. Or have you ever seen somebody who's shaking, got the shakes? That's traumatic. Someone overdosing and then you're told that you need to inject them if that happened. I didn't inject them because I'm not a doctor and I was just terrified but somebody was, were they overdosing or were they, they had the shakes and they were unconscious and they needed to be injected to bring them round, I think that was it, I don't think they were overdosing, yeah. Like *Pulp Fiction*. All of this, *Pulp Fiction* I watched years after I was doing all that kind of stuff so I was like "what?" it's real. For it to be recognised in films this kind of stuff must happen all the bloody time and it's sad.' (USG 01)

Role differentiation

Effective CL operational management requires role differentiation, for example cutting and bagging to expedite supply by matching skill and dexterity. Role differentiation also assists in task allocation, management and apportioning blame when things go wrong. Over time runner/dealers are expected to master all skills:

'So, I would do the white, he would do the dark, it would take us a good couple of hours. Especially me. When I was up there I wouldn't have my glasses or contacts or anything and I'm being so careful – to get the weight right.' (USG 01)

Role differentiation by gender is variable but seldom matters during cutting and bagging:

'I was treated like a boy, I know there shouldn't be any gender differences but I was treated like a boy. Like one of them. I could do exactly what they were doing. Nothing was off limits for me. Obviously girls are objectified a little bit more obviously with the language and stuff like that.' (USG 01)

Building the line

After arrival, the critical business requirement is to build the line. Some lines are pre-established; others must be built from scratch. At this stage business prowess and entrepreneurial skill are foregrounded as all aspects of marketing and business management are utilised to move products to market, build customer bases and reach end-users. Success demands all lines expand their marketing user-database using tested techniques:

- cold calling by text; on foot to targeted locations; on sight via 'recognition' or prospecting;
- buying in other lines;
- swapping of user details;
- buying in users contacts;
- word of mouth;
- targeted marketing.

Cold calling

This strategy has multiple variations, for example locate a user's number and simply send an unsolicited text (cold calling) identifying one is open for business. This also includes walking the streets and prospecting at recognised locations:

'First two weeks it was a bit complicated going into the betting shops and going into the job centres and these sort of places and to the homeless shelters, it was hard.' (USG 06)

On-sight recognition involves walking around trying to recognise potential users (prospecting). Once identified, they are approached with introductory offers or product samples alongside a branded card with phone details. Experienced runner/dealers will differentiate between different types of users and seek to build a line (database of users) of the best-quality and most reliable users. One CL manager described prospecting thus:

> 'Trying to just recognise Cats. There's a differen[ce] between homeless Cats and ones that are homeless and ones that actually smoke. You can tell by gestures, their hands, the way they move, their mouth, everything you can tell. You can actually tell who's just a normal homeless person, you can tell. When you've been seeing it for so long you know the difference. One hundred per cent the user is the better client. They are the ones bringing you the money. A homeless person will come to you once in a while and he's short when he does come so it's different, cos he's got no money, always short.' (USG 06)

Once entered into phone databases, Prime-users are allocated an asterisk or colour-coded to designate Premium Customer status. This designates high value/frequent purchases, elevated trust or possible onward-selling of bulk product. Lines containing Premium Customers are highly valued. Inexperienced runner/dealers often build lines using multiple names to later find duplicates or homeless people or infrequent users, deemed second-rate. Professionals are Premium Customers:

> 'Everyone smokes crack. All the professionals smoke crack. When we would go and sell drugs and whatever they weren't your typical down and out drug user, they're professionals in their big houses on their big salaries.' (USG 01)

Premium Customers are considered to be demanding:

> 'They smoke it. They wash it up and they smoke it and then they always come back to you and tell you that it wasn't pure because they wash it up themselves and then whatever is left they mix it with bicarbonate of soda and then put it on the heat and then whatever is left is the purity of it, what is actually the real drug so they will always come back to you and say, "No, that was that" and "This was that". I'd say, "Don't argue

with me, what do you want me to do?" They were the hardest customers to deal with.' (USG 01)

Middle-class users hosting parties will often double up by buying in bulk.

Utilising improved customer service

Sleek and effective customer service, where users are valued and treated well, generates a large and loyal customer database, improving customer retention through 'businesslike services' – meaning the difference between customers searching for you, and you searching for customers; between success and struggle (Johnson, 2015; Johnson et al, 2013).

Marketing

The objective of marketing is to increase product sales and market share. Acting as a series of crafted techniques and methods, it orients products to users thus increasing market loyalty, for example:

- **Word of mouth**
  'That was just like word of mouth. Tell people it was really good. Tell them we give amounts, that kind of thing.' (USG 01)

Users are openly utilised to market products by way of an extended business transaction which brings benefits of free drugs:

> 'But normally they'd get a little extra of the stuff that wasn't that pure, but they don't care, they're getting it.' (USG 01)

- **Free samples**
An effective way to nudge into the market is offering free samples:

> 'It's such a market down here. There's new users starting up … they'll come down here and start giving out free testers. Here you go, have a free tester, pass it on to your mate. And the dealers will say, "OK, I'll give you 50 for every phone number in your contacts". So they are paying 50p for every line or number and then they've got all those numbers. Then they

bump a bulk text out saying I'm on 335 so people are selling the numbers on their phones to drug dealers.' (Police 13)

▣ Group text

Group texting is a direct marketing tool achieving effective results:

'On that line over 100 users.... If everyone picks up £10 you've got 100 contacts that's £1,000, something like that.' (USG 03)

This text will communicate important data such as product, quality, and price:

'They send messages out saying "got the peng" as in I've got the nicest drugs, the purest – the peng. That's what we used back then, I don't think they call it that now. So, it was like "I've got the most amazing food" – food is drugs and they'd pay drug users, we would pay drug users with drugs to spread the word that this is really good. It was a lot of advertising as well getting the drug users to advertise among their own group.' (USG 01)

▣ Special offers

Some bulk texts offer time-limited deals, for example Easter or Christmas Packages. Some offers only last two hours leading to a scramble among users to call in quickly to acquire the bargain:

'Special offers would go out [as] bulk text messages "for an hour only", or "buy five get seven" or something like that just to get more customers so they're passing on the numbers. "I've got somebody that's offering more", "Okay, give me their number", so they are going to come back to that person, they're going to have that number. Or they would send bulk text messages out, "Got new food, it's great, got the peng de de" and then you'd pay.' (USG 01)

▣ Business cards

These are professionally printed and distributed containing CL phone numbers. Most are branded with logos often containing multiple numbers leading to the same CL:

'There's a CL called [Name] line. They'd make actual business cards with a picture of a man mowing grass and their number – "call [Name] line". One man had loads of boxes from Vistaprint with cards. We stopped a dealer in this alley and he had cards on him, so they're drumming up business by handing out business cards.' (Police 10)

■ Upselling

Market expansion occurs by widening customer usage, for example making offers attractive enough so that single-drug users become poly-drug users. This is most commonly achieved by selling crack cocaine to long-established heroin users. Alternatively, the quantity of purchase may increase from one rock to five.

■ Using social supply networks

Drug supply also involves social supply whereby local users will gift or sell small amount of drugs to friends and associates. This mitigates risks for those unsure or unwilling to interface with runner/dealers. While only very small profit margins are made through such deals, one user can, if requested by friends, act as a mini-distributor with a tight social circle. A runner/dealer reaching a social supply user might then achieve bigger sales than an ordinary dealer.

■ Building user loyalty

Improved customer service generates reciprocity and trust, for example prompt arrival; hassle-free transactions; contactability; instant recognition; forwarding other users' details; offering introductions; providing local intel re police movements, CCTV locations and so on.

For runner/dealers this includes: knowledge of users' needs/preferences; willingness to give drugs 'on tick'; improved product quality/quantity; improved demeanour; better money-handling; doorstep deliveries:

'Yes, he delivers to your doorstep when you need it. Don't need to go out. Straight to the house. Yes – there are different levels of customer service and how it links to business.' (Police 10)

Another officer commented that branding became important with some lines associated with professionalism and customer service:

'Actually, it's like shopping. If you go into Waitrose, you know you'll get certain brand quality – but if you into a sketchy shop, it's not going to be such a good quality.' (Police 13)

Some levels of customer service are viewed as paramedical intervention, that is, urgent delivery of drugs when needed. Many users refer to withdrawal from drugs as 'being ill', so empathetic service is viewed favourably:

> 'He uses him for his customer service. He's absolutely fantastic. He's never late. If he's feeling ill and has got no money, he'll get it on tick. If he gets a call saying "please help me out" he'll come round and help him out. Because of that, [name] is loyal to him. And that's really all he uses and because of that, he'd come and deliver straight to him.' (Police 10)

All CL operations suffer intermittent supply interruptions leading to customer loss. Branded lines offering better customer service are more likely to win back customers with free or cheaper drugs:

> 'Sometimes they do have to go somewhere else. We took [name] out recently so there was a gap. I think if it did shift, then they'd try to get back in using free gear rather than violence.' (Police 10)

Management risks

A CL manager is skilled in identifying risks associated with line building, for example risk mitigation is an acquired skill signifying street capital, for example getting someone to hold drugs for you. Managers know that the initial stages of line establishment are crucial and misjudgements now are costly later. A skilled CL manager must therefore mitigate all risks, establish and secure lines to commence profitable returns. Early risks here include retaliation from an existing/rival lines; over-exposure of marketing generating police activity; failure to create a market share; transposing profits back to the parent gang.

Throughout this process police activity is common as upper-level CL operatives are involved. Similarly rival CL operatives often take this opportunity to enact robbery as maximum profits can be obtained. Profits are usually returned by car with operatives retaining small parcels of cash to keep within money laundering rules:

> 'Every other day they either come and get the money themselves or we meet them halfway. If returning in a car, there's a certain amount you're allowed to have on you

without being questioned, so like £200/£300/£400. So if they stopped us it's not a big amount, it's separate type thing. I know that still goes on now, I've learnt, and this wasn't when I was doing it.' (USG 01)

Some CL profits are returned via train. Here a runner/dealer (later a high-level CL operative) regretted a missed opportunity for intervention:

'So, one time I was going on the train back to [town] with a load of money and I got stopped by the Transport Police because I didn't even have a train ticket and I was a missing person at this time, missing child. So, they asked me my name and I said Sarah Smith or whatever, here you go, here's a fine, blah blah, Jesus Christ. But then I wanted them to know who I was and take me home at that point, I wanted them to. Yeah, a lot of money.' (USG 01)

Money is also returned to parent gang via Royal Mail:

'They send money in the post as well. So, like in a big package, birthday present, whatever, they're sending it in the post to different addresses in case they were stopped or whatever.' (USG 01)

This function is often delegated to CL Hub managers:

'So, we were always supervised. The little runners on the ground which I started off as are always supervised by the soldier, let's say. He's not quite a big man in the gang but he's got a little bit of recognition, they rate him a little bit so he would always be up supervising with us and trying to oversee things as it was either out of ten days of the week or whatever, so he'd get the money, package it up, go to the post office, or pay a crackhead to go to the post office and send it. He was older than what you are but not as old as the Olders.' (USG 01)

One CL manager spoke glowingly of enjoying collecting profits at weekends. This can include involving several managers and adopting cloaking techniques:

'No, we would always go up there, but not me personally. There was six of us from London that went altogether, so everyone had a part to play. The best journeys were going to collect money … even though you could get arrested for money laundering. People say when you're in nice cars it's a bit hot, but it's not the truth. I think you could be in any type of car, if you're with the right person you're all right. I like to roll around with white girls when I'm driving. Baby on Board sticker at the back is better. Yeah, it's better. So, it's different. There's different tactics. The Game has changed now a lot.' (USG 06)

Case Study: Early problems – USG 03

'My heart was beating, I'm not going to lie, I'm completely new to it and I'm not a gangster at that point, I'd just finished school but I wanted the money. I wanted the money. I'm not going to lie, I wanted the money. It's a lot of money for a 16-year-old. I've never heard of a 16-year-old being paid that kind of money in a week. So, I was like "yeah, I'm going to do it". So, we went up there, the first day I felt so uncomfortable. Very uncomfortable.

'He had a phone he threw away but he had our numbers. So, he would phone us and tell us, "A customer is coming for three and four, get ready, go and meet them at the church" for instance or "at the park" – all within a five-minute walking radius. Everything was local. Rarely you'd go past that. If it was further we would have a driver.

'I did run into a problem after three weeks or a month, I ran into a problem. One day we had a whole batch, I'd say £1,300/£1,400 worth of drugs, all pebbled up, all in little rocks in a bag on the table and I got a phone call from the Older. He said to "Yo" I can't remember the amount but let's say he said "five and six" I'm like "okay". "Go to the church, they're waiting for you now", "No problem". I took it. I put it in my mouth. What you usually do is you put it in your gums or under your tongue, so if the police stop you, you can swallow it. It's hard for them to get it. I took it and put it in my mouth. When I walked out my partner he was sitting down and he got a phone call from the Older and the Older told him to go and hit one as well … to go and do another transaction.

'So, I've gone to walk out, I'm at the main door, something is said to me, "Go back inside and wait for your friend" so as I turn my friend has come to the door so I've looked in his hand, I don't see anything. I said, "Where's all the drugs?" and he said, "Oh, I left it on the table" and we're in the customer's house, there's three of them there, this is only seconds, all of this happened within less than a minute, less than 30 seconds. I've run inside to the front room, all I could see is £150 worth left. Nothing on the floor. Everything is just gone. So, now we've lost over a £1,000 worth of the Older's drugs and I turned to my partner and I told him, I knew we were going to get in some real trouble for that so I said, "Look, you've got to tell the Older that it's not my fault. I got up and I left there, it was your responsibility because you were the last in the house. You've got to tell him", and he's like "okay".

'He phones him and tells him, it's on loudspeaker and the Older has gone completely berserk and he's like, "Okay, go and sell the little bit you've got and then come back down to London". So, we come back down and I think fuck, I didn't want to be there any more, I felt so nervous. The police were everywhere. The police know what you're doing. They're not stupid. They will stop us. No matter what the excuse is, I'm here to see my auntie, when they do a background check and see that you're from [London borough] they put it altogether and think you have to be selling drugs so they're watching us.

'So, I went back down to [London borough]. I let him go and talk to the Older because it was his fault. I knew it was going to be serious. I said, "No, the Older isn't hurting me. I didn't do nothing wrong". I was really scared because this guy is ten years older than me. I just didn't want to play around with him. All I know is that my friend got beat up real bad with a baseball bat. The Older, he phoned and pretended that everything is okay. "You all right? Do you want to work again? Why don't you come back up, you can work with us," he said. "Don't worry about your friend, I don't want your friend but I want you because I know it's not your fault. I want you to continue". I just said no because of how they had beat my friend. I said no. I just gave him my little money left for the week and I'm fine, I'm going home.

'After that experience I got a taste for the drug life. It was too tasty. Too much money. I remember the first week I came back to London from going OT because we'd come back down on the weekend to get the drugs, so we'd be out for a couple of hours and then we'd go back up, the first time I came back down I worked in my area, [Town] in Dorset, and the boys, they were all around me, they were like "you disappeared, I haven't seen you in a week, where have you been?"

'Yeah, just for the first week. The first week before that happened. I pulled out £500, you know, and I was like "look" and they were "whoa, where did you get that from, I know what you did, bring me, I want to be involved". It gave me a really big respect, really big because I wasn't doing what my age was doing, I was doing what the big guys were doing making their kind of money. I bought eight pizzas, four bottles of Hennessey, half a weed and I just gave it to everyone.

"Drink, have a little party on me". Everyone had a lot of love for that. People still remember it today.'

Finance: making money

The key driver for CL networks is maximising profit margins through supply. Financial returns for one line can vary depending upon the age, reach, longevity, coverage, extent, locality of the line; ability to reduce margins, cut costs and the frequency of supply. Profit margins are maintained by criminal exploitation of young people and user-dealers.

Income generation varies from hundreds to several thousand per day. The NCA noted one line made £21,000 per week (NCA, 2015) and report lines making over £5,000 daily (NCA, 2017b). Individual lines can generate profits above £800,000 per year (NCA, 2019a).

In 2015 a single line sale generated above £25,000 (NCA, 2015), and by 2017 lines were sold for £50,000 and £30,000 (NCA, 2017b). Leasing arrangements undertaken for around £10,000 a month can produce revenue streams of £5,000 daily (NCA, 2017b). Accurate data on such transactions remain vague. Profits depend upon market coverage, user numbers, dealer numbers and number of operational lines:

> 'But as well you might not be making £5,000, you could be making a lot more especially if you're not in one restricted area, more out, not the towns but the whole, how many workers you have. A rock is a tenner. So, if you were to buy more, a lot, let's say five and five you could have ten for the price of eight or something like that.' (USG 01)

Calculating weekly profits is done by locally based Hub managers. This involves calculating incoming income from users; outgoing payments to staff; any 'float' or balance needed to cover living costs; break–even points; final net profits. Phone recording of transactions is not favoured. As lines can have several managers/operatives working shifts, losses arise easily. This causes conflict. Often experienced operatives have strong skills at mental arithmetic. Managers can mitigate losses by passing deficit downline to runner/dealers then force them to recoup losses. Others retain details mentally:

> 'Everything is in my head. I used to just keep track of everything but that's my week. Everyone operates different on

their week. Me, I think I used to lose a lot in terms of money on my week. Everyone does, but I think my week was a bit, I don't know, I just used to ... it's different. I used to be more [caring]...' (USG 06)

One USG respondent was boastful of his workers, market coverage and profit:

'Already, it's about fuckin' 30 or 40 bags, yeah? It's a team of eight, there's about 30 or 40 bags we're bringing in. £1,000, Yeah, I work with n****rs from all over, knowhatI'msaying. As I say, there's a team of them, man, it's not just one man, they've got bare youts working for me man. I got bare youts, it's not a joke to me. I'm out here getting doe, you understand. I'm not playing games out here. From the south of the river to the east of the river, you understand what I'm saying?' (USG 10)

Another ex-CL manager used coded language regarding his line but talked of job-sharing:

'Yeah, 500 of each, so in £10 shots, 500 whisky and 500 brandy I left him with. We used to take turns in weeks so one week would be mine, one week would be his. That's how we were doing it. Saturday and Sunday together made £400. Monday it made £600. Tuesday it was £800 and kept going until we started making £2,100 a day, and then it just became crazy and then we were constantly picking up half a nine of each and just getting through that.' (USG 06)

The coded language of dealing refers to money deals. Slang and terminology is regionalised and localised with drugs commonly termed 'food':

'No, no, we were picking up, half a nine is a lot in terms of whisky, Z, I don't know how much a Z goes for now, maybe it's £1,400. A Z is basically like, at my time, it was £1,100, or £1,200 and you would bag that up into £10 shots. And then you can take £1,200 away and your profit would be £1,400 or whatever. So, a Z is £1,200, we had four Zs so that's what half a nine is. Yeah. That's four Zs together equals half a nine. Yeah. And we had the same with half a nine of brandy as well. No, brandy is the brown, heroin. But we were cultural people so we used to call it a [adan] and [milo] so it's different, that in

Somali means light and dark. So milo is dark. So, that's what we used to call the whisky, we used to call the brandy [adan] and [milo] just so people don't know. We used to say it over the phones and stuff. That's what we used to call it. I started making a lot more money. I remember it never got higher than £1,200 or £1,100 it would always stay between that, but by then our line is doing 24 hours as well so it was good. It gave us that edge as well.' (USG 06)

One reformed operative acknowledged that extensive financial returns gravitates upward and down through the hierarchy with money laundered through small businesses:

'[the bosses] … they're making up to £8,000 a day now. It's really like that. Yeah, it's crazy now. And the top, top people who are laundering the money, a lot of it, you see these bagel shops keep popping up everywhere, bagel shops, hairdressers, sunbed shops, nail shops, all of it's going into stuff like that. So, there's so much money, so much revenue, it has to go somewhere, it's not a pile of cash. So, these top, top guys they're established people. They are not just Road Men sitting in a house buying trainers. It's so much more than that. At the bottom, the people putting their lives on the line, the front line workers are poor little young exploited children. They are happy with the little bits they are getting because it's not nothing as I was getting, they were getting money so they can buy a pair of trainers for £100 and that's good for them. That means everything to them.' (USG 01)

She reports that since leaving CL profit margins have increased significantly:

'Yeah, because the money that is being made has gone up. So, I suppose these older lot can afford to give the little boys and girls a little bit more. They were done, or they still are done in rocks, so a tenner.' (USG 01)

Paying runner/dealers

An effectively managed CL must ensure regular payment to runner/dealers. Expectations are this is handled efficiently but in practice it is often intermittent, in cash minus any deductions:

'No, no, we used to do everything ourselves. There's like four or five of us and we each had a week and then we also had some kids with us as well. Yeah, pay them by day. I can't remember, could have been £100–£80 a day and they can get essentials. They've got perks on the block so they can buy weed or Pizza Hut to get through their shift. The limit would be ... because the line is already losing out in terms of making deals, so three for £25 or six for £50, because people are coming for deals so we're always at a loss in terms of ... knowwhatImean? And our profit really comes from brandy (heroin) so it's a bit, the whisky (cocaine) just gives it a tip, so it was a bit different. So these kids, giving them £40 and then paying them it's a lot and a line had to be making a certain amount for us to actually be able to not feel that as much. But I would feel that more if I was just moving a Z a day, do you know what I mean?' (USG 06)

One ex-CL operative revealed resentment about being underpaid:

'We were bringing in at first £3,000 a day, let's say ... a lot of money. We weren't getting a wage out of that. The very first time they decided I could go home after two weeks it was "here you go, babe, thanks for that" a box with trainers that were size ten – I'm a size five. Disrespect! But what was I going to do? More and more it may be like £50 or whatever, or "here's a bit of change". No more than that. They are getting £3,000 a day sitting at home doing nothing.' (USG 01)

Laundering

Profits are laundered, cleaned, washed, managed carefully and fully accounted for. Deposits are made into savings accounts of family and friends and churned quickly through nail bars, hairdressers, barber shops, small garage-repair shops or cafes to distance operatives from the money trail. Recently examples have emerged of localised laundering through bank accounts of young people and school children whereby they are enticed or coerced into opening accounts which then receive several thousand pounds. By the time parents become aware cash is relocated or withdrawn.

Moving up: building CL experience and skill

All CL operatives strive to operate their own line – a process called Moving Up. First they must build skills and street capital to progress. However, there is no timeframe for this and movement is highly situated and subjective. Several influencing variables are identifiable, which when mastered will help elevate status: Loyalty; Efficiency; Honesty; Availability; Management ability; Investment. Operatives quickly become experienced in all aspects of the customer base:

> 'Oh, yeah. And now, before I was young anyway, but now I could spot a drug user, even if they are a surgeon, you know. You just know. They're everywhere.' (USG 01)

Some advance to line management quickly via emotional intelligence, sills or smarts:

> 'I think there's never a kind of template that fits everything. They went to this warrant and a 19-year-old man from London was there and a 15-year-old kid, and that kid was controlling it. The 19-year-old was kind of a bit docile, a bit not quite with it, everything about that 15-year-old kid pointed to the fact that he was controlling what was going on.' (Police 06)

Some operatives with deep exposure to USGs recognise their own personal leadership qualities, or withdraw to become indie-trappers. Some Youngers try to take over from Olders as CLs have opened routes for fast-streaming advancement where Youngers thrive. Olders respond to this with violence, as one commented:

> 'Trying to rise up, thinking they're bad boys. Gun shot dem pussyholes!' (USG 09)

Market consolidation and expansion

Evolution of CL business models (see Table 2.2) includes changing dominant strategic outcomes, from maintaining the Status Quo – formalising – professionalising – diversifying. Movement between Models #2 and #3 generates multiple opportunities for market expansion leading to adaption of business practices and changed business models – all driven by profit maximisation. As model evolution accelerates, business principles (see Chapter 1) elevate in importance, and finesse. However, for most, market expansion remains dominant.

Maximising line profitability presents several business options for employment individually, in tandem or comprehensively, by adapting the marketing mix. Each is tested for efficacy (see Table 4.1):

Table 4.1: Options for line expansion

Activity	Description
Improve customer service and professionalism	Offering improvements to the dealer/user interface with a focus on customer satisfaction and loyalty
Expand product offerings	Retain the same market but expand range of products supplied and/or quality of products
Expand market coverage through multiple lines	Open series of branch lines in the same market area or fresh new markets
Split the line	Halve the line or split with mates
Consolidate with other lines	Strengthen branded lines by taking over smaller or less effective lines in same location or across wider markets
Build patch loyalty	Increase user loyalty to line/brand
Hostile takeover	Taking control and management of rival line by force
Staffing adaptation	Changing staff roles and staff usage by evolving business model
Re-invest	Plough profits back into the line

Improve customer service

Adjustments to the 'Four Ps' – Product, Price, Place, Promotion (see Chapter 1) creates multi-variate matrix of options which when tweaked can radically alter customer service. Through model evolution Professionalism becomes critical to the business model and casual working arrangements disappear, as noted by one manager:

> 'No, no, it's much more rigid. As you climb the scale people do it more respectfully towards a proper business, how a business should be run. You're up at eight o'clock, you finish by eleven o'clock at night but you can guarantee within those times you're working. If you've got something that you need to handle in that area then you phone them in advance, let them know in advance, go and wait for something else to come up. That's highly regarded. At lower levels where you're

doing weed, you're your own boss, they don't have that many customers anyway. On a white line I can serve ten people in five minutes.' (USG 03)

Expand product offerings

Largely associated with Model #4 – Market and product diversification – here adjustments include retaining the same market but expanding product ranges and/or the product quality.

This pushes boldly towards expanded market share by: upselling different products; increasing product ranges; better quality ranges (different grades or strengths); offering the same product to different customer groups, for example offering crystal-methamphetamine to the recreational party crowd; or simply offering more products, for example moving into MDMA or Fentanyl. Market diversification is bounded by end-user social positioning and habitus, expectations and recreational habits. As one CL operative candidly expressed:

'I'm thinking of moving into steroids and Xanax.' (USG 10)

Expanding market coverage through running multiple lines

A fast route to expanding market share is to operate more lines into the same single location, sub-region, or in fresh new markets:

'[Name] was in charge running Django line but it also goes under different names. But its linked to different networks, so it could be three people running it, all joined together. He'll do Django, then Max his friend will do Max, and another mate will be Pricey. They'll do things together, all run different lines but will do things together successfully. Or it could one day be Max and then other days Django, so there are all different ways around it. Obviously that's who he is affiliated to. He was driven around in his car by a drug user.' (Police 16)

Branch-off networks

If wholly fresh lines are unavailable or if market demand exceeds supply then branch-off lines might be initiated:

'Biggest line at the moment? – the Peckham Guns 2 and they've got branch-off networks – all busy.' (Police 10)

Case Study: Expanding market coverage by opening multiple lines and adapting staffing – USG 06

This case study from a USG Older and CL manager reveals the challenges of opening up a new line in the Midlands after job-sharing a line with friends on rotation. After realising using black runner/dealers was a risk he switched to recruit local white boys:

'My new line in [area] just blew up, it just blew proper. Started going crazy. And the people that were selling it over there were locals, were nerds, if that makes sense?

'When I've came over I'm with a few people from London because I brought some of my London friends with me and it was proper different, it was good. I was getting two different incomes, because keep in mind, once I've done my week in my area in the borough, I've got four weeks until it's my week again. So, I would make £8–9,000 from my week, and then I've got a month to wait but I'm still getting a lot of money, to get £8,000 a month, so it was like I was a service manager. It's crazy. Yeah, so then I went to [area] because I wasn't doing enough. I wanted to start something else, I had the money, it's mine, I'm starting it, it's mine so I went there and took a couple of boys from London. Started that line. That line was making about £3,000 a day – crazy, and quick as well, within three weeks the line was popping but it came with lots of problems that area. You feel comfortable in your own borough, you know? I know who's who. I know what cars are what. Even the different class of Cats. There they were sarcastic, not trustworthy – look like they will set you up themselves if you say the wrong thing to them.

'Yeah, so you're not in control. It was different. I was building rapport, I was the nice guy, I would always give them deals if they come short or whatever they are. I just did because I was doing the hand to hand myself at the beginning. When I started getting kids in there and then my kids don't actually stay there, they're from London, they're like "you know, this place is a bit crazy". So then I'm trying to get local little white boys or little skater boys to go round to certain areas, to the parks and stuff and I would catch little boys smoking weed telling them, "Do you make £150 a day?" and one of the kids stood up and said, "Yeah, yeah, of course" so I said to him, "Come and let me chat to you" so I started speaking to him, getting in his head in terms of brainwashing or coerce, or whatever they call it.

'I started speaking to this kid and I said to him, "I like the way you are, have you got any more friends that are like you?" and he's like, "Yeah, yeah, [name] is like me", I said, "Bring [name]", and they'd come and see me, I'd take them to a cafe, speak to them both and I'd tell them I will pay you this money, come and do this line it's nine to nine. I'll pay you this much and they were like "all right".

'It only worked out for a short time until their dads came in caravans a week later looking for us. Not caravans like white vans and stuff – looking for us and it was crazy. Yeah, but they could never find us. We were always in like Canary Wharf and penthouses, we're not in Lincolnshire. But that line lasted about nine months and then I turned it off. I made a lot of money. Me and the boys made a lot of money out of that line.'

Splitting the line with a mate

Splitting the burden with friends ensures regular downtime:

> 'I got seven days in a week from my week and I would do everything. Come Saturday and Sunday I'm using that money for the reload for the next person, but they will already have theirs but that money would be there for the third person to do their third week. He can go get his food while he waits for this guy to get through his week. I would go with whatever profit I had, like £8,000 after I spent on trainers, and I would actually relax and do nothing, and go back.' (USG 06)

Line consolidation

Model #3 notes line consolidation brings economic benefits to those seeking local market domination:

> 'Like I said, it's all about making money.' (USG 11)

This brings economies of scale permitting managers to shift staff from one line to another. Trap houses, bandos and cuckooed properties can be rotated more easily; travel arrangements can be simplified with grouped travel arrangements established.

Line consolidation creates market disruption or local or regional turmoil. While parent gangs try to keep this managed things can move suddenly catching people out, for example alliances shift; old lines of accountability and networking no longer fit; trust changes. This brings market fractures creating suspicion and distrust. This generates violence in host towns and reverberates back upline.

Re-investing back into the line

Expansion of a county line drug supply network revolves around networking links and financial capital for re-investment, as in this example:

> 'I remember my friend saying, "I need a partner. I know you do this money thing … I need a partner" and this was the first chance to be a boss properly. I had my own line before where I had workers but I mean in terms of white and B, crack and heroin, this is my first chance to be top of the food chain, to see what was going on. I said yeah. I worked it. After serving customers for two months we had £1,000 and he said, "Invest back into the line, be a partner and we'll just take everything 50/50, all the profit 50/50". I said "no problem" and gave him back the money. From that moment I got my godbrother involved and got a couple of people involved. We ended up having four workers, two cars, rotating in [area] and they were just rotating selling drugs. One would come down and one would go up, a 24-hour line. Generating a profit of about £900 a day.' (USG 03)

Re-investment varies depending upon maturity, long-term outlook, family commitments and so on.

Patch loyalty

Patch loyalty involves developing user loyalty to the line alongside awareness of, and loyalty to, the specific patch operated by that runner/ dealer. This is different to loyalty to one runner/dealer as lines can have several dealers working the same patch, or branded line, thus they seek loyalty to the dealing patch. Within this context shifting user loyalties in a competitive market generates violence:

> 'Another time loads of dealers came onto their patch. The first boy came back and said, "You've let 'em onto our patch". Didn't take it out on the dealers but they forced their way in and stabbed two of the users and hit one round the head with a hammer. So three users in there, all attacked cos another dealer – whether they were trying to rob the dealers or just take it out on the users – for letting them onto their patch. And that has become more and more common. It's all gang-related stuff. Patches and loyalty, I suppose. Being loyal to that network, otherwise you'll pay the price. All the users want is to use.' (Police 10)

Hostile takeovers

Management means constant appraisal of competition via intelligence. Any rival line considered weak can be targeted for a hostile takeover. As an acknowledged risk this reinforces managers' desire to ensure their own CL is tightly controlled. One respondent details a CL operated by Jamaicans from London which was taken over by Albanians:

> 'We had intelligence that in that line the person had had their phone taken, been beaten up, had their drugs taken from them and then Albanians then took over that line and customer base. So the Albanians done identified this dealer, waited for him, beat him up, took his drugs and phone. They then had a perfect customer database so they've got the phone, got all the customers in the database. They sent out texts to all users in there "best of both 24/7, Dave/Gina", and in one fell swoop had the intelligence. Line taken from him and new people with considerable clout… But it's not often that that happens because there would normally be retribution for that. We didn't see any repercussions against the Albanians. No. No. but that is a common theme now as well.' (Police 02)

Such actions generate retaliation – often deferred – or played out upline:

> 'They know not to take over, but if they try to take over, then obviously it's gonna get sticky, innit. We're not gonna sit here,

you have to retaliate and it comes at a price, it always comes at a different extent. One time maybe they run off, then the next time someone could be ended up dead, stabbed, because these days you get a lot of young youths that you see that are carrying shanks and that.' (USG 12)

A move to user-dealers

Evolving models from Model #2 to Model #3, from Model #3 to Model #4 is not pre-determined and some models get stuck. Progression is sometimes a business necessity arising from a series of factors already affecting the line:

- declining profitability;
- need for greater control of staff;
- local hostility;
- level of attrition among current staff;
- need to blend in more regarding ethnicity or age;
- lack of local intelligence.

To achieve successful market expansion these issues must be resolved. Maintaining competitive advantage is now paramount. Resolution of these problems is best achieved by changes to staffing arrangements leading to a change in business model. Staffing changes at local Hubs can create significant impact in profitability. Profit maximisation is now best achieved by turning local users into user-dealers (Coomber, 2006; Potter, 2009; Coomber and Moyle, 2014; Moyle and Coomber, 2015; 2016). Primarily this greatly improves local intelligence and permits opportunities for tighter line control (see also Chapter 2).

CL operatives employ users to achieve strategic advantage. Motivations include:

- cheap local labour working for less and generating savings;
- users are disposable if caught;
- having local area/user knowledge = local intelligence;
- ability to expand lines through local networks;
- less likely to set up a line themselves or run off with money;
- being vulnerable, controllable and compliant;
- usable as hired muscle;
- ability to blend in as often same ethnicity;
- easily manipulated via debt into working for free.

Dealers assume users are untrustworthy so address this via tight control, including supplying limited product; demanding constant reporting and surveillance; physical and mental intimidation.

Multiple motivations also exist for users deciding to become user-dealers: though often choices are constrained with many feeling intimidated/pressured. Motivations include:

- generating income or obtaining drugs to sustain their habit;
- a desire to perform a regular 'purposeful' role as opposed to shoplifting, burglary or begging;
- an opportunity to earn a level of 'respect' among the user community;
- a reason to move around the area and reduce isolation;
- provision of perks such as a push-bike or food voucher;
- a crude belief they are forging links to local power-brokers or edging closer to them;
- obtaining a regular drugs supply without the normal difficulties;
- building knowledge of other users to later trade as intelligence;
- ability to use personal networks to build the line and add value.

The creation of a cohort of user-dealers results in some becoming elevated among their peer group, creating a user-hierarchy which might not have previously existed. In this way the homeostasis of the normally docile user community is ruptured. The fragile equilibrium is fractured and trust evaporates. This has further exacerbated localised violence.

Case Study: User becomes a user-dealer – User 04

'I did it for about a month. Well, it was one of my friends … see, I was round there quite a bit and he knew the person who was running before so he just asked us. Well, I was going there to score as well, knowwhatImean. So we built some trust up, knowwhatImean. I got paid in cash or gear but I took the gear. I preferred the drugs, yeah. I just wanted to get my own gear. Yeah. I used to run for them. They'd say, "Do you want it in shots or do you want it in money?" I used to get the gear as it was easier. You know, like, it was there all the time. That's what made me want to do it so you don't have to go out shoplifting. To be honest, I was thinking – well, if I don't do that, I won't get into trouble with that. Obviously I could get into trouble running – a lot more trouble, knowwhatImean.

'I'd walk, or I'd have a push-bike, yeah. Half the time it was walking, half time push-bike. But really most of the time the people were so close. They were only down the road. I'd go back and forth all the time unless I was out in which case it was just given. I don't like to carry a lot. Sometimes about ten and ten, or 20 and 20. It all depends. That could be one or two drops. It depends on what people buy. I'd do it all morning. It was a while ago but there was a choice of people always about. Now when I wanted to get something a few weeks back I really struggled to get it, knowhatImean. It all depends who's about or working the block, then you can get it.

'I never lost the money or got into debt, but there was a time I said [to the dealer] that I got robbed but I never got robbed. You do that. The person running tends to get into trouble with the dealer, knowhatImean. So a few times I'd seen the Old Bill and that. I never used to nick big amounts, knowwhatImean. It was little things like three and three. A fellow I used to work with ... some of these guys are really violent ... I knew someone come back and he got robbed ... made him strip naked and made him shit, then looked up his arse and that, knowhatImean, in case he'd plugged it. There are some nasty people out there who do these things. You don't wanna get involved, if I'm honest, it's a nasty game. Definitely trouble.

'Quite a bit of drugs round here though, perhaps not so much now. I've heard it's harder to score now because the police took out a few people. There ain't as many as there used to be. Before I used to be able to score at six or at seven in the morning. Now you're lucky if you score before 11 in the morning. There's the odd person, but ... not a lot of 'em [dealers] but if they do come down then they come down from London and come early. The local people is down here early. And they come down until they run out then they go again. It's not constant like before – so they [the police] are doing a good job. When I scored it was from local people or guys coming down from London.'

Closing the line/moving on

At times a CL manager will decide a line is not worth keeping or will sell it on. Several factors influence this decision, notably profitability and increasing risks:

> 'I was making money but didn't like to stay there, no. I started the line and got out of there. I wasn't there, I never stayed there. I ended up giving the line to two little boys at the end. It just became too hot. My boys kept getting arrested and me just driving up there to sort shit out. Was just becoming long.' (USG 06)

In Chapter 5 I move on to consider how each county line is tightly managed and controlled by a County Lines Control Repertoire which involves criminal and sexual exploitation and debt bondage.

5

Controlling the Line:
Exploitation and Sanctions

This chapter considers how CL managers employ strategic and tactical actions to control their lines to keep them active and thriving: firstly, through exploitation and; secondly, via the County Line Control Repertoire which provides multiple tactical sanctions for CL operatives to control the line.

Exploitation by street gangs and organised crime networks is UK-wide, and the NCA Briefing Report (2016) noted 80 per cent of reporting areas confirmed exploitation of children aged 12–18 by gangs. Within county lines, exploitation of both adults and young people is fundamental to all CL business models and is essential to achieving the profit margins making CL models a profitable enterprise.

Forms of child criminal exploitation (CCE) can take different forms and also operate within general criminal behaviours. Within CLs, however, it can include: grooming and selection, recruitment, running drug lines, interlay carrying drugs, hiding or carrying weapons, money laundering and so on. Increasing job differentiation within CL models offers specific roles for young people and as models evolve exploitation can magnify, not least because young people are exploited by way of mitigating risk for older USG and CL affiliates.

Exploitation is often targeted towards the most vulnerable who are exploited by way of risk mitigation and risk avoidance strategies employed by Olders. A USG Older with years of acquired street capital can detect such vulnerabilities lying beneath street swagger, bravado and attitude. For local charities and agencies, however, such 'in-your-face' presentation can mask vulnerabilities. Moyle (2019) invites us to reconsider vulnerability within the nexus of victim/offender and revisit the definition and application of the term. Windle et al (2020) in their most recent work, '"Vulnerable" kids going country', talk in-depth about the perception, definition and interpretation of 'vulnerability'. They further note that young people involved in running county lines frequently present front line practitioners with a hard-bitten street-tough exterior that mitigates against viewing them as either vulnerable or victimised. It is likely that such presentations represent adherence to the street code (Anderson, 1999) and to street capital and immersion into the social field, which over time inhibits ability to 'code-switch' (Anderson, 1999, Harding, 2014: 197).

Child criminal exploitation

Child criminal exploitation (CCE) is still an emerging term and not yet widely recognised or used. The national Home Office Guidance on child criminal exploitation states:

> Child criminal exploitation is common in county lines and occurs where an individual or group takes advantage of an imbalance of power to coerce, control, manipulate or deceive a child or young person under the age of 18. The victim may have been criminally exploited even if the activity appears consensual. Child criminal exploitation does not always involve physical contact; it can also occur through the use of technology. Criminal exploitation of children is broader than just county lines, and includes for instance children forced to work on cannabis farms or to commit theft. (Home Office, 2018)

In other words, CCE involves a child 'being exploited and receiving something in return for completing a, often criminal, task for someone else' (Home Office, 2019). Three component elements are commonly involved in CCE: a) pull factors: children receiving something as a result of completing tasks, for example money, status, a sense of safety or drugs; b) advantage, financial or otherwise, to the groomer; c) control: grooming and threatening the child (Home Office, 2019). The Children's Commissioner report Keeping Kids Safe (2019) calls for child criminal exploitation to be made a national priority.

Aside from the government definition, the Children's Society (2019: 4) offers a pithy definition from young people: 'when someone you trusted makes you commit crimes for their benefit'. The report, Counting Lives from the Children's Society (2019) sets out this agenda effectively noting there is no statutory definition of child criminal exploitation. They note that children are targeted via social media and face-to-face contacts with those experiencing or presenting vulnerabilities at increased risk. This includes those distant from their families; under-performing or excluded from school; growing up in poverty; or those with learning difficulties. The report also notes that CCE can be easily masked or hidden by how young people present or 'act out' along with issues such as age, gender, ethnicity and background. Agencies can often fail to recognise CCE due to such masking characteristics, and thus responses to CCE vary hugely from child to child and across agencies.

In 2018 the Children's Commissioner for England, Anne Longfield, noted 30,000–50,000 young people could be affected by the expansion of over 1,000 branded CLs and over 2,000 individual CLs (cited in the Children's Society, 2019).

The report by the Children's Commissioner titled, 'Keeping Kids Safe' (2019) makes several statements about susceptibility to CCE among young people and USG affiliates. Reporting on research into 25 Local Safeguarding Boards in 'high-risk' areas, the research identified a dearth of local information on levels of gang activity, little proactive planning by stakeholders and insufficient numbers of Serious Case Reviews into gang-related killings. The report estimates around 27,000 children in England identify as a gang member, with only a fraction known to children's services. A reported 34,000 children know gang members who have experienced serious violence in the previous 12 months.

Child criminal exploitation in county lines can often commence with recruitment to the line. Robinson et al (2019) identified that criminal exploitation also occurred in the county lines networks they studied in Merseyside and Glasgow. They further noted the challenge of young people self-identifying 'exploitation', pointing out some of their research participants readily acknowledged they were being 'used', but rejected 'victim-status' labels while emphasising the positives of county lines running. Grooming techniques are favoured by some but this can also include more straightforward intimidation or coercion:

> 'So we'd been to the letting agency and said we had concerns that she was being cuckoo'd and blah, blah, blah. They said, "There's the key, let yourself in." So we went in, walked up the stairs and she's at the door with some black guy standing behind it. He's seen me and legged it. So we ran up the stairs and he threw himself outside the top window. He had 70 shots down his pants. Whenever we go up, we go front and back so we've got some cover. He's landed and my friends had a big fight with him and he's bust his leg. He's a 14-year-old lad. And basically, he's fully admitted he was up near a park

in Croydon and a car rocked up and said, "Do you wanna earn £200 a day?" He said yeah. So they said, "Meet me here later and I'll drive you to an address". He just got dropped down here by car. He's probably never been out of Croydon or London before. Well, they said to him, "Do you fancy going to an address five minutes down the road?" and then once he got in the car he said, "Where are we going?" They said, "You're going down to [DISTRICT], mate". He told his mum that he was staying at his cousin's home. I think it's the initial "oh, wow, I've got £150 in my hand" but before you know it, you're stopped by the police with a couple of shots in your hand then it's…. And you lose a couple of the shots then it's, "Right, you owe us. You've been nicked. So you've got to work that debt off". You're constantly in their debt.' (Police 13)

Operatives are aware the threat is there, and is most likely to be carried out:

'Yep, well, it's all intimidation. They know where they live so they say if you don't work for me, I'll go round, I'll kill your family, I'll do this and that and you think, well, they could be bullshitting you or it could be about to happen. They end up in that cycle.' (Police 13)

Missing children and recruitment

The connection between gang involvement and missing children, that is, children who go missing overnight from home or from care (Missing People, 2019), remains under-researched. Definitions are tricky in this sub-topic and it is important to determine if one is referring to a child missing in care or a looked-after child?

The Children Act 1989 defines children in care (looked-after children) thus:

A child is looked after by a local authority if a court has granted a care order to place a child in care, or a council's children's services department has cared for the child for more than 24 hours. (Children Act, 1989)

A child who is 'missing from care' refers to 'a looked-after child who is not at their placement or the place they are expected to be (for example, school) and their whereabouts is not known' (Department for Education, 2014). In 2017–18, over 11 per cent of looked-after children in England were reported missing on at least one occasion. Also looked-after children are more likely to have repeat missing episodes, for example in 2017–18, this averaged six missing incidents, compared to 2.6 missing incidents for children who are not in care (Missing People, 2018: 8).

'Repeat missing' as a term also poses definitional problems with varying definitions used across different police forces. Some define 'repeat missing' as 'three times plus' in a 90-day period, but some define it as anyone missing more than once. Some forces lack any definition at all. Identification of 'repeat missing' remains critical as it sets the threshold for commencing inter-agency intervention (HMIC, 2016). For a more detailed exposition of this topic please see Missing People (2018).

According to Rees et al (2011) from the Children's Society, 80,000–100,000 children aged under 16 run away overnight each year. The Catch 22 report *Running the Risks* (Sturrock and Holmes, 2015), offers a comprehensive overview criticising scant government guidance on this issue. They also note that missing episodes if identified early and understood can be a critical warning sign and potential intervention point. However, all too frequently interventions emanate from the criminal justice service ignoring exploitation and victimhood. The Catch 22 report rightly concludes that gang involvement and going missing-from-care are strongly linked to CL, fear, intimidation, interpersonal relationships, relocation and the care system. Central too are concepts of debt and criminal exploitation, however, 'missing episodes linked to relationships and sexual exploitation tended to be specific to females' (Sturrock and Homes, 2015: 63). Research by Firmin (2010; 2011) informs us that girls and young women can be affected by gang activity and criminal exploitation through personal relationships with gang members even if not themselves gang-affiliated.

Beckett and colleagues (2013) identify that risk-taking is increased through association with peer groups, though for many risks are not fully assessed or managed (Farrington, 2003). The Catch 22 report identifies exploitation; recruitment and coercion as overarching themes emerging from their research into missing children, each linking to criminal/sexual exploitation within CL and USGs. While concepts of recruitment are nuanced it is clear various push/pull factors determine decisions to go missing, notably domestic conflict and perceived need to acquire street capital.

Links to the care system and relocation policies are also elements facilitating or exacerbating missing episodes.

The UK Missing Persons Bureau (NCA, 2017c) reports that data for missing-from-care episodes was collated from 37 out of 43 forces in England and Wales for 2015–16. In this period some 43,564 incidents of going missing were recorded involving 10,681 children (noting some children go missing multiple times). Of these 3,470 children from London were reported missing from care. While data quality for this data set has many limitations it illustrates the enormity of the challenge of children missing from care.

The CL business model requires regular availability of young people as recruits into the line. This constant supply is needed to ensure business is neither slowed nor interrupted. Children going missing-from-care are vulnerable and at risk of targeted recruitment by USGs for exploitation into CLs (Sturrock and Holmes, 2015). This issue has, however, been slow to reach national policy and public debate. The All-Party Parliamentary Group (APPG) on Missing and Runaway Children and Adults, chaired by Ann Coffey MP has, alongside the independent charity Missing People, sought to raise awareness of this issue. The APPG Inquiry (2016), and the APPG Briefing Report (2017) both report that grooming for criminal exploitation is not routinely identified during missing episodes; young men are often reported as 'no apparent risk'; with those going missing thought to have elected this outcome. Both reports advocate authorities utilise improved understandings regarding child sexual exploitation to better understand risks and threats.

In 2016 the NCA (2016) noted sexual exploitation of young females was under-reported while recognising missing children were vulnerable to exploitation. By 2018 (NCA, 2019a) pupil referral units, special educational needs schools, foster homes and homeless shelters were all identified as key locations for recruitment into county lines.

'Sent away' children

A key contributing factor to CL recruitment is placement of young vulnerable children in care settings many miles from home. Young people can be housed in long-term or temporary accommodation scores or hundreds of miles from parental homes, leading to isolation, depression and increased vulnerability. The APPG for Runaway and Missing Children and Adults (2019) identified that in 2012 approximately 46 per cent of children's homes were placed out of borough. In 2017 this had risen to 61 per cent.

The APPG for Runaway and Missing Children and Adults (2019) makes a series of bold claims:

These 'sent away' children become magnets for paedophiles and 'County Lines' drugs gangs, who find them easier to exploit because they are isolated from family, friends and social workers. Local authorities are unwittingly becoming recruiting sergeants for 'County Lines' gangs by placing so many children far away from home. Councils may also be inadvertently opening up new 'County Lines' operations because relocating children, who have been groomed to sell heroin and crack cocaine, can create opportunities for criminals to expand their reach into rural parts of the country.

Chair of the 2019 Parliamentary Inquiry into 'sent away' children, Ann Coffey MP stated, 'it is a national scandal that local authorities are unwittingly becoming recruiting sergeants for county lines drugs gangs by sending so many children miles away. It must stop' (Marsh, 2019).

Stakeholders in this study often reported that London authorities responsible for placing children in such accommodation often did so without ever having visited the accommodation, checking suitability, or liaising with host authorities. Stakeholders reported they were often unaware a vulnerable child had been placed within the host authority, with this only coming to attention after interception by police or social services.

'But what you're finding with children's homes is staff getting placement of young people where information has been omitted from the risk assessment, sanitised, so they get the young person on behalf of the out-of-area placement and then suddenly find out that young person is grooming their kids. Then go back to the placing authority who said, "Oh, yes, they are, sorry, we didn't put that in the..."' (Stakeholder 06)

Non-regulated care homes

Not all care homes are fully regulated by Ofsted inspections (a requirement for those housing under 16s). They thus appear to operate 'off radar' generating increasing concerns among professionals. Described by the APPG for Runaway and Missing Children and Adults (2019: 2) as 'the frightening twilight world of unregulated semi-independent homes for older children, aged 16 plus', many police forces now express concern about increasing numbers of vulnerable children in such establishments. Criminals and known offenders are often housed in the same accommodation further raising risks. It is common for young people housed in such homes to go missing and become easy targets for sexual/criminal exploitation.

Katie Razzall investigating these homes for *BBC Newsnight* (Razzall, 2019) described the homes as 'rogue homes' noting about 5,000 looked-after-children are currently located in these so-called 16+ supported or semi-supported accommodation with children 'abandoned to crime gangs' – an increase of 70 per cent in ten years (Locum Today, 2019).

> 'We had an Albanian network take over a drug line. It came to light that a young female was working for them as a drug runner. Arrested her and with large quantity of drugs on her and she told us that she had been made to sell drugs by this Albanian group then disclosed a number of sexual offences and kidnap saying that she'd basically been put or told to get into a car and driven to us but also driven down to [Town]. Taking advantage of her completely. Definitely had some sort of hold over her.' (Police 18)

Those accommodated in this way are deemed to receive 'support' not care as defined by the Care Standards Act 2000 therefore the home is not subject to the comparable checks and inspections required by registered children's homes with support often inconsistent and infrequent.

The safeguardinghub.co.uk website (2019) reports that there are approximately 110 Ofsted regulated children's homes in London alone with three times as many non-regulated homes in London. They further cite the costs provided by the National Audit Office in 2014 that the annual cost of a residential placement was approximately £135,000 adding that 'where this type of money is concerned, there may well be temptation by some to drop standards in favour of filling places' (safeguardinghub.co.uk, 2019).

As sexual exploitation operates within USGs, it also operates with county lines networks. Robinson et al (2019) found strong links to prostitution with young women coerced into selling sex as well as an extended element of criminal exploitation surrounding county lines. Vulnerable young people (male and female, adult or child) can be subjected to different forms of sexual exploitation. Additionally this form of control can be targeted towards those working for county lines as runner/dealers, or delivery mules and so on, as well as targeted towards end-users and drug dependant. Forms of sexual exploitation can include:

- being forced to hide and carry drugs internally;

- forced removal of drugs from inside body cavities;
- forced strip-searching and inspection and digital penetration of body cavities;
- creation of 'ucking' videos as digital artefacts used for 'hostage-taking';
- filming of sexual assaults upon males and females, including against those aged under 16;
- rape or group rape of male/females;
- forced line-ups or 'train-lines';
- gift girls;
- posting and circulating videos of sexual and physical assault;
- sexual assault of cuckooed users;
- forced sexual favours to pay off debts;
- survival sex and use of sex as payment for drugs.

Gender roles in county lines models

The role of girls and young women in county lines is broad and varied. In some ways CL appears to offer equal opportunities with possibilities of entering into more contractual relationships and business operations. Certainly some young women become CL managers while most revert to gender-specific roles lower down the hierarchy which signify depleted levels of trust – or situational short-term trust. Female roles within the hierarchy of the USG social field and within CL models depend greatly upon acquired levels of street capital and social skill (Harding, 2014, see Chapter 8, the Social Skills Spectrum). Those with higher levels of social skill and trust find positions higher in the USG or crew hierarchy. Skills are utilised for administrative and business functions to facilitate transport, accommodation and so on:

> 'Even hiring out rooms and flats and you've obviously got to have payslips, and this, references from jobs. When we were in [Town] some girl hired a little place for us. None of us could have done that at that point. It's always girls that do that kind of thing. They get paid for it though.' (USG 01)

USG affiliates and CL crew operatives in this study were generally disparaging of girls and young women, relegating them to untrustworthy sleeping partners or sexual conquests. One officer concurred:

> 'The way they treat girls too is bad – just as disposable garbage. I think too that's about branding themselves. We had one

guy on his phone – a Nigerian guy … so I'm going through his phone and you can see this ordinary girl trying to have a conversation with him and him replying saying, "Bitch, unless you're sucking cock, I'm not talking" … and that's on his phone. That is the way they treat them. That's the initial level – not the level it goes up to, where they then film them too.' (Police 06)

Over time exploitation can be replicated, and victims can also become abusers:

'We had an investigation into a young girl who was moved out of London because she was at risk of CSE from Asian gangs up in London, but what she was actually doing now was she was recruiting other girls that she was in placement with down here and taking them up to London to be sexually abused by this gang. So you looked at her and you went oh my God, what's happened to this girl is horrific, you know, she's clearly a very damaged person and she is a victim, but then the problem is she's also become … a procurer … she's taken that – Yeah, and she's getting other kids involved in this, so very, very tough to make some decisions about what should happen to these people sometimes, and it's not always, well, if we get a 15-year-old person they are a victim and it's difficult sometimes.' (Police 06)

Within county lines, girls and young women are controlled by gender-based sanctions, often sexually oriented, involving sexual assault, rape, group rape, forced line-ups and so on. These are at times filmed and shared to shame and control the women. Such actions and digital material is used to coerce them into drug dealing or carrying weapons or simply transporting drugs to Hub locations. Deceit and manipulation is also used to the same effect.

Sexual exploitation of females by the males is, however, a normalised and expected aspect of trap house life:

'I was still this boy's girlfriend so sexually I was off limits but other girls that would work and come up, do drops would have sex with all of them and stuff like that. A lot of times there would be, the soldier who would be up there, he would have other little friends up there with him and they'd take turns having sex with the other girls who were up there and that kind of thing. Just kind of your typical, what you'd expect.' (USG 01)

Some young women in county lines are manipulated and made compliant through drink or drugs. Over time, however, some go on to become groomers themselves. On occasion this can is done as a strategy of self-protection; that is, passing on the abuse to someone deemed more vulnerable. One stakeholder respondent had worked with both such scenarios, noting girls working county lines are often more reluctant to engage with safeguarding agencies or to discuss their involvement:

> 'Give her a bottle of voddie and she'll do what we want…. Some girls are groomers – they are … into county lines. Social media is used to control. Girls don't want to talk about it. They are judging of staff, embarrassed and won't engage so much. Girls feel they will be judged and embarrassed and told off.' (Stakeholder 13)

Gift girls

One positive control mechanism within county lines is the provision of 'Gift girls' to male operatives who have turned in several shifts at a trap house and now present as bored, bolshie, in need of control, or deserving of a favour and reward. Here CL managers arrange for girls to be brought to the premises to be 'gifted' to the boys for sex. Examples were given in this study of men arriving outside Secure Accommodation facilities or care homes in the late afternoon to collect young girls (aged 13 plus) by car. Procuring usually is premised upon invitation to a 'party' in London or outside London. In reality no such party exists and girls are plied with alcohol and drugs to ensure compliance before being raped, or gang raped, then returned back in the following Monday.

The gendered exploitation of girls, including CSE, is now more widely recognised. Local police also noted it is acknowledged by those operating CLs, and some felt CL operatives had been instructed to refer to exploitation if arrested as a risk mitigation strategy:

> 'Yeah, as soon as you get someone coming in found with drugs and they are saying they've been forced to do it they are treated as victims of trafficking and modern slavery straight away but it's then gaining the evidence to get a charge for those offences because as soon as you start looking into their allegation it's

not always consistent. If they say, for example, I was picked up in a car on this day at this time in this location and we go there and do some enquiries there's nothing to support that, no CCTV and the phone data doesn't always match what they're saying and I think straight away we're on a back foot and you do struggle. That being said, if it's like a brief that they a being told to say or if it is genuine we're certainly not finding the evidence to support.' (Police 18)

Human trafficking and modern slavery

The Children Act (1989) stipulates a statutory requirement for authorities to work together to ensure safeguarding and welfare promotion of children. However, criminal exploitation including within county lines networks is closely aligned with offences under the Modern Slavery Act 2015. Adults, including CL managers, who traffic or exploit children can be charged under this act. Increasingly the NCA and police seek to do just that. Police report that the stigma of being viewed as a 'child abuser' or trafficker' is a moniker the CL managers and USGs actively seek to avoid as this goes down badly within prison. Post-sentencing Slavery Trafficking Prevention Orders are also now within the CJS toolbox. One overarching aim here is to force adaptations to the behaviour of CL managers.

Child trafficking is defined in the United Nations Palermo Protocol as the 'recruitment, transportation, transfer, harbouring or receipt' of a child for the purpose of exploitation. In the UK, trafficking is regarded as a form of modern slavery (Dent, 2017; HMICFRS, 2017). The trafficking of children is a process comprised of two distinct stages: the Act and the Purpose. This is the 'recruitment, transportation, transfer, harbouring or reception of persons, including the exchange or transfer of control over those persons ... for the purpose of exploitation' (Protocol to Prevent, Suppress and Punish Trafficking in Persons, Especially Women and Children, supplementing the United Nations Convention against Transnational Organized Crime ['Palermo Protocol'], 2000).

While such protocols might be legislatively available, this does not necessarily mean girls arrested for working county lines feel safe or are willing to divulge details to the police:

'For reasons I'm sure you can appreciate, they are very unlikely to give formal evidence against that network. So obtaining the evidence to look at the slavery offences is very, very difficult.' (Police 06)

Police would consider any such evidence; however, it is but rarely provided:

> 'We would safeguard that person and work with the councils to move them so that they're not able to come back and set up again. But we would look to use the circumstances of that to aggravate their sentencing. But the reality is, that is very rare that we'll get somebody standing up to say I will give you formal evidence to that effect, so yeah it's difficult sometimes'. (Police 06)

Even if a court case is not successful for a modern–day slavery charge, the police would use that intel to elevate the county line to one requiring special attention. Curiously under–18s do not have to prove coercion upon arrest or detention by the police.

The key route to addressing these issues is via the National Referral Mechanism (NRM). According to the NCA, 'the NRM is a framework for identifying victims of human trafficking or modern slavery and ensuring they receive the appropriate support. The NRM is also the mechanism through which the Modern Slavery Human Trafficking Unit (MSHTU) collects data about victims. This information contributes to building a clearer picture about the scope of human trafficking and modern slavery in the UK' (Home Office, 2016a, 2017a). There were 2,118 children referred into the NRM in 2017; a rise of 66 per cent on the previous year (Missing People, 2018: 7).

Anyone suspected of being trafficked for profit can also be referred to the NRM, and this includes a number of children recognised as victims of modern slavery. The NRM Statistics (2019) show increased referrals of children having risen by 48 per cent across all different exploitation types from 2,118 in 2017 to 3,137 in 2018, with criminal exploitation highly prevalent.

Those involved are frequently both vulnerable and damaged through trauma and possibly fail to realise what is happening at first, though responses vary depending upon situations, personal agency, level of threat and intimidation.

Nationally prosecutions using Human Trafficking and Modern–Day Slavery legislation have been slow to materialise, though in 2019 two successful prosecutions regarding trafficking of young people to make a profit within county lines models made national headlines and helped to establish case law.

Local police in the study were keen to utilise Modern Slavery and Human Trafficking offences for prosecution, however, locating evidence to secure a prosecution is not always easy as evidence is required linking victims to phones and movement of people for benefit. Obtaining a successful prosecution regarding Human Trafficking is not always straightforward as one police officer noted:

> 'Yeah, I think, we ... so we had a recent Albanian network and a couple of females were arrested; they made disclosures in interview that they were being forced into this and so on, and so on, so we released them from custody, did a load of work around their allegations, then the problem is you download the telephones and they'd have videos of them wrapping up loads of drugs and some accounts given in interview, the checkable facts weren't correct and they've made allegations that certain things happened and we can prove they were in a different place at the same time. So yeah, it's difficult. We've got a very, very robust recording of the crime and investigation but sometimes the investigation actually doesn't bear it out.' (Police 06)

Police officers recounted that among CL operatives it is now widely believed that if runner/dealers claim to be trafficked victims they will be released, making some officers more sceptical of claims of coercion or trafficking:

> 'If you spoke to the guys on my team, they would say that in their experience it has become quite well known that if you come in and claim that you've been trafficked and so on, and so on, the likelihood is you will be released from custody.' (Police 07)

The complexity of working with potentially coerced victims of human trafficking was well articulated by one officer:

> 'I think that there has certainly been a number of false claims of it. But then sometimes what you have is, and be aware of, is that as in the sort of CSE elements, your victim isn't going to be of the best character because that's the nature of it; they recruit these damaged young people. So you've got to be alert to the fact that actually when you get this victim in front of you, they may have previous offending, their character might not be the greatest, there may be elements of their life that you look and think, oh crikey, but you've got to turn that

to your advantage and you've got to say well, yeah, that's part of the methodology, they recruit these young damaged people. So you can't say, oh well, they're not a reliable witness, because they've got previous for this or that; that's the whole idea of it, but I think that we're very good at going through every element of it, you make an allegation, we investigate it, we see if we can kind of get the evidence to support your claim and if we can't so be it, but we've been through it, you know.' (Police 06)

Citing duress under the Modern Slavery Act is not uncommon. One officer noted human trafficking and modern slavery issues were considered more suited to young victims with older dealers thought to have more agency:

'Her problem is she entered into the agreement willingly. That was her problem, so he said, "Do you want to work for me selling drugs?" She said okay, and then 24 hours later she was a user, she short-changed him so then he worked her like a dog for the next six days, walking 15–20 miles a day and she went through her shoes and stuff. Then she got caught. So it is difficult to prove coercion because she's older, about 30, with previous for drug supply as well, heroin and crack so she don't stand much chance. No, she doesn't but you see, users they don't make the best decisions anyway, do they, so you can kind of understand. I feel a bit sorry for them actually. They're a pretty kind of wasted bunch.' (Police 02)

Victim/offender nexus

The duality of victim/offender status and agency is acknowledged by this reflective member of a USG who became an active CL operator:

'I was never part of getting the big bits. I was finding younger people to come up to [name] and sort them out, asking, "Have you got friends?" and get more vulnerable young people, it was me. I turned into that person.' (USG 01)

Few runner/dealers are aware of the extent of their exploitation. As one female CL operative/manager later noted:

'So, we're expendable. I know this now. At that age I'm thinking, "He's a good guy. He's just trying to help me out". He's never going to do that, you know. I grew a lot of respect and a lot of trust from that particular Older and through that I got to meet a lot of his friends in the area because he's come back, He gave all of his money and he's telling me these little 16-year-olds they're up in country, they're doing it big, you've got to give them respect. They've lost nothing. No problems from the customers. They're doing it correct.' (USG 03)

The County Line Control Repertoire

An effective business model with a profit objective requires all risks to be mitigated, and ineffective behaviours, practices, or staff to be monitored and managed via rules, policy, governance and accountability. Business in pursuit of a competitive advantage will tighten all these mechanisms through increased command and control to make the business leaner, meaner and fit for competition. Evolution of CL from Model #2 to Models #3 and #4 require just such practices. Looser, casual business practice evolves into sharper more professional practice. Many operatives fall short, fail to appreciate the new rules now operating and must be brought into line.

Significantly the use of exploited young people as runner/dealers, use of local dealers and the increased use of user-dealers generates multiple problems of compliance and control. Compounded by variegated trust, police informing, gossip, grassing, rival gangs, competitive rival lines, short-changed drug deals, substance misuse and debt, the lines now present a constant management challenge. A loose line will fail, end, or be taken over. A strong line will thrive and bring rewards. This doctrine underpins the concept of the County Line Control Repertoire. Moreover any failed line, outstanding debt or disrespect brings reputational decline and street capital deflation which cannot be endured:

'… this idea that that whole tier (of vulnerable users) is being leaned on in a way that has created a little bit of tension, because I've picked that up. I think that's part of what is sitting behind this upsurge in crime, is that these guys that were just basically running a kind of covert drug line are now flexing their muscles and getting more strident, getting more confident and they're getting tighter, smarter and more adaptive in their business models.' (Police 04)

Control is required within each different level of the CL hierarchy, notably from CL managers to district or Hub managers; from Hub managers to runner/dealers; from runner/dealers to users and user/runners. The different techniques of control operate as a menu or repertoire of sanctions which can be utilised. Each sanction presents as both a variable which can be moderated in its weight or dosage, and also as a strategic action for the CL manager. This repertoire of sanctions operates in CL drug supply networks acts in the same way as the sanctions repertoire utilised by USGs within the social field of the street gang (see Harding, 2014: 72–9). The County Line Control Repertoire permits informal social controls to be enacted, including positive and negative sanctions, to assist in controlling, events, actions, behaviours and to avoid potential situations. They can be subtle or direct and dangerous.

Figure 5.1 graphically represents the circle of violence, debt and profit which forms the basic economy of the county lines model. It visually demonstrates the key actors or players in CL illustrating how debt in particular is established as a principle bonding criteria between each actor/participant. As such alongside 'disrespect', it is now the prime impetus behind the invoking and exertion of the County Line Control Repertoire (See Table 5.1). Indications are that in the last two or more years control has become tighter as competition has increased.

Figure 5.1: Circle of violence, debt and profit

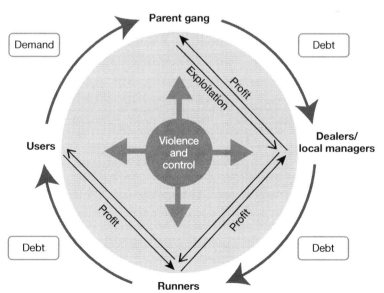

Table 5.1: The County Line Control Repertoire

Type of control/sanction	Description	Most likely target/beneficiary
Positive		
Working conditions	Adjustments to the working conditions of CL operatives	Runners/dealers
Gift girls	Provision of girls for sexual favours	Runners/dealers
Favours	Provision of 'chicken change'	Runners/dealers
Negative		
Using the 'trapping mentality'	Demand adherence to the concept of trapping and codes of loyalty and brotherhood	Young runner/dealers
Rumour/gossip	Use of rumour or gossip to suggest someone is a grass or informer or is untrustworthy, for example working for a rival crew	Everyone
Fear	Threats of potential violence to the individual, their family or friends	Runners/dealers/users
Intimidation	Cumulative and multiple threats which may or may not be carried out; reference to previous violent incidents; visual presentation of guns, knives or weapons	Runners/dealers/users
Use of drugs	Use of medical cosh/snaring a young person into drug use to achieve compliance	Users – some runners/dealers
Docking of wages	Wages taxed or reduced as a penalty	Hub managers/ runners/dealers
Physical violence	Use of physical violence, including through the use of weapons; use of group violence or proxy use of others	Runners/dealers/users
Robbery	Use of robbery as a deliberate targeted sanction against a rival individual or crew	Runners/dealers
Debt bondage	Use of debt, or fake debt, to create a servile relationship which might lead to human slavery	Runners/dealers/users
Use of enforcers	Specialised individuals skilled in employing sanctions used against a target specifically identified by CL managers	Serious high-end cases

Working conditions

Positive control techniques offer rewards to runner/dealers for efficiency or loyalty with improved working conditions, gifts or group-bonding treats. Favours and gifting might include moving them from a bando to flat; increasing wages; allocating shorter shifts; paying for an evening take-out meal; paying for trainers; purchasing an Oyster card; buying a push-bike to ease local transport problems.

Using the 'trapping mentality'

Young people involved in CLs generally originate from the same socio-economic background sharing the same habitus. Joining a USG brings expectations of joint socialisation and adherence to common bonds and rules. In CL networks this means bonds of brotherhood and shared values regarding making fast money. It also includes loyalty to the line, to the crew/team. While highly situational, variable and temporal, it nonetheless creates a mindset of compliance and duty which holds sway over younger minds, operating a form of subtle mind manipulation. It predominates minds, assuages fears and provides an overarching *raison d'être* for involvement. This common mindset can be invoked or manipulated by Olders:

> 'The way you're manipulated and the way you're broken down and you're made to think that this is what you're worth, you're made to feel that you're not better than anything else and you're never going to do anything else, it's torture mentality. When you're in that it's just mental torture and the days just drag on and drag on, a day feels like a month, and a month, it's awful and these kids now who think "I'm going to be making money", no.' (USG 01)

Some CL managers claim to treat their crew like family and constantly reiterate this to their team in the expectation that any potential problems will be kept 'within the family' and subdued quickly:

> 'Well, they know not to step out of line. I've been doing serious business but I treat them like family.' (USG 03)

Rumour/gossip

As in the social field of the USG, trust is a scare and highly prized commodity. Acquiring trust brings dividends of Intel – information, access, opportunity and so on, which in turn lead to economic benefits, or status advancement. Withdrawal of trust means instant deflation of street capital and must be avoided to avoid vulnerability. Rumour and gossip are powerful strategic actions which when used effectively damage or destroy personal stocks of street capital leading to victimisation or exclusion.

Fear and intimidation

Users fear being targeted for cuckooing or retaliation. This alone becomes a coercive driver for some users to become a user-dealer as risk mitigation. For others threats are openly used. Threats of retaliation are now also commonly directed towards partners and family (see Chapter 8). Some user-dealers report intimidation into dealing:

'There's a 40-year-old in [town]. We've had a couple of warrants out on him. Last year he was eventually forced into running drugs for a county line and they threatened to throw acid into his partner's face last year. The bloke forcing him to run is inside now but he's nasty. He was using him, forcing him through intimidation to get whatever he needed in terms of running drugs. He was mid-40s from [country]. He could be very intimidating through his size and demeanour – a big black guy. He said essentially he knew he was working up a drugs debt but he needed his fix. So he ran up a debt and eventually the guy said if you don't go out and deal for me to work off this debt, I'm gonna throw acid in your partner's face and I'll do this and that. He managed to cut down his habit to about £10 a day but he needs to get out of [town], cos when he walks out the door there's guys walking around offering him stuff and giving their number. It's so rife that he can't kick that last bag.'(Police 12)

Case study: Fear and intimidation – User 12

During a ride-along with two police officers in [town] a white male user was seen in a state of distress and when stopped, quickly jumped into the police car uninvited, clearly seeking sanctuary. I was already recording interviews with the police and this incident was captured on the recorder. I remain uneasy at the thought of capturing such data without the respondent's consent. However, I feel this unprompted street exchange indicates the fear generated among the using community by CL operatives and perhaps also the dilemma of frontline police in working with this community. Such interactions are rarely if ever captured by research and I argue there is value in bearing witness to this type of conversation which never normally reaches beyond frontline officers. For this reason I have decided to report this dialogue after editing all possible references.

The individual is well known to the police as a member of the using community. He is described by them as a persistent liar who struggles to tell the truth. In this incident the user was visibly shaking and crying with fear. He was breathless at the start of the conversation. His words are panicked and repetitive. It is not known if he was on drugs at the time. The opening question from the police was, 'Are you all right?'

'No, I'm not all right, I don't mind telling you I'm worried. There were loads of 'em waiting down there, trying to get me hands and stab me. They tried grabbing me. It's not good. They all witnessed it. In this shop here, I had to hide in here. That dealer fella across the road – [name] has paid them two to stab and batter me basically. And they tried to get me out of the shop and they're waiting at the end. They're on their phones, watching. I have to get out town. Bastards. Yeah, I have to go [desperate]. I'm stuffed. I can't go anywhere, it's ridiculous. Oh, mate.

'He found out I was talking to you guys. They found out – we know what you're doing, boom, boom, boom. Perhaps it's because we spoke earlier, I don't know, and he says that I've been telling you about them. I don't know. It's about being found out, basically. And that one I was with, yeah, he set me up. I came this way and they were hiding in the alley waiting for me. It was lucky I came this way and they were trying to grab me since. He's part of the set-up! They've been waiting down here – waiting for me to leave. Oh, God! I can't go home. They know where I am. I'm dead. [Desperate]. I'm telling you now, I can't stay anywhere round here. I haven't had my medicine yet.

'You can ask in that shop what they've been trying to do. They've been hiding round here, they've been on phones. They tried to grab me out of the shop. I don't know but they know enough to wait for me. "We know you've been talking. You've been talking to the police. You've set us up". This, that and the other. They've been trying to get me out of the shop. They've been waiting for me all this time. That [name] bloke has been walking around. You can ask them in the shop, they witnessed it. He was in the shop shouting, "Get out, I'm gonna stab you!" Boom, boom, boom.

'I can't stay in this town. I can't. If I do, I'm dead. I don't know what to do. This is what I'm hoping you can help with. I don't know what I'm gonna do, I can't stay here. I'm finished. There was quite a few of 'em waiting … waiting for me to come. And they tried to make out that they'd brought drugs off of [name] and they weren't happy with it and they were just upset with him and it was OK for me to come out of the shop. But I see them waiting and hiding. They keep watching. They're on the phone. They wanted me to leave. There were several white guys from this town. They'd been paid obviously by [name]. They were users. They were gonna beat me up and stab me – the rest of it, yeah. Go to work on me. He's paid 'em to do it. I know who they are, but no names but I know who they are. I cannot stay here in this town. I haven't had my medicine yet – I need to get my medicine. You can't leave me there. I'm dead. You don't understand, that's what I'm telling you.

'I don't know how but they know. You can ask the shop what was happening. I know I struggle with everything but it's happening, I know what I saw. I can only tell you what was said. "We've known you've been talking" is what was said. [....] "You've tried to set us up and put the police on us – boom, boom, boom". What that [name] was saying, he must have paid them drugs or whatever to have them do what he wants done to me. And they've all been trying to get me out. The people witnessed him getting very angry and say he was going to do and do that. Now they're gonna to be lookin' everywhere for me. I can't stay here. I don't even have a phone at the moment. I can't stay in this town. I'm terrified by it.

'Well, the police are always chatty to me. I could quite easily have been seen. I said to a few [of] 'em, "You can't keep coming up to me like this" cos quite a few of 'em came up to me and stop me in the street and wanna talk to me. I knew it would happen sooner or later. But it was very intimidating how they got me by the [step]. If I'd gone the other way, I wouldn't be here now.'

The dialogue speaks of several keys issues:

• CL operatives use local users as hired muscle to intimidate other users. The use of a proxy is a purposeful control techniques for CL operatives.
• The user might now be intimidated into leaving town thus uprooting him from his user community and engagement with substance-misuse agencies – deemed a powerful result for any CL operative thereby strengthening his reputation and status.
• Challenge for police working with the user community regarding veracity and mendacity arising from mental and physical addiction to drugs.

- Challenge of obtaining/verifying community intelligence and 'grassing', illustrating how grassing is viewed within CL and risks involved.
- Possibility regular police stops of users might compromise user safety if witnessed by others.
- Potential physical violence accompanying county lines.
- Time required for police in dealing with this incident, including: removing user from immediate vicinity; taking user to get his methadone script; liaising with other agencies to get him rehoused; recording the incident; investigating the incident.
- Ongoing repercussions and reverberations arising from this interaction.

Medicinal cosh

One control technique is to keep users happy and compliant by providing them with a ready supply of drugs. For cuckooed users this amounts to a medicinal cosh to prevent theft of drugs or money or as a reward/incentive for efficient dealing.

One CL manager noted operatives will encourage runner/dealers to sample products they sell. This provides a dual benefit of passing off any drugs as personal while bringing increased manageability and control:

> 'Also, something that you may not be aware of, they encourage you to sample the drugs that you're selling. I never ever, ever tried crack cocaine or heroin, they never got me to do that but a lot of people do and you're told to do that because if you're caught by the police and they piss test you or whatever and you're stuck with drugs you can say personal use. If it's in your system. A lot of people don't know that so that's how a lot of people develop habits as well. Me, I always thought it was "don't get high on your own supply". No, because then as well if you've got someone under the influence of drugs you can take the piss out of them that bit more.' (USG 01)

Docking wages

An attachment of earning or docking of wages is the most common control mechanism as it is quick, effective, widely understood and rarely challenged. It further supports the illusion of a functioning legitimate business with bona-fide employability T and Cs:

'I never had to get physical. They lost things time and time again. I said, "Do you know what, I'll just take it out of your pay", and they'd continue. So, I learnt from the experience how to conduct business more wisely.' (USG 03)

Physical violence

The links between substance misuse, drug dealing and violence have been more thoroughly explored in the USA than in the UK (Moore, 1990). As with USGs, physical violence is widely utilised for control and sanction but one officer noted violence against users was moderated to ensure they remain fit for work:

'Basically they've then got free labour then and dealers are more motivated by money, I think. If they beat ten bells out [of] the user they can't use them to work any more. a) they're sort of cutting off their bridges with that person. And, b) they might not feel well enough to carry on working so they don't tend to administer serious violence. I think, as I said, they want to set them up for a fall because they want free labour. They want to make as much money as they possibly can.' (Police 18)

Reasons for physical violence vary but include theft or short-changing on deals. In scenarios involving users, violence is demonstrative and fast, usually a hard slap or punch. For breach of trust by a runner/dealer, retribution is harsher. Interestingly this CL manager points to saving face among his peer group as motivation for harsh treatment:

'I had a youth work my line. He was young, he was 15 and he knew my little brother so I said, "Okay, I'll go with him". So, me and my little brother, "Okay, you know my little brother so you must be all right, my brother is doing this thing as well", and he ended up stealing from us. He stole from us. He lost a package of drugs so that was £800 he lost and then he came to one of our houses, a friend of mine's house and he was stealing. I don't know if he lost the drugs or sold them then kept the money. He wasn't the only one. There was another friend that did that as well. A friend my age. A friend of mine, I helped him out and he ran off with the package. We had to deal with him severely, very severely. He got put in hospital. I had to. I didn't want to because I know him as a friend but

(1) if you're a friend why are you stealing from me, and (2) my partner expects a set behaviour from me. If someone stole from me and it's my responsibility he expects me to deal with it. So, I had to. To not lose the respect of my peers.' (USG 03)

Enforcers

County Line crews linked to USGs have access to enforcers for high-level or serious infringements. This might include major issues of ongoing disrespect, or where people need to be 'taught a lesson'. This will act as a serious communication and boundary-setting for others:

'Yes, and they don't always get 'em so it doesn't always happen but we've seen people who've been filled in – proper. Either cos they've been thought to have been – or they have been robbing people. Robbery runners. Cos the users need their drugs and they think if I can rob somebody of their drugs, I don't need to pay for it. And only users in front of 'em so it'll probably only do 'em about three days or four days. They'll share it with their friends then it's gone. They can't balance themselves or spread it out. If they've got it in front of them, they'd just use it.' (Police 13)

'The one with a ponytail got hit with a hammer. That Older had just popped round to see 'is mates and he got battered by an 18–20-year-old black male, fit as an ox, who can barely stand up. He was airlifted out, didn't he? Well, it sends a message out to the others though.' (Police 10)

Being robbed

Described by one CL manager as being an 'occupational hazard though. It comes with it'. (USER 01), as a control technique, robbery is ubiquitous and accounts for considerable violence accompanying county lines. As strategic action (Harding, 2014) robbery provides personal and professional advantages:

■ **Targeting rival county line activity:**
• disruption, or take-down, of rival lines;
• establishing pre-conditions for hostile takeovers;

- showing strength among rivals;
- consolidating lines/market share;
- generating intel regarding CL activity, for example number of workers, product quality/quantity, market share and so on, with some being acquired through violent interrogation.

■ **Targeting individual, personal or crews:**
- demonstration that a rival (possibly within your own crew or USG) is unable to manage the business;
- control of one individual or crew;
- fake robbery as a means of control and creation of debt bondage.

Robbery provides benefits of easy economic returns, acquisition of product/drugs, including mobile phone databases. It can destabilise rivals; take them out of the Game; end rival dealing; and control individuals, for example Youngers getting too powerful.

Post-event recriminations are frequent, and interrogations of users and runner/dealers can be brutal. This study uncovered examples of young men tied to scalding radiators as a way of making them talk or to divulge knowledge of the actors involved or their role in the robbery. Users too can be subsequently targeted by runner/dealers and violence will be passed down the chain or hierarchy.

Debt bondage

Any young person working in county lines drug supply networks, or any user supplied by CL networks can quickly fall into debt through naiveté, inexperience, or just as likely arising from a calculated strategic move by another to out-manoeuvre or control them. Reasons for falling into debt include:

- skimming money or drugs from Olders;
- short-changing Olders;
- losing money or drugs;
- failing to honour loans;
- shrinkage in dealing;
- mis-reading the weights.

Debt increases vulnerability while diminishing respect and trust. Vulnerable people in debt will be quickly exploited through methods of control – either criminally or sexually, or both – in a process known as debt bondage, that is, where those in debt are bonded in servitude to those to whom the debt is 'owed' (as some debts are perceptional, others are fake).

Cited by the NCA (2017b; 2019a) as a key element of county lines, debt bondage is known to:

- pull people into working in county lines to pay off debts;
- perpetuate or deepen their involvement in CLs;
- generate and exacerbate associated violence within CLs;
- contribute to users accepting dealers within their properties to staying on in their properties;
- contribute to users becoming user–dealers.

It is acknowledged by some young people in USGs and county lines but widely under-played or neutralised by them as a risk. When debt bondage occurs, or is set in motion by Olders, it can be sudden and swift with responses ranging from harsh to severe. Following physical violence, those in debt will be forced to work to pay off the debt (which is often magnified and increased by 'spurious additions and arbitrary interest payments'):

> 'Just shows you the control these networks have over people.' (Police 04)

There are a growing number of cases where debt has led to homicide, even for seemingly trivial amounts of money.

One CL manager noted how robbery led to debt bondage:

> 'Not get robbed. Occupational hazard though. It comes with it. And you know you're going to get slapped up if you are. And then you're working for free, working for free anyway but do you know what I mean? If you were getting money, you're not getting paid until you've worked off what you've lost type thing. If you're not getting paid anyway, but you're given an even harder time and you owe them even more. The thing is as well as being robbed by your drug dealers and your rival gang members you're also being robbed by, on purpose, so by your team would send somebody who you don't know but who is affiliated to rob you. So, you haven't got robbed, you haven't lost them any money because it's gone right back to them because it's them that's robbed you so they can put you in a situation where you owe me, that's what happens

a lot. That didn't happen to me but that happens every day now. I'm not paying you. I'm not paying you and your friend, and the other one because you all shouldn't have got robbed.' (USG 01)

Fake or set-up robbery

This occurs when a CL manager or Older arranges for a CL operative to be robbed of their drugs and money – thereby instantly plunging them into debt bondage:

> 'It's very clever really, isn't it? And you can't argue and even if you know that they did it as well.' (USG 01)

This operates as a calculated management control mechanism and strategic action to diminish rivals, and gain competitive advantage. This is usually undertaken by proxy so managers can claim or feign ignorance and distance. Fake robbery (set-ups) result in instant street capital deflation. Those losing out are now highly vulnerable due to street capital deflation and also because they must now work harder, or for free, to get out of debt bondage. They will be subjected to further threats and possibly physical violence. They may now lose their status in the line or be demoted:

Case study: Robbery – USG 01

'What you've got to realise is how are you going to know, if we're moving around from spot to spot, where we are, what we have on us at the time, because how it works is you have to get the new stock replenished. Some people would bring it up or somebody would go down to get more drugs. So, we were up there at this house, they came. How did they know we were there? It's an inside job! It always is an inside job, no matter what. Always somebody within your circle, within your team is giving information out to other people because we'd just had a [re-up] we had so much drugs on us – so everyone is under suspicion. There was a girl up there, obviously I had drugs internally stored, and there was a girl up there who came up with the boys, I ended up having a physical fight with her and being stabbed twice in my chest. I didn't know she had anything on her. I didn't see. I was terrified because she's a really big girl. She's so scary. If I saw her now I'd faint. Really big girl. Physical fight. She obviously had a weapon on. I was sliced twice in my chest. They took the drugs from us. They had guns on them, what can you do? There were two cars, I'd say about nine of them. They all just piled in? Literally. Booted off the door.

'In the house at the time was me, the two boys and the drug user. He was crying his eyes out, he was terrified. I was the only one that got actually hurt that time but we used the woman that I was telling you about who used to shoplift, she took me to hospital and she said, "Oh, my niece, she was playing around with my kids and they've scraped her with the nail clippers", they cleaned me up and I went right back to the man's house afterwards. No questions asked. No social services. No where are your parents? Do you know what I mean? Nothing of the sort which wouldn't happen now, would it, at all? But nothing of the sort at all.

'So, that happened then but we stayed there. For whatever reason we stayed there, it kind of made sense that we stayed at this man's house now looking back because maybe a week later they were back again, that lot and this time the young Turkish boy I told you about he got shot twice in his groin in the middle of all of that struggle. I think he was two years older than me so about 16/17. He was a bit older than me. He got shot. I don't know, [why they shot him] you know. He wasn't confident. He wasn't cocky. He wasn't a fighter. From what I can remember he wasn't resisting because he wouldn't have resisted because we were scared. Maybe because they could. I don't know.'

Risks

Running/dealing brings multiple risks of being robbed but also of dealing to undercover police officers:

> 'Every time you're going somewhere you're thinking, "God, are they going to try and rob me? Are they going to be with the police?" which kind of brings me on nicely to the other boy that I told you who got killed recently who was working with us. So this was when the Turkish boy wasn't with us after he got shot. We used to take it in turns and it was slow. And one time I said, "Please just do it for me, I know it's my turn, please just for go for me, I'll do the next five", and he said, "Okay, that's fine". Obviously we always had knives on us, guns on us, weapons of some sort on us. He went to do the shot, it was quite a big one. It was something like ten and eight or something like that so it was quite a big one, he never came back. So, I was waiting for an hour, two hours, I thought he's

dead, that's it, he's gone, he's dead. Three hours, four hours and then we heard two days later he'd been arrested. He'd sold to an undercover police officer. He obviously had the drugs on him and he had a gun on him as well. So, he served a prison sentence for that. He got deported back to Jamaica because he was born in Jamaica and then recently he got stabbed to death in Jamaica.' (USG 01)

Test dummies

Using test dummies is now a recognised risk management strategy regarding robbery. CL operatives prepare a parcel of fake drugs then send a runner/dealer in expectation of arrest or robbery. This helps to test a new market or foil robberies based upon local intel:

> 'They might send someone down as a test dummy with a load of fake … they've done that, I've know[n] that a few times as well. They send in with a fake parcel. To find out who's going to rob them, first. Because it's not always the police that's their biggest worry, it's getting robbed. It happens a lot. So they normally send them with fake stuff, so if they get robbed they haven't lost any money. They've got a bag of coffee or sugar or whatever. Or if the police catch them and nick them, yes, they might spend four hours in the cells, but they've haven't got any drugs because there's no drugs.' (USG 06)

Debt impedes recovery

In addition to debt generating violence and exploitation it can also impede recovery for users:

> 'The feedback that I get from people in these situations, it's always they feel they can't get out, it's really difficult for them to actually find a way out. Because obviously the drug use is illegal, what they're doing is illegal, and they're not certain how to get away from it, and that is a real problem for people, particularly when what they want to do is their recovery. So, they may come in to start recovery, maybe making progress in recovery, but if they've still got debts and obligations, it's really difficult.' (Stakeholder 11)

Responses and acceptance of violence

The evolution of violence now exercised within the Sanction Repertoire or the County Line Control Repertoire has generated a sanguine acceptability of normative violence:

> 'It comes with the Game, it's the lifestyle, this shit comes with it. So if you want to be on this ting, then this comes with it, innit, you're gonna have to be part of what it is and deal with the consequences. Every action has got a reaction, buddy.' (USG 09)

Others recognise that violence can occur among runner/dealers over relatively small or insignificant issues. However, one respondent quickly noted he would not back down in such an event:

> 'It's mostly small things that fights could start over. Just a wrong look, but apart from that, it's just about making money, but obviously if you get these little dickheads who want to say something, then we're not afraid to take it wherever it goes.' (USG 12)

Younger runner/dealers were much more aggressive as to how they would face violence or anyone thinking of targeting them for violence:

> 'I'd smoke the whole family. Yeah, so you know what, all you pagans out there, all your bullshit, you think you can try and lean on Man, to get man's bread and that, you know what? Man's got something for you man, yea? And it shows, yeah, break it for them man, yeah. A 16, a 16 16 Digi. Man's got that for you 16's, yeah. Not no hand ting, 16s. I won't fuck with him man, yeah. Man's not out here to play games. He's talking about an 18 gun ... blast.... Smokin' season. Smoke dem n****rs. Yeah, taking from my fuckin' bread and my thing and my line, no, then I'm killing n****rs, bruv.' (USG 10)

Some USG affiliates appeared well seasoned in terms of adaptation to constant threats of violence and mitigating risk:

> 'Yes, of course, it's a two-way street, like whatever I'm dishing out, I expect it to come back to me, but to be fair, that's life that we live, I really don't give a fuck.' (USG 10)

However, he also demonstrated that he was already wearing body armour. His response when asked why talked of risk mitigation and protection from rivals. His comment notes a sense of empowerment but also of having to keep constant observation and vigilance (MeerKatting):

> 'Well, why do you think blood? Well, it's protection, innit? Sometimes Man coming for n****rs, understand. I'm the one that does the coming now. I'm the one that does the fuckin' Meerkat checks, you understand what I'm saying? It's just safety measures, you understand, safety precautions. From Opps, Enemies, Pagan, you understand? Feds.' (USG 10)

Increased criminal confidence

Senior police officers articulated their concerns that street gangs and CL drug dealing crews had evolved over the recent years with a rapid escalation of confidence and sophistication over the last two years. Police identified that users were being heavily 'leaned on' by the county lines crews. Some officers described this as a 'step up', not only in sophistication of business tactics but more 'extremely confident now' in their ability to exert control over users:

> 'Absolutely. There is a confidence. We've had a couple of instances where our users have pushed back against that in a physical way.' (Police 10)

Officers were uncertain as to why this user pushback was occurring:

> 'I don't know if they're fully cognoscent of the consequences of what they're doing? I think that's probably it. I think it's maybe a bit of bravado. I'd be interested to find out why that pushback is. Because it's early days yet but I've started to tangibly notice a little bit of a sort of pushback from ... maybe it's that overconfidence of the gangs, I don't know.' (Police 10)

Defending the line

Once established it is imperative to maintain vigilance and to defend the CL from potential hostile takeover, shut-down by police, loss of line to rivals or through mismanagement.

CL operatives recognise violence is ever-present at all operational stages notably in controlling the line. One respondent noted CL work meant an abrogation of morality and preparedness to set aside a personal moral compass to keep business going:

> 'Well, I've been on both sides. Man I did sell 'tings to people. Then Man managed to try and take my kids from school, you know what I'm saying. So look, it's not all roses, you knowwhatI'msaying, like people have died over the stupidist shit, £20, £30, £100, where people's houses are getting burnt down and people's families are at risked, feel me? Like it is what it is man, you can't really have morals, morals ain't for Road Life – it's a negative, Bruv.' (USG 07)

Violence was confirmed as a routine activity:

> 'Yes, of course, man, all the time. It's gone from tying people up, kidnapping, it's gone from trying to get man's kids from their house to their schools. It is what it is, man, you've got to get in there and you've got to get in. Some people want to hide, if people are hiding, what else are you going to do?' (USG 07)

When asked if violence arose through desire to protect the line, responses were strongly affirmative stressing the nature of the social field, that is, street justice is openly available as other routes for conflict resolution are unavailable:

> 'Course it is, it's all about the line, man, it's all about the line, without the line, what else is there? I can't go to the government to help, can I?' (USG 07)

> 'The statistics don't really convey the violence that goes with county lines.' (Police 01)

Within the USG and CL the imperative for violence to defend lines is normalised:

> 'Even though we're selling and everyone is making money we have problems with people. We were always getting phone calls, saying "we're riding out to do this", "we're riding out to do that" so we would go and fight people, do these sort of things.' (USG 06)

'It depends on what scale you want, man, like violence, to us, is just life; you know what I'm saying? It's life, man. For someone to get stabbed up, it's an everyday thing, man, like for an ordinary man, it's a shock, but for us, it's someone got stabbed.' (USG 07)

One street gang member and dealer summed it up simply as the street code statement as follows:

'It's kill or be killed.' (USG 10)

Violence is readily engaged to protect profitable lines from diminishing returns:

'He's gonna protect his line because that's all he has, his line becomes his job, you understand that. Man will die over money. Once you've affected my line, if my line stops and if my line normally [rings] out a thousand times in one day and it goes down to a hundred times in a day and someone new moves on the block, no, you've got to go and pay him a visit.' (USG 07)

The propensity for violence among CL networks arises due to the habitus of the social field which codifies the type of response deemed a credible action. As most CL operatives can reference a shared habitus of poverty or gangs, then violence is an elective from the normative repertoire. Habitualised experience then shapes further action making violence a constantly credible strategic action:

'Yes, whether it's selling drugs, whether it's doing kidnapping, robberies, anything, working with other dealers, whatever it is, if you've got something that I want, you know what I mean, I'm gonna take it. I started getting involved at about 14, by the time I was 15, I was serving four years, in prison for GBH.' (USG 07)

Several street gang respondents with access to firearms scoffed that guns might somehow be absent from county lines:

'Well, like my n****r said, I've got to have my stick on me everywhere I go, but you see what, the stick's so big, so I make the girl carry it, yeah. A big Louis Vuitton bag, you don't even know what it's coming from, yeah, to, you know, bare gun shops getting nicked, yeah. Come on, we're not playing games, we're not out here to play, it's fuckin' real life shit, it's a dog eat dog world. You get it? Yeah? There's people out there, grinding nine to five and there's Man out here like Man making 30 or 40 bags a month. Come on, my guy.' (USG 09)

In Chapter 6 cuckooing is considered as a way to reduce business costs and retain competitive advantage. This highly exploitative strategic action includes different techniques by dealers to gain access and different techniques by users to retain control of their property.

6 .

Cuckooing and Nuanced Dealing Relationships

The first half of this chapter considers the complex set of inter-personal relationships between the user community and CL operatives starting with cuckooing and the development of a cuckooing typology. The second half of the chapter considers the views of both users and dealers as they offer insights into their often complex relationships and how they feel about county lines.

What is cuckooing?

The term 'cuckooing' borrows from the habits of the cuckoo bird which takes over the nests of other birds for its young. Essentially it is a form of criminal exploitation where vulnerable people are conned, coerced, controlled or intimidated into sharing, providing or offering up their accommodation to criminals (often drug dealers) who then use it to base their criminal activity (often drug dealing). Methods vary, however, intimidation and violence often underpin this. It is now widely associated with CL networks.

An alternative simple definition of cuckooing is provided by HMICFRS: A 'tactic where a drug dealer (or network) takes over a vulnerable person's home to prepare, store or deal drugs. Commonly associated with exploitation and violence' (HMICFRS, 2019b).

Cuckooing (Butera, 2013) is not new, but for years remained 'hidden' within housing or policing reports of 'crack dens' (Robinson and Flemen, 2002), largely overlooked or unrecognised as criminal exploitation and downplayed as a 'type of manipulation'. From 2000 onwards its profile was raised with the BBC describing it (2008) as 'a new type of crime which involves a drug dealer befriending a vulnerable individual who lives on their own. Like a cuckoo, the dealer moves in, takes over the property, and turns it into a drugs' den'.

For certain criminal groups it proves an effective exploitation technique. Widely utilised within CL models, its recent expansion indicates widespread shifts of CL models to profit maximisation and competitive advantage.

The term itself it not 'flagged' within policing systems so no specific quantifiable data is retrievable from constabularies. The NCA first referred to cuckooing in its 2015 Intelligence Assessment (NCA 2015: 4) noting some CL operatives entering into relationships with vulnerable women to access their premises. The 2017 Assessment (NCA, 2017b: 12–13) notes 77 per cent of police forces (33) reported documented cases of cuckooing linked to CL networks and that it remained the dominant method of obtaining access to suitable dealing locations:

> 'Yes, the cuckooing aspect. That's got worse. Definitely.'
> (Stakeholder 11)

This NCA Assessment confirms CL operatives target vulnerable individuals for criminal exploitation. Once access is gained the duration of the cuckooing episode varies from hours to several weeks.

Within CL cuckooing offers several benefits: reduced financial overheads; risk mitigation to avoid detection; easy access to local user networks; potential boost to local workforce; localised intelligence, for example dealers, markets, drug quality/quantity, dealing locations, CCTV positions, police activity.

It is not, however, risk-free as it involves sharing accommodation with vulnerable users often with physical/mental health issues. Such groups are considered unreliable and untrustworthy so they are tightly controlled. Successful cuckooing involves close contact and relationship-building which requires different skill sets, for example people skills or maturity; or, conversely, ruthlessness.

Spicer and colleagues (2019) identified four cuckooing typologies centred on different practices based upon host-dealer relationships observing many blurred lines regarding exploitation and complicity (see Table 6.1).

These typologies often underscore the complexity of various relationships between users and dealers. In their recent work on county lines, McLean and colleagues (2020) found evidence supporting all typologies in Merseyside, except coupling. Noting inherent ambiguity Spicer and colleagues cautioned against 'over-simplified binary notion[s] of willingness or unwillingness on the part of local residents' (2019: 14)

Table 6.1: Four cuckooing typologies identified by Spicer et al (2019)

Parasitic nest-invading	The archetypal cuckooing practice whereby the vulnerable are targeted and their homes accessed under false pretences and then used for dealing
Quasi-cuckooing	'Cases where notions of willingness and consent to host dealers were more complex' (Spicer et al, 2019: 11). This could include initial invites to stay or deal, or 'reciprocal renting' (Coomber and Moyle, 2018 :11) but which often later soured or dealers became unwelcome.
Coupling	Where sexual activity/relationships with female residents are used as the premise for access and later dealing from the property
Local cuckooing	A 'highly localised' cuckooing practice, often by local dealers imitating the practices of other gangs/crews, that is, appropriating the homes of those living in the same areas

while further cautioning about 'problematising simplistic understandings of how cuckooing manifest[s] and [is] experienced'.

An attractive business strategy?

A triumvirate of issues make cuckooing an effective strategy. Firstly, the environmental eco-system: properties belonging to drug users witness habitual use and sale of drugs. Secondly, informing authorities of drug usage on premises usually means interrupted supply. Thirdly, threats of violence are often met with compliance. Such factors alongside relationship-building means host-dealer interactions are complex, intertwined, nuanced, and often mutually-supportive, symbiotic and co-dependent.

Among user communities cuckooing is well established and in areas with a high-density of substance misusers, dealers can pond-skip premises breeding fear among users that it is inevitable. This widens insecurity, even leading some users to vacate premises.

Candidacy and social field

Potential targets are often 'visibly assessed' by CL operatives for 'vulnerability', for example dysfunctional domestic/family backgrounds; recent/enduring personal crisis; limited mental capacity; depression; disability; educational limitations; financial worries/debt; isolation; gambling, drug/alcohol addiction or dependency. Character traits such as susceptibility, gullibility, openness to manipulation/control (possibly through age, stature, gender, physicality, disability or mental impairment) increases potential candidacy. Those housed in conditions considered unmanaged/unsupervised, for example Care Homes, Supported Accommodation, Houses in Multiple Occupation, run-down private-rented bedsits, are deemed ideal candidates. Here the very visible housing conditions articulate the personal crisis embracing the individual, bearing witness to their vulnerability.

As when prospecting, CL operatives loiter outside drug treatment centres to identify vulnerable candidates or 'show face' they are present and ready to sell/serve up:

> 'Outside our office were people just hanging around in cars; quite obvious they were dealers, and again, we'd let the police know. But sometimes they do get targeted. I guess that's one of the problems of an agency located in the area, open and suitable for users – it becomes known to the dealers.' (Stakeholder 11)

Vulnerable 'candidates' exist on the margins of society, living in poverty, with limited financial opportunities and hustling to survive. Addiction, reliance upon medication and limited inter-personal relationships amplify vulnerability. Chaotic personal relationships and living arrangements are common, that is, sofa-surfing. Nonetheless vulnerable users find mutual support sharing food, benefits and drugs. These circumstances create in-group bonding which simultaneously segregates them from mainstream society pushing them towards criminality or exploitation:

> 'These people are clearly often very vulnerable and although they're using, they're victims. Essentially victims of the system. They're on heroin; they've got mental health issues. They're very, very vulnerable people. They are all ages from reasonably young people up to people in their fifties, sixties.' (Police 10)

These vulnerable groups constitute a shared social field whereby hustling and 'getting by' is accepted and validated (Fields and Walters, 1985). Society's rules are bent, broken or circumvented with lives 'off the cards' not liable to authoritative scrutiny. This social field overlaps significantly with that of CL operatives as both groups are immersed in eco-systems of drug supply/purchase/use. Commonalities create unspoken social bonds whereby certain behaviours are credible or familiar. These social fields, however, differ in terms of their rules. For CL operatives knowledge of the user social field gives a dominant upper hand in the shared sub-field of drug supply as they recognise users have constrained options.

Cuckooing also takes the form of 'Mate Crime' – a form of disability hate crime associated with fake/false friendships whereby guile, deceit or calculation is used to obtain advantage over the disabled person or to control/deceive them (Thomas, 2013). It is most common among those with learning disabilities and is linked to grooming and exploitation (Landman, 2014). In many cases, vulnerability, and reduced capacity, inhibits ability to cope with, or risk–assess, situations. This leads to judgements being impaired, poorly informed, short-term and risks overlooked. CL operatives can be seen as offering relief and solutions to such enduring conditions. Some vulnerable people are familiar with 'Tuesday Friends' – users posing as 'friends' who arrive each Tuesday to help 'spend' benefit money.

It was noted in this research study that there was a high level of awareness of cuckooing among the user community, though for many it was a source of anxiety:

> 'They're worried about getting robbed. They've always got something. And that always play[s] on your mind.' (User 04)

Ability to assess vulnerability means skilful employment of street capital, and witnessing parental drug misuse creates further proficiency:

> 'They are looking for vulnerable people whether from a single-parent household, no supervision, no money, being bullied – vulnerable ones to get on board, to groom them – "I'm your best friend", "I'm your boyfriend", and now you're in, it's abusive, that's who they're looking for.' (USG 01)

Cuckooing typology

CL operatives have established a typology of approaches to situationally adopt determined by: location; the presentation of the vulnerable individual; urgency of finding a base; potential for successful access; the operative involved.

Techniques are adopted to fit the situation using street capital. Ineffective choices suggest rusty or defunct skills. Ongoing assessments made regarding dosage and calibration also rely upon street capital. Importantly this includes assessment of duration. Degrees of deception and crafting of an initial narrative becomes an important element to relationship-building with socially skilled actors more adept at framing stories (Goffman, 1974) aimed at obtaining cooperation. Techniques for gaining access include:

■ Slow approach over time

Building relationships over time such as a 'Tuesday Mate'. This approach is often used and operatives establish a nearby Hub and 'hedge their bets', for future moves.

■ Guile and fake friendship

Including identifying locations where vulnerable people spend their day, for example 'greasy-spoon cafes'. One CL manager used considerable skill to commence a conversation before inviting herself back:

> 'Yeah, we drove down, had a look around. Noticed a lot of homeless people, lot of drug users. Obviously I'm sent to flutter my eyelashes, talk to people, find things out. I started on this particular drug user, I called him Buttons because he would always [eat] chocolate buttons. He would tell us where to go and we would give him drugs and then the line just literally started from there. He brought his friends, other cousins and stuff like that so started working on the line up there. I got us into somebody's house. There was a man in a cafe where we always used to go. Obviously he had special needs, learning needs or whatever. In a wheelchair, in that cafe every single day, all day. You know those people. You recognise. So, obviously "Go and make friends with him". All right, I went and made friends with him. I used to sit and talk to him. They're still establishing the line up there at the time, like the users and stuff and giving out free samples. We knew that it was kicking off so we needed a base, we needed somewhere to be. He liked *Hollyoaks*, he liked *EastEnders*. He talked to me about that, buying me cups of tea all day. "Okay, I'll come to your house. Let's watch the soaps. Let's get food from Morrisons". Easily done. I was in his house. No questions asked, and within an hour or so, there were six of us. Easily done.' (USG 01)

■ Tip-offs

Tip-offs from other users also facilitate cuckooing opportunities. Often users' desire favours with new runner/dealers and they provide information in return for 'freebies'. Sometimes done as revenge against users they dislike or want controlled; or to deflect attention away from them as a target.

▓ Introduction or 'passed on' by other users

Here introductions can occur through normal interactions, again often meaning drugs in return for a favour:

> 'Well, normally it can be through a friend, or not really a friend. Say my friend Bob knows this drug addict, he might bring one of them, "Ben, meet my mate, so-and-so," and then one day so-and-so will turn up by himself. "Oh, he c[a]me in once before with my friend, I'll let him in." Then so-and-so will turn up the next day with two of his mates, "Meet my mates," and then before you know it, they just intimidate him.' (User 06)

▓ Coat-tailing

Here a runner/dealer enters by force on the coat-tails of another user to whom the door was opened. Users become proxies or foils and are paid in drugs to 'front up' this action:

> 'Last night I had this man at my door at one o'clock last night. He goes out with that mad girl, [name]. As I opened the door I could see a shadow and it was him waiting to rush into my house. See [name] – when she was nicked at my house she blames me for it, so she was waiting to rush into my house with him. It's not ideal having her nearby.' (User 01)

▓ Open proposition

Sometimes referred to as cold calling. Here potential users are approached by operatives as a 'nitty' and followed home from a Job Centre or Needle Exchange. Open propositions follow to serve up:

> 'Two guys that lived there, just drug users and we just propositioned them one day and said, "You can have a free whatever you want – if we could stay in your house". No problem. They had two children as well. That was no problem. Crack cocaine and heroin, both. They weren't intravenously using though but the woman, her baby was pretty young, she was bad. She was like skin and bones, she was so bad. She wouldn't eat; used meal-replacement milkshakes and stuff. Before that we were going to Wendy's Cafe to charge the phones, a wash in the sink and all. We were never questioned. Nobody ever asked us what we were doing. We'd buy a cup of tea or something, because we'd have change, they'd give us

change, like "Get yourself food" or whatever but I'm talking about £20 for the week for the two of us. So, we went in and out of that before we had somebody's house to use.' (USG 01)

▪ Enticement

Users are enticed by offers of (what often starts off as) 'free' drugs, sample bags, special offers, two-for-one deals, increased quantity, improved quality, short-term deals, 'take it or leave it' deals. Immediate availability free-at-the-point-of-service, clinches the deal:

> 'We went to another house, a chalet. This was a single woman, with five children, all of them were taken into care. She'd come from London to get herself sorted out so she could get her kids back. Obviously we come on the scene, were offering this delivery service, we're offering these special offers trying to get the line to grow. Her habit went way out of control. She was really nice, but ended up in prison due to her habit. She would shoplift to get even more drugs because we took the piss out of her. She was so vulnerable. When it was her by herself not like the woman and her partner we could say, "No, you're not getting anything today, what are you going to do about it?" type thing, so she would shoplift and give us trainers in exchange for drugs even though we were living in her house.' (USG 01)

▪ Tandem work with care staff

One unpleasant example of cuckooing was revealed in a previous research project in Lambeth, south London. Research revealed a local care worker with responsibility for the daily personal care of an 80-year-old disabled man with dementia had set up a fake care-management arrangement with her son. The female middle-aged care worker would collect the man daily from his flat in Brixton and take him 'out' for the day. During this time her son would weigh/wrap/bag/deal drugs from the premises until they returned in the late afternoon. During the time away from the flat the mother would sit on the Circle tube line all day with the gentlemen while she read magazines. The elderly pensioner would regularly go to the toilet where he sat.

Cuckooing frequency can vary or properties can be rotated. Some runner/dealers stay only an hour to 'serve up' for users, almost like in-house catering. Such addresses become problematic for neighbours. Runner/dealers also know when properties locally become vacant and will move in.

186

Cuckooing Control Repertoire (post–access)

Having gained access, the Cuckooing Control Repertoire offers multiple techniques to manage and control the premises to facilitate drug supply. Techniques have much in common with those utilised by men controlling women using domestic violence as in the Duluth Power and Control Wheel (Duluth Domestic Abuse Intervention Project, www. duluth–model.org).

The repertoire includes:

■ **Control of domestic environment**

This includes using physical domination and emotional control of the house or flat such that it is clear who has control. It might also extend to controlling household interactions and finances:

> 'Yeah, yeah, I put him up and he turned nasty after a while. Started taking over … go and get this, go and get that … get me fags … everything … to me and [name] he was just a horrible, horrible man.' (User 09)

> 'The guy in question was a vulnerable chap recently moved down from [name], for exactly the same thing. Now when I spoke to him afterwards he said, "I don't know how the hell they have tracked me, they've followed me". So somehow the gang that were operating where he originally came from had managed to find out where he was. Don't ask me how. I didn't get into that. But he was adamant it was the same group of people. So we get two calls, one from the housing provider, one from him. We do our usual thing – a late-night knock. We managed to get in without alerting anyone. The drug … the vulnerable victim has been chucked out of his room essentially and is on the landing, just curled up. His door, his room is shut, so he just does the thing. We get into the room, there's a young drug dealer in there, I say young, 20s, he had not a great amount, I think it was about 18 wraps but he'd managed to stuff them into his arse cheeks before we got in, somehow, I don't know how, and he had essentially threatened our vulnerable person that if he didn't give him his room, if he didn't do some deals for him down the street that he'd get knifed. Clearly we arrested the chap. We then took the vulnerable victim … we phoned up the housing provider and said, "Have you got any other rooms for this chap we can

take him to tonight because he's clearly not safe where he is?" They were brilliant.' (Police 10)

'Certainly the two I know of who were cuckooed were frightened and anxious, yes. I think it was scared more than anything. Especially if they can't avoid it if someone has gone and kicked them out of their room, that's bad enough.' (Stakeholder 08)

■ Threats of violence and intimidation

This includes displays of violent temperament, shouting, swearing and physical intimidation:

'Mostly commonly, yes, it's normally a knife, yes, of course it is. I don't really so much hear of guns much. Not unless it's the blacks from London. But a few of the Travellers and what not, normally it's knives or just pure fear. Sometimes it's not the attack that scares you, it's the thought of when they're going to do it, you know?' (User 06)

'When they had that incident and the guy had a shotgun and they had to search the property, and remove everything. He threatened them with a shotgun and they thought he had stored it in [name]'s home. So we went round, he was ... they pulled everything out and put it all back again and the gun was found in the garden down the road.' (Police 10)

'Threats and violence, yes, that's what they do, don't they? Once they get their foot in the door, if they can do that they will! If you're in a room on your own and there's only you and him and three of his mates, what chance do you have? They all have knives and that. They're not going to come down here with nothing on 'em, know what I mean?' (User 04)

■ Fear

Fear of police, the probation service, social services or of prosecution prevents users reporting or taking action. Others fear the physical presence of the runner/dealer:

'Some people are really rigid and won't let us in. Others? Well, this woman who is vulnerable re drug use and mental health, did let us in and the drug dealer was standing there with a

Samurai sword in his hand. I don't think he realised we were police until she opened the door then he see us and he it put down. I think the thing for her is fear over anything else and she's probably got herself into a bit of trouble for allowing this a second time. We dragged a young girl out of there as well. She gets herself into certain situations. Like there was a black male, 6ft, a big built guy, quite intimidating for her and he's got weapons, and we pulled out 550 shots – that's £10 wrap. So you're looking at around £10,000 of drugs. That's a lot.' (Police 10)

'Once they're in, you pretty much have got no way of getting them out. Unless you call the police, but then if you call the police … do you know what, a few people … is it worse off going to prison or living on the outside as a grass? I don't know what's worse, because I got labelled as a grass and it sticks, you can't get rid of it. They done Mum's cars, I've been attacked in town and there's nothing worse than walking through the High Street and someone's shouting out "snitch", or "grass". You know if you don't want them sort of people … it's embarrassing being known, associated with that sort of people.' (User 06)

■ Physical violence
One elderly pensioner user told of a violent relationship with a local runner/dealer:

'Oh, he's just horrible on the gear and that and he was just horrible to me. On the white 'n all that. Making me try to weigh up the gear and that with [name]. [Name] has to wrap it and I had to do the weights. The size 'n that he'd go, "Nah, that's something off and you'll have to pay for that". When he was doing them up. He was just putting it on me to pay for it. He had one of my pensions, took my card off me and everything. We've had all that trouble. But it seems everywhere I go he seems to just turn up. He hit me. In town he hit me in the car on the arm. He said, "You're lucky I didn't reverse back and run you over". They were down by the [pub] when we were walking down he drove right up on the pavement at us. We moved out of the way, he got out and came across to us and whack. I took it on the jaw like. I was 70 recently. He hit me in the eye and it came up and my eye is still wrecked a bit there. Yes, he's horrible. Just a horrible man. He's a nutter, mate. He's a white guy. He goes around in his [name] van. I don't know if he's still dealing or what. But yeah, he just turns up out of the blue when we're out and bout. He keeps pointing and that.' (User 09)

'Knives, tends to be a lot here. I've heard of cases, in the past where there were hammers and beatings involved, but I think the knives tend to be the main thing that comes across. Of course, it's quite difficult to identify. As a drug service, we get targeted, dealers try and target us. In terms of they want to be around sometimes our service, to try and pick up clients, or see who's coming in.' (Stakeholder 08)

■ Pacification

One effective management and control technique is to pacify cuckooed owners by making readily available the source of the addition – be it drugs or alcohol – to achieve user pacification and compliance. Drugs offered may be increased in quantity, quality and availability, often meaning users no longer have to source the drugs themselves, removing anxiety. With prospects of improved availability, other problems and unpleasantries are relegated making pacification a transition phase before other controls are required:

'No, it's just that they're well known in the area, they're users, just using. And people often come down and say, "Look, can you put me up in your address and I'll give you three or four shots". They don't work, so they've got no money, so they say, "Yes, come back, you can use our gaff" and they'll say, "We'll give you three or four shots while we are [in] your gaff". This will feed their habit while they set up in and deal from the address. Then when they're in there, they can't get shot of them.' (Police 10)

■ Medicinal cosh

Aligned with pacification is the more advanced repertoire technique of providing drugs as a medicinal cosh. This moves beyond pacification to ensuring users remains in a semi-permanent drugged-up state. Supply is now readily available and cheaply acquired. While some users welcome this and comply, others have this forced upon them through stealth and guile. Heavy or regular dosage/supply of drugs ensures supplication leaving dealers free to move unhindered by challenge or interaction.

As other users or runner/dealers join the house freely this permits 'gas lighting' whereby the user's memory can now be questioned and ridiculed. A medicinal cosh reduces risks of informing or recalling details. Some users claim to have been kept in a zombie-like state which soon becomes normalised.

■ Withdrawal or control of drugs

An alternative technique is to withhold drugs from dependent users, including prescribed drugs.

■ Control of interactions

One young female CL operative reflected that her role made her act contrary to her nature, but attempts to demonstrate compassion were subject to control:

> 'He made me so sad, he really did. I'm the biggest cry baby ever, I'm the biggest softie. All of this kind of stuff, and I'm not trying to make excuses for it because I've done what I've done, you're forced to act that character. You're forced to be somebody who you are not because you're scared or because you're trying to keep up this bravado for whatever reason. That's not me, I'm not that kind of person and that got me in a lot trouble. I tried to stick up for him. He used to have Meals on Wheels delivered to him all the time, so every day they'd let him out of his room to speak to his Support Worker, go in the living room, and then we'd wheel him back and he'd be locked up for the rest of the day. She had no clue. He could have asked [at] any point? Why didn't he? He was terrified. He knew what was going on. He saw what was going on. He could have got himself out but he didn't. But so many times I'd say, "Let me just take him out. Let me just wheel him around", and I would get assaulted and he would see it, he would cry, he would feel bad because I tried to, but I was crying because I said, "It's my fault you're in this situation."' (USG 01)

Such situations illustrate the missed opportunities for practitioners to identify when domestic situations have altered.

■ Holding hostage

Some users refer to their engagement with CL operatives as being held hostage:

'I was lucky to get my flat back. He had me hostage in there for three months in a way till I escaped … with the gun in that. Yeah … well, they found that, eventually. We had armed response teams come round. And the big knives he had.' (User 09)

The NCA Intelligence Assessment 2017 (NCA 2017b: 13) notes that of the 33 forces reporting cuckooing 21 per cent (7) reported forms of modern slavery with vulnerable hosts detained against their will or denied access to parts of the property.

■ Framing of users
The Cuckooing Control Repertoire contains inventive techniques such as framing users for criminal actions:

'No, he tried to put the gun charge of little [Name], didn't he. Tried to put it all on him. I said, "Mate, don't you be taking a fuckin' gun charge – are you mad? Fifty bullets and a gun, are you going to take that charge. You're fucking nuts."' (User 01)

■ Put to work – dealing and wrapping up
Some CL operatives require the cuckooed user to perform tasks. Some users are happy to do this voluntarily in expectation of drugs. Task allocation depends on runner/dealers but this comes with risks as users are not considered trustworthy, so must be surveilled. Others just answer the phone. For some users roles are forced upon them under duress.

■ Generation of further violence
A cuckooed property used as a dealing Hub becomes a target for robbery which in turn generates significant violence. Vulnerable users are aware of this and CL operatives point to this possible outcome suggesting users 'work with us' to create a more effective team, to reduce likelihood of attack by rivals.

■ Ongoing intimidation
The Cuckooing Control Repertoire continues even after operatives move out. Previously cuckooed users accept they are on a waiting list for a return visit:

'[Name] keeps coming round in his van staring at me and he came round with his crew from the pub the other night. He came round to get the wheelchair and some stuff he had at mine and he took the wheelchair and said to me, "You'll be in that fucking chair soon. I'll make sure of that". He's making threats to me.' (User 09)

The Cuckooed User Response Repertoire

Users exploited by cuckooing also have a Repertoire of User Responses available to them. Some options, if actioned, help them regain control and enact more agency. Although available, options might not necessarily be actioned immediately until risk assessed. Assessed risks will change daily making assessment very challenging.

Each repertoire option constitutes a strategic action though in reality such choices are often constrained and each brings different consequences, for example staying away or moving temporarily leads to disrupted friendship networks or disrupted treatment pushing users to unknown dealers. The User Response Repertoire includes the following:

■ **Compliance**
Some users are complicit in their relationship with the CL operatives, clearly deriving benefits from the hosting arrangements. It is likely this relates to hosts operating with greater capacity and agency. For police, it is crucial to establish victim/offender relationships or duress to determine possible prosecution as opposed to pathways out and rehousing.

> 'It's much more reciprocal than most people think. But then you have the people that are complicit in a way in that it suits them, they maybe get some free drugs, you know, and so on, and so on, and actually … or they maybe get paid for what they're doing, and so yes, in a sense they may have elements of vulnerability about them but they're much more complicit and able to make some decisions around what's happening to them.' (Police 06)

■ **Compromise**
Some users will compromise with CL operatives and accept a medicinal cosh or drugs believing they now have access to a steady supply of cheap/ free drugs from a known source, without having to leave the flat to score. Rent will be paid and violence, at least towards the user, minimised.

Other forms of compromise include starting a sexual relationship. As a strategic action this might bring benefits of free drugs and violence avoidance – though naturally this is not guaranteed. Some users admitted to conscious employment of this strategy. Other felt this happened naturally without strategising.

■ Complain
Here users complain to other users/family in the hope that intelligence will eventually reach the police. The police are likely to raid the premises and:

> 'More than likely, take the door off, I would've assumed.' (User 06)

■ Cashing in
Some users acquiesce to their new situation and comply through a state of helplessness or fear. Others merely comply with any new demands and simply wait for the 'visitors' to leave:

> 'Yes, I have, it's happening now. No, not me. No, I know some people it's happening to. They just take over your house. They intimidate the people into taking over their house and when that happens, what do you do? What can you do?' (User 06)

Others will accept the benefits provided by the runner/dealers and cash in by running favours, working and acting as a user-dealer.

■ Casting off
Here users 'pass the buck' by passing on runner/dealers to more vulnerable users – usually done by implying covert surveillance operations are underway on the property. The cuckooed user suggests a new premises as a favour to help relocation. This ensures a triple benefit of ridding them from the flat, passing them on to rivals and being paid in drugs for the favour.

■ Calling in
Here users call in to visit their housing landlord to 'share' details of their experience or make it known to them. Opening up to agency staff emphasises user vulnerability.

In this study, the local charity working with the homeless for more than 20 years has many alcoholics and Class A–using clients. Staff are aware of the cuckooing situation and adapt daily routines to undertake house visits:

> 'It's a lot of house checks. The staff do it by during the day then we do two checks throughout our shift – when we start our shift and when we finish.' (Stakeholder 08)

Not all clients will open up to staff about cuckooing issues:

> 'It's difficult to say really. I suppose it depends on their own
> robustness really. We become ... I know there's several cases
> where we've become aware of it because the person has been
> quite fragile emotionally, and they've basically unloaded and
> opened up in the sessions, and given more information,
> whereas I would think a person who is more robust, and feels
> they're able to cope and deal with it, would take longer to
> actually feel that yes, it is time for me to be able to try and get
> some sort of support, or help.' (Stakeholder 08)

■ Conspiring

This usually involves liaising with rival dealers to get the property raided.
This high-risk strategy is probably a last resort involving snitching to rivals,
passing on details regarding money, security, personal movements, drug
supply, quantities and suitable times to 'call'.

■ Counteracting

Here users try to retake the property by force, maybe in tandem with
other users. Again this is very high-risk and only undertaken if users stand
to lose more keeping the dealer on the premises, for example being on
licence/bail. This strategy might be undertaken if dealers are young and
inexperienced. This strategy can bring retaliation.

■ Calling the police

Informing police that your property is being cuckooed and used as a
dealing Hub brings police response. Such engagements need careful
planning and timing. This option takes two forms:

a) Direct Informing. This brings problems of possible arrest for the user
   and brings the possibility of retribution from runner/dealers.

> 'Obviously a lot of people grass. People we speak to who will
> just grass on everybody – I've got someone round at Dave's
> house, or there's this person down at so-and-so's house. We'll
> rock up and try and get in. A lot of results are where we stop
> people and say, "Right then, what's going on? Who's about
> today?" "Oh, yes, so-and-so, he's down at Old Angie's house",
> "And where's Jimmy?" "Oh, he's down their home". Yes. If
> you call the police then you're in trouble because you've got
> them in your house. Either you've conspired with them or

you're allowing them in so you're already involved, aren't you? So, do you call the police and get yourself in trouble or just hope for the best?' (User 06)

'A lot of 'em have grassed – they'll often just talk to use cos they're intimidated or they find them to be a rude abrupt person. So they'll say go get that person, he's an arse.... He's dangerous or something like that.' (Police 10)

One user noted being labelled a grass brings retribution from other users whose supply is interrupted noting they will shout across the street and draw attention to informers.

b) Soft grassing. Users choose to moderate their risk and exposure to cuckooing by informing the police to get people out. This strategy might also increase their risk if caught out. Variations of this strategy include deliberately passing their keys on to the police. Keys might be offered with minimum information or no information other than a suggestion that the police call round or use the keys if they wish. This operates as a tacit agreement and expectation of police involvement.

'I stopped [Name] once and asked her if anyone was in her flat. She said no but I could tell it was a lie. So I said, "Gimme your keys and I'll check". Then she said, "Actually I think there is someone in there doing drugs". So we walk in and there is a woman in there frying some chicken and she sees us and goes "whoa" and freezes. She's got about a grand of notes in her pocket and there's a load of uncut on the table.' (Police 10)

■ **Calling it quits**

Some tenants casually leave the property and stay away. Others tenants request to be moved by their landlord until things die down. Local charity staff identify that sometimes clients are moved because of cuckooing. They acknowledge that this is also highly disruptive to clients in recovery and those seeking to manage their habit and their domestic life:

'People are very guarded in what they say about that, and again, we only get a partial picture of what actually is happening. We are aware that certain people feel they have to leave the area for a short while, and then come back when they feel it's safe. Some people have had to completely be transferred out completely. Because they've been threatened. That their place has been cuckooed, and it has got to the stage where police had to intervene, and they had to move away.' (Stakeholder 08)

■ Capture
Here users will elect to get deliberately caught by police which permits police involvement without being considered a grass.

Additional outcomes

The effects of cuckooing do not simply end at the door of the user. Impacts can be felt in other ways and by other groups:

■ Overdosing
Increased frequency of encounters and access to readily available drugs of increased purity can lead to overdosing. (Refer to Public Health England and Department of Health (2017) for statistics.) Some users referred to this as a consequence of deeper involvement:

> 'Yeah, I know of them. Definitely. I know a few people actually this has happened to, yeah. Quite a few people. [One guy] he's a lot older than me but he'd have a lot of people coming in and they just bullied him … well, I don't think he was all there, to be honest. He had problems really, but they just took advantage of him. And you had people standing there … one of the dealers got caught there, if I remember rightly. Yeah, someone got caught there, but he ended up being kicked out. People died in that house – yeah, two people died in there from an overdose.' (User 04)

■ Distrust among users
Users informing to the police generates police intelligence alongside other problems, so some inform by proxy. This furthers distrust among the using community who blame each other for their arrest. Others bear grudges and will occasionally 'dob each other in' in order to switch police attention from themselves or to rid themselves of troublesome runner/dealers, especially those who have cuckooed their properties.

■ Prostitution/sex work
The links between county lines drugs networks and prostitution/sex work are complicated. The NCA Intelligence Assessment 2017 (NCA,

2017b) identified that the use of premises associated to sex workers by CL operatives is reported in 33 per cent of force questionnaire returns (14). Many women working in the sex industry are doing so to fund their own drug habits (Moyle et al, 2013; Sanders et al, 2017, 2018). As such they also vulnerable and liable to be cuckoo'd.

> 'A lot of our prostitutes are Class A drug users and vulnerable to cuckooing, just as vulnerable as any other. We have a local prostitution problem. We did a diversion scheme with them over the past six years and reduced it down from about 60 individuals to a hardcore group of about ten. These people are funding their habit through prostitution, but then there's the link to county lines where their addresses are being used by dealers. This is street-based, which is really rare nowadays. Most of our work is in relation to brothels at the moment.' (Police 04)

In this study local police were aware of new pop-up brothels appearing in the vicinity (Saghani, 2018). The links between drug misuse and sex work are well established (Sanders et al, 2017) and local police were supportive of local sex workers often offering exit pathways. Some women chose to inform on CL operatives and exchange intelligence, probably as a risk reduction strategy. Sex workers are also used as proxies to access a user's property for cuckooing including acting as intermediary between users and runner/dealers. The arrangements can, however, be mutually beneficial for all concerned.

> 'This older guy had runners in his flat. He had runners down in Ashford, he moved to Medway and continued it here. He's just an old boy who allows drug dealers into his house. He's in his 70s, this guy. He came to our attention as we got called to the address. He always has young London lads in there. Recently he has a prostitute living with him. She pretty much has moved herself in, but he just seems happy with having her there. He doesn't seem to have any issue with these young lads sitting there with knives, or going in and out selling drugs. I don't know what he gets out of it. He's not a user either. He's vulnerable to some extent and will engage but he seems oblivious. Can't see dementia or anything. He's never mentioned family or anything – it might be company more than anything.' (Police 06)

Users with agency

Other forms of residential arrangements are identifiable and operate differently to those discussed earlier. Frequently these alternate arrangements only occur where the users operate with a greater agency than the more vulnerable user groups. This might involve a user or two users living together as a couple offering their home as a potential flop-house. This might operate as a sort of criminal Airbnb:

> 'Remember, I mentioned [Name]? He's from this area. He started off as a runner and he now has earned his stripes and has his own contacts. So [Name] and [Name] are contacts of his and they are also on the contact list of every county line phone we have ever seen. So that address is obviously copied on cards and passed around on pieces of paper so they know that that's a secure address and contact. If they won't house them, then they know someone who will.' (Police 13)

Some users will market their home to runner/dealers using social media and listing favourable aspects of the property:

> 'Also what I've seen on county lines is a text message which reads as follows from a contact for example called, Savvy. It will say… "Hi Ace. Just to let you know my place isn't known to the police. It's never been raided before. It's tucked away nice and quiet. I can also do a bit of running for you if wish."' (Police 13)

Such promotional arrangements might be offered by users who are not necessarily viewed as the stereotypical drug user, that is, they might maintain a job and a heroin habit:

> 'So users will happily promote themselves cos they know it'll bring in free gear for them. So for the dealer, the risks here are relatively low cos they've never been raided. They may only have been stop-checked once by the police in 15 years. Cos they are under-the-counter heroin addicts.' (Police 13)

This arrangement typically benefits both the user and CL runner/dealer. The police quickly point out, however, that this will also negate the likelihood of the user claiming victim status or coercion.

'And it shows, from a criminal point of view that they've gone out of their way to allow the county lines to operate [so tougher sentence if caught].' (Police 13)

By offering up their premises for short-stays, users achieve benefits of cheap, readily available drugs. They also achieve elevated status and improved networking contacts. Crucially such promotional arrangements give users greater agency and more situational control.

Here violence is likely short-lived. Regular runner/dealers rate their stay with others. This arrangement offers minor income, stable drug supply and eventually increased status.

For runner/dealers this arrangement offers security and usually a higher standard of accommodation. Local intelligence can be shared, for example regarding local police movements. Not all users are skilled at conducting this arrangement so it is favoured by those functioning better in society or hidden as users. This arrangement allows users to prepare for arrival and inform others of arrival. This boosts their credibility and status as intel is more accurate and trusted. This can be beneficial increasing local status and street capital.

The NCA Intelligence Assessment 2017 (NCA, 2017b: 13) identified some cuckooed addresses being used by multiple CL networks simultaneously. This fits with hosting operations. There are no reports of violence associated to this model. Use of caravans, holiday lets and serviced apartments and Airbnb are also reported from this study. This represents diversification and attempts to isolate bagging and production operations and to reduce risk.

Case study: Cuckooing – User 05

This case study focuses on a mature drug dependant male with severe physical disabilities. The flat owner had a previous history of heroin and crack cocaine use. He lacked independence and was isolated. Police located a London drug dealer in his property with over 100 wraps. The dealer appeared to be an upper-tier or middle-manager supplying/managing a range of junior runner/dealers.

'I'm sick and tired of being on all that stuff. I'm not on heroin any more but I'm just tampering with crack cocaine. I can stop if I want but I only have manageable amounts. It doesn't really give a good buzz – only when you go on a bender, but I tend not to do that. I don't have to buy it regularly but just as and when I want. I don't have a regular dealer but I know how to get it.

'I had a couple of bad fellas staying here, you knowwhatImean. They came and stayed and tried to take over but it didn't work out. The lad who was here from London? ... well ... I don't know how it happened. I opened the door. I didn't know him beforehand but I knew him name was [Name]. Well, one day he just turned up, he asked if he could spark up around here and I let him in. He was here for about three weeks. It's the same person every day, but when he was here he was quiet. He'd be here for three hours, four hours, maybe less.

'Well, he just served up, as far as I know. I let him. He was trying to serve up from here. I didn't tell him to get out. He gave me a shot just to sit by and watch. You're never gonna stop it unfortunately. But you'll get one dealer off the street and another will turn up. I've had about 20 dealers' numbers on my phone at one point. Then I change my phone but they still get my number somehow, I don't know how it happens. I haven't spoken to anyone so I guess someone just passes it on. Even though they don't know you, they ring me. They're just trying to sell normally not to get put up or anything. I don't have to get back to them, it's all by text.

'I know some users have their own pad and dealers will try to take that over, so you've got to watch. I know a few friends where that's happened. You just know all of a sudden they're running the place. It lasts as long as it goes on for – a week, two weeks, three weeks ... it can be a long time. They don't pay rent or nothing but they do give you some gear. I'd get just a couple of shots, a couple of stones. Crack. He'd give me that at the start of the day. The quality, well? The rocks are not all that ... not all that at all. You might as well burn a ten-pound note, Ha Ha.

'I didn't take shots before he came. I took stuff but not every day. When he was here I think my drug taking got worse. Yeah, I got two shots each day. I do it in one go, knowwhatImean. I would've taken three if he'd offered 'em. I guess I might have been manipulated to keep me quiet.

'During the day he'd just sit and play with his phone. He got a lot of texts not calls. I think he had people to serve up for him – but I don't know who that was. He never got me food. I think he just wanted this address as a base, I suppose. He'd go and buy something, pizza and stuff, but he was staying here at night. He'd often get McDonald's. He'd come in at any time of the day, stay a few hours and go. I'd sit and watch TV. He never had his own key, but I often have the door unlocked though.

'In terms of his money, it varied ... varied. I can't tell you how much he had on him cos I didn't always see. He'd have a wad sometimes, making several hundred a week, I guess. After three weeks, two others arrived and stayed in the back room. Occasionally I'd have a couple in the room, but I'd never seen 'em before. He never tried to talk to me or had relationship[s] at all really, he never tried to help me. I was quite happy to have him here for a while.

'Eventually, I was getting pretty pissed off towards the end, knowwhatImean. But I didn't really say that to him. I didn't know how he would react. I wasn't really scared and I've not come upon violence ... I've got people ... I can make a phone call and have people here quickly if I need to. But I was getting pissed off, yeah. I really thought he was taking the piss. I wasn't intimidated by him. I think it was his first time with an older person. He was only 15 or 16. I thought he was older as he told me he was 19. He was from London but I don't know where. When he was not here I don't know where he was. I don't know if he was part of a gang ... well, part of a London gang probably.

'It's been going a long time. Gangs have been dealing for a while. Sometimes they serve up in the street too. Now they serve up more from people's homes. It's worse now than even five years ago.

'In terms of people coming into my home and dealing from here.... Yeah, well, it's not happening ... I'm gonna make sure of that. I'm just going to say NO. I've got a big family so I have people I can call on. I didn't have visitors coming to the address.

'I can still get gear if I wanted it. My drug taking is less now as I don't take it every day. In a week I'd take a couple of shots. So since he left I've gone down from two shots a day to two shots a week.

'If he came back tomorrow with the same sort of deal ... I'd say no. My health is worth more. You've got to get it into perspective – my health is worth more than all that, knowwhatImean.

'Well, if you've got a drug problem, it's very hard. You can't help them. If you've got a drug problem it's too tempting to let that person in. It's up to the person to stop it.'

Although not fully evident how this arrangement came about it was clear that it was perceived to be mutually beneficial by the user. The user had employed methods of neutralisation (Sykes and Matza, 1957) in order to re-frame the arrangement as a bargain through which he could obtain both drug supply and company.

Reflection

In this research study most CL operatives viewed the vulnerable people they cuckooed as pawns and playthings who could be easily manipulated. However, one young female CL operator reflected during interview on those she has cuckooed noting with regret that:

> 'Do you know what, they're all really, really lovely people. I couldn't tell you anything bad about any of the drug users who I was staying with. I couldn't tell you anything bad. Nothing. None of them were aggressive. None of them were rude even though we were awful in their own houses. The ones that we stayed with anyway.' (USG 01)

In the next section I consider the views of the user community, a group almost wholly ignored or deemed irrelevant by wider society. Often a tricky set of interview respondents, they were nonetheless insightful, friendly and informative. I then articulate the views of dealers regarding users before reviewing how dealers feel about involvement in county line networks.

The complex world of user/dealer relationships

Over time the user community has frequently been demonised and pejoratively characterised as compulsive 'junkies' (Lloyd, 2010), 'outsiders' (Taylor, 2008), whose addiction compels them to be irrational and desperate for their 'next hit' (Coomber, 2006: 90). If not viewed as 'problematic' they are often viewed as 'vulnerable' and to be pitied. For some, their very presence signifies neighbourhood degeneration, diminished community values and ontological insecurity (Innes, 2014: 17). For detailed insight into the drug using community see Young's *The Drugtakers* (1971); Agar's *Ripping and Running* (1973); Pearson's *The New Heroin Users* (1987b) and Parker and colleagues' *Living with Heroin* (1988), and regarding crack see Bourgois (1995); Williams' *Crackhouse* (1992).

Coomber and Moyle (2017), Spicer and colleagues (2019) and McLean and colleagues (2020) all identify greater nuance between being an exploited victim or an active perpetrator while decrying often simplified and singular media narratives of users as hapless victims. In reality users are both victim and offender simultaneously – (as are many runner/dealers), though agency or presentation often mask both.

Perceptions of dealers can straddle both the negative: 'Pushers' (Coomber, 2006); child exploiters (NCA, 2015); traffickers (Dorn et al, 1992); engaged in exploitation, manipulation and violence (Coomber and Moyle, 2017; Coomber and Pyle, 2015; Coomber et al, 2014; Spicer et al, 2019); or the more positive: 'individual entrepreneurs' (McLean et al, 2020); 'subcontractors' (Windle and Briggs, 2015b), or 'grafters' (Moyle and Coomber, 2015).

Views from users

The user community operates as its own social field with its own rules of behaviour, ways of being, codes of practice, manners, identifiable actors, habitus, doxa (value of the Game); illusio (worth of the Game) (Bourdieu, 1991: 22–5) and accepted concepts of social fate or trajectory.

Critical to this social field is skill and knowledge regarding drugs, how they work, their psychological and physiological effects, safe dosage, usage techniques and so on. Such skills can mean life or death so this knowledge is much valued within the community. Skilled users become 'old heads', central to knowledge exchange, often helping out those less skilled. This ensures drugs knowledge acts as 'street capital' within this community.

As in all social fields, the social field of the user is not homogenous but is stratified and hierarchical (see Parkin's work *Habitus and Drug Using Environments*, 2013). Skilled users acquire street capital skills of recognising attributes of other users, for example reliability, vulnerability, emotional intelligence, reliability, experience of using and so on. Respondents talked openly about how some drug users were 'scummy' or 'deadbeat junkies', while others were 'reliable' and 'more trustworthy'. One using couple were quick to differentiate themselves from those openly begging for money in the High Street:

> 'The users all know each other, mmm. See, we've been together 20 years, they know us. You built up.... See, some of the people we know were friends first, then sent us out and some do it the other way round, knowwhatImean, cos that's

the best way to do it because there's distrust in everything. We don't mix with all the riff-raff. You know the ones who sit outside and beg. We just keep ourselves to ourselves. We're users, we use it to keep away the pain, the stomach cramps, to keep us mobile. If we can, we'd come off it tomorrow but it's not as easy as that. I wish it was. But if it was easy there'd be way more people doing it.' (User 02)

Users' views on dealers

Throughout numerous interviews users talked openly about the practice of dealing, those involved, its presentation, how dealers control both users and lines. They were keenly aware of recent changes resulting from CLs:

'Oh yeah, yeah. Every time you take one off, another one takes their place – always! They know they can use young people – they make so much money.' (User 04)

Their ages:

'I've got tattoos older than the boys doing the dealing and running the lines.' (User 11)

The capricious nature of the dealers:

'There's many. They [the dealers] move the goalposts when they want to, mate.' (User 10)

The volume, age and risk of runner/dealers:

'Yeah, it's rife here, fucking rife! Well, yes, you see, it … it's dangerous, it's shit. You see, I choose it myself. I got arrested and even done my meth in the police station. When I came out they [the dealers] straight up offered me a spliff and I said, "Nah, that's it for me now". I've got two children. Fair enough, I smoke crack now and then … but county lines, yes, there's hundreds of 'em down here. They're youngsters. They're getting robbed out there, there's knives being pulled out – soon there'll be a murder around here.' (User 06)

Making money to buy drugs

Poor communities hosting established heroin markets become exposed to (and often actively support) criminal activity such as acquisitive crime and the illegal market economies arising from this localised criminality (Parker and Newcombe, 1987; Seddon, 2006).

Those active in the social field of the using community strategise how best to raise funds to maintain access to, and purchasing power for, illegal drug use (DeBeck et al, 2007). Strategies include sex work and criminal activity such as burglary, theft, robbing other users, street begging, hustling (see Chapter 8). Most common is shoplifting:

> 'I've been to prison now eight or nine times for theft and shoplifting, more or less to get the money to get gear. I've got 40 convictions – well, 46. I can sell it on straight away really. I've got customers all across [name]. If I steal from [town] I've got people in [town] [town] town] to sell to. Yeah, most of the time I nick to order. But you can also just nick stuff people want every day like working stuff, or meat or razors. Yeah, that'll go easy – stuff that'll go quick. That's the high-end goods that people want, yeah. Meat, yeah, you gotta stick it down yer trousers or in your jacket. I was doing it in my trousers years ago at one point, weren't I? Everyone else was doing it. I'd go along with other users so I just followed the lead. I started nicking bottles with a girl called [name]. She's dead now, through drugs. Her and her cousin used to go out in their car and nick bottles of spirits and I just done the same thing; they took a rucksack and it went on from there. I'd sell 'em for £10 a bottle. Now it's about £7, I think. Everything's gone down in price. People are selling £50 stuff for a tenner now. Even if it's 70, 80 quid now you'd just pay a tenner. You'd get it for nothing. That's what I thought. What am I doing all this for, it's pointless. Here I am sitting in a prison cell – what for – for £30. It ain't worth it.' (User 04)

Quality of drugs

User respondents were vocal on the highly variable quality of drugs locally:

> 'It varies enormously, shame.' (User 01)

Users are also aware that different runner/dealers sell different products, often mixed or diluted. More long-term users test products before use, but often need greater quantities to get the 'hit' they desire:

> 'It varies. Some people get it and mix it with whatever they can, just to try and get an extra penny. Some people don't. So that's why you should do half a bag and test it first. Some of it only just does the job, it stops you from being ill but then you get something the same size that's just over half a bag and it gives you a slight buzz, so it varies depending upon what is being taken.' (User 02)

Despite an abundance of runner/dealers most users think quality has declined recently:

> 'It's got worse, if I'm honest. It used to be OK. So many big dealers keep getting nicked so you end up with the little ones running around trying to make the bags up. They get a £10 bag and cut it in half and try to mix it. They're the ones you've got to watch – the little dealers, who are doing it to get their stuff. So they'll charge you £10 for a bag but what you're getting is actually a £5 bag mixed with something else. So they've made £20 out of a £10 bag – so that's a £10 bag for them. So all along the chain, someone is making money and the smaller ones are doing it to feed their habit. They can't afford it. So it's the smaller ones who are more likely to give you the shit stuff and the stuff that'll put you in hospital, if you're lucky. If not, you OD – that's the smaller people.
>
> 'The big people, they're not so bad. They don't need to cut in half. Some do, but the majority don't. So you're better off going to the bigger ones for the better quality and less risk than for the little ones who mix it with whatever they can get. If it's not stringers? What they do with a string is they put something in there that looks like it or a cigarette end. When you get it you can't really check it till you get home. When you get home and you've got about five pieces and you open 'em, you find a couple are good but then you've got a bit of mud or a cigarette end and they'll put something in it and there's nothing you can do about it. You've just lost £50 and that's your last 50.' (User 01)

Experienced users differentiate between runner/dealers and middle-management CL operatives just starting a line or dealing from nearby Hubs. They are sometimes referred to as bigger or non-local dealers, as opposed to local runner/dealers.

> 'No, they are only here to sell. It's the littler ones that are the users. You see, they've got to get their stuff so it's more risky. So we try not to go for the smaller ones, we go for the better quality ones, the bigger ones.' (User 02)

Transactional trust

Trust can be considered 'the making and breaking of cooperative relations' (Murji, 2007: 795). Murji notes that while risk is the key definer for markets, trust is 'the analogue' for networks. Edmunds and colleagues (1996) identified trust relationships operating at three different levels in drug markets including between dealers; between dealers and buyers; and between buyers. They found that variance in trust levels was most significant between open/closed markets.

Universally within the drug using social field, trust is scare and usually calibrated in relation to potential harms such as personal safety; product safety; transactional security and confidence. To address these harms users try to build trust and loyalty as best they can with known runner/dealers:

> 'Yes, if you can trust 'em. We normally go to the same people. I know what I'm getting and so on.' (User 02)

While regular runner/dealers are preferred, this is not always possible:

> 'It depends and varies. It depends if they've [police] nicked 'em.' (User 02)

Transactional trust appears much aligned with risk assessment and risk mitigation and if assessed carefully, generates greater confidence between user/dealer. Experienced users talked of 'knowing' the risks, or at least recognising them. Levels of agency differ as to whether this knowledge is ever put to practicable use. Users talk of learned strategies to build trust which if employed over time pay dividends offering tangible benefits. Buying from a trusted dealer offers benefits of:

• a regular or known face;

- a trusted and safe product;
- a better, reliable or assured quality of product;
- a regular date, time or buying location;
- a speedier and often a more sociable transaction;
- possibility of buying 'on tick';
- possibility of being given a larger quantity;
- a normalisation of the transactional process.

Where possible, experienced users employ strategies to build trust to benefit from these outcomes, which then acts as transactional risk mitigation. If achieved this reduces overall levels of stress before, during and after transactions helping normalise transactions as routine commercial activities.

Health assessment and risk mitigation is forefront for many, but not all, purchasing users:

> 'Yes, I feel it's safer at present. Cos I can go to you and get something off you and do a £10 bag, and do half a bag and not go over[dose] and then go to someone else and not realise that his stuff is stronger and then go over. You can die from an overdose. That's why I tend to go to the same person. Build up a trust.' (User 01)

Trusted runner/dealer arrangements are considered highly desirable as in the event of withdrawal, they are reportedly more likely to be empathetic:

> 'If you've got no money and you're ill [withdrawing], they'll maybe give you one, just to make you better. That's the trust you can build up. Not all of 'em but some of 'em. If you're a regular customer and you spend money regularly with them they don't mind lending or giving you something just to make you better.' (User 01)

A further advantage of a trusted relationship is runner/dealers will offer drugs 'on tick' or free in return for later payment, though this is situational and dependent upon other variables:

> 'Yeah, or give it to you for nothing. It depends how much you spend, whether you're regular or whether they trust you. We try not to do that. And you don't realise it's happening and then they come to your door, or they come in and demand your money.' (User 01)

'Yeah, yeah, but normally it depends who it is. Yeah, we try
not to. Besides they can give you something for nothing. But
it can get you into debt.' (User 02)

Dealer switching

Areas with multiple, simultaneous county lines are more complex.
Multiple lines into one area dilutes transactional trust as runner/dealers
alternate so frequently. This outcome was eventually recognised by
CL managers in earlier CL models. Later CL models (see Chapter 2)
operate from localised dealing Hubs to make building trust more integral
to transactional interactions. This benefits all concerned and some CL
operatives strive to develop this as a unique brand selling point.

Multiple lines operating in an area brings increased competition
flooding markets with more choice of supply routes, dealers and products.
This might temporarily lower prices but simultaneously increases user
risks. Switching dealers becomes attractive, even if temporary. However,
users switching loyalty to new arrivals leaves trust-building to commence
afresh. Reactive-switching can arise from necessity, for example dealer
got arrested. Proactive-switching occurs when new dealers boost product
quality upon market-entry to secure fresh customers. If trust is quickly
established and maintained this transactional arrangement may endure.

Multiple supply routes means potential transactions from multiple
runner/dealers which brings inherent risks to be managed:

- unknown or insecure provenance of drugs;
- variance in product quality;
- increased transactional activity of user;
- altered transactional terms and conditions;
- potential fall-outs and disagreements;
- possibility of covert policing or increased police surveillance of user.

Outcomes arising from these issues often upset the local equilibrium of
the user community, leading to localised volatility. Again within each of
these variables, trust must be re-negotiated over time.

Risk mitigation

For drug users risk management means constant assessment to minimise
harm. These assessments are either:

- situational – including attempts to identify product provenance, strength, quality; number of complaints; or
- anticipatory – the dealer's career, skill and experience in serving up; relationships with other users; market base and networks.

Situational assessments, usually undertaken via hurried conversation between user/dealer are compromised by situational variables, for example location of the deal, if transactions are under surveillance; speed of transaction; number of other users; trust levels and so on. Anticipatory assessments are undertaken by intelligence gathering among users' over time.

User consumer behaviour thereby constitutes daily risks relating to purchase, product, use and personal safety, each inter-relating and interchanging daily presenting users with multi-variant risks requiring constant re-evaluation. This process of evaluation and risk mitigation is akin to a process of neutralisation (Sykes and Matza, 1957). Mitigation strategies are heavily influenced by street capital and experience (habitus of the drug world); peer influence, and drug dependency and habit.

Each consumer is constantly placing themselves at risk and even their mitigation strategies generate further risks (see Table 6.2). As a result risk mitigation becomes risk displacement. Risks are elevated or relegated within a risk model which is constantly revolving and changing each day.

Parkin in *Habitus and Drug Using Environments*, notes 'drug users must remain transitory and ever vigilant of authority that seeks to displace, disperse and criminalise their injecting practice' (2013: 234). They are thus constantly reviewing and memorising possible drug consumption locations including public and private spaces. Regarding public consumption of

Table 6.2: Risk management for drug users

Mode of risk facing user	User perception of risk	Mitigation concept
Transactional safety	Situational; short term; multiple variant risks	Street capital skill in building trust and confidence; using familiar/known dealers; using peer recommendations
Product safety	Short term; variable; dependent upon and subject to availability	Cumulative street knowledge and experience; test purchases
Usage and safety of using environment	Short term; variable	Knowledge and frequency of significant locations versus limited ability to plan and urgency
Personal safety	Reflective; longer-term; variable	Highly variable; street capital and experience; limited ability to plan

heroin, Parkin notes the role of 'old heads' in harm identification and risk mitigation, noting novice users are at greater risk.

Public injecting and use of drugs

In his contributions to public health sociology on drug dependency, Tim Rhodes (2002) argues the risk environment is a useful way of considering how social networks interact with harm management. Risk environment for Rhodes is constructed through interplays of physical, economic, social and policy variables which operate at either macro- or micro-risk level. Here public consumption of heroin is governed by 'situational necessities' by Rhodes and colleagues (2007: 276) such as inter-relationships arising from drug dependence, homelessness, drug cravings and unexpected access to drugs or injecting space. This is aligned with urgency to avoid detection or interruption, and privacy to conduct intimate acts. These can lead to inadequate preparation followed by rushed injection of badly prepared solutes. Parkin (2013) notes the harms arising from injecting heroin include overdosing, injecting alone, bacterial and viral infections, unhygienic locations and police arrest. A proliferation of CLs might increase public consumption and visible injecting. Competition for using known injecting spaces becomes pronounced (Coomber and Moyle, 2012; 2015). In this study public injecting was clearly visible.

Some users prefer drug consumption in private settings. Where user groups work together to purchase drugs, the expectation arises that one offers their home as a consumption location.

Home use for drug consumption

Bringing other users into your own home is highly situational and must be carefully risk assessed. The focus here becomes harm reduction through shared resources for preparation/administration (including not being left alone) to reduce potential overdosing. Home use for drug consumption can be offered as a favour, necessity or to garner status. It provides opportunities for peer-group bonding, swapping customer feedback on dealers, info-sharing on dealers' movements, drug quality, police activity and so on. Parkin notes (2013: 233) that peer injecting is often undertaken by dyads (close friends/associates/ sexual partners) and offers forms of social capital via providing injecting assistance but also coping mechanisms for those withdrawing or 'recovering'.

Skill is exercised to determine suitability for invitation with judgement acting as street capital:

> 'Instinct and over a period of time. Know what I mean? You do little tests. You might, you can't 100 per cent trust 'em. You do things like you put 'em on your bag, you give 'em a little bit of your bag and then you just see if they come back and help you out when you're ill, see what I mean? And you build it up by that kind of stuff. It's the ones who turn up at your door knowing that you've just been paid. Yet when they get paid, you don't see 'em. That kind of people.' (User 02)

Philosophically noting his judgement goes awry occasionally he quickly reframed this as a positive learning experience:

> 'You can't really trust any of 'em. Yep, we've had valuables gone missing. When that happens, you just batten yourself down and it's another lesson learned.' (User 02)

A further potential risk is that over time a user's address becomes common knowledge and users trade such details for drugs. Known address become targets for dealers seeking new dealing Hubs. This targeting includes placing drugs through the letterbox of an unknown user – only to call back later and demand payment. Police recognise this circulatory exchange of information:

> 'That [the users address] is always known. They "know" people and if they give a user a bag that'll get whatever information they want out of them. Information? They just wave a bag of downers at you and you'd sell 'em your grandmother. It's not hard for them to find out who lives where.' (Police 14)

One user noted how this knowledge can bring unwanted complications:

> 'Where I've lived before I've had 'em coming round my home at 3am chucking stones at my window. They are after you all day. They wanna serve up from my home and use my property.' (User 10)

On occasion a user's residence becomes a common using location for multiple users, for example rented social housing. Renters operate open-door policies allowing user/dealers to call round anytime. Transferring keys becomes too tricky with unreliable or uncontactable users so flats are left unlocked:

> 'This property was left unlocked and the resident is not there but the flat is used by others. They don't live there so don't bother to lock the doors as it's too much trouble to do so and swap the keys around.' (Police 01)

For some this is also a risk mitigation strategy to avoid unnecessary hassle, although equally it can be a risk-generating strategy.

Staying safe

Paramount concern for users is to 'stay safe', during drug consumption but also to avoid arrest and also avoid violence. User respondents advised that safety and 'staying safe' was variable and often short-lived. For some it was desired but remained elusive. It could be easily compromised depending upon numerous variables and the urgency to achieve a drug supply hook-up. Concepts of 'staying safe' is therefore situational with some referring to it as 'staying as safe as you can in a difficult or dangerous situation' (User 02). Users operate learned risk mitigation techniques to minimise potential threats.

Techniques for risk mitigation by users varied with some users actively liaising with police, for example asking them to undertake personal welfare checks to ensure cuckooing is reduced:

> 'These officers do welfare checks on us anyway so they're always popping in to check we're OK. And they find out who's sitting there. And to make sure nobody is using us.' (User 01 and User 02)

Consumption performance and situational script

For many users, consumption is heavily related to drug use, the consumption environment, the setting, other players involved, rituals and so on. As Deighton (1992) noted, performance can be central to consumption. The rituals of serving up heroin, for example, relates to what Schank and Abelson (1977) call a 'situational script' – essentially an improvised but pre-determined sequence of actions and reactions which both script and define well-known situations. Here actors know the roles to be played and improvise accordingly. Within this ritualised consumption certain locations may be resignified as important places, for example the alley at the back of the shopping centre as a locale for serving up. Such shared consumption practices define many illicit drug consumers creating micro-markets with identifiable subcultural practices and experiences. The using community therefore often forges alliances of shared interest and support but also of social solidarity, sometimes enduring, sometimes transitory, but which revolve around shared consumption interests. Maffesoli (1996) refers to the 'emotional glue' which binds together these consumers (who would otherwise be lonely and isolated) in a process of sharing emotional space and sentiment which he calls 'proxemics'. Such proxemics and situational scripts are reassuring and constitutive. A CL operative seeking to maximise both his brand and levels of customer satisfaction will practise immersion into this world and demonstrate ability to 'serve up' in all situations. Increased drug consumption can also lead to increased localised violence (Jacques and Allen, 2015).

Increased frequency and volume of drug consumption

Users widely reported that CLs had increased the volume and number of runner/dealers in their area. One consequence being that users who traditionally just consumed either heroin or crack cocaine now often mixed both:

> 'The using got worse. There's not so many dealers now, but there are more people doing it. There are more people doing snowballs – y'know. brown and white. A lot of 'em used to just do a bit of gear and may have the odd pipe … now, it's just snowballs. Everyone I know is doing snowballs … snowballs.… And it's making people worse. A snowball? … basically you get the rush and after that you get the droop, but with this it's really much more intense. But it messes you up … I used to slam it. You can do it on foil. But most people will bang it up. But I'd do it on foil, to be honest. It's an extra good hit, to be honest. But it messes you up.… I know people who do all this body moving and all that [he imitates jerking].' (User 04)

One user detailed the effects of a snowball:

> 'I use a bit of both, mostly the dark. Yes, you either do the brown separate and the white separate or you do them together

in a snowball, both together in a syringe. So you get your up and down and that. It depends how you take it, if you take it before the brown, it'll give you a rush. If you take the cocaine it usually works stronger than what the heroin, so ... it gives you a rush then you take the brown to get back down. Sometimes it works differently for different people, whereas for me the brown gets me up and mobile. The white doesn't. So to make me mobile, like I am now, then it's just the brown. But if I had just the white then I'm under me covers. Like when the police said, "Oh, you're up and about". Normally I'm not, I'm just the covers.' (User 02)

The ubiquity of CLs and the volume of dealers make it almost impossible to come off/stay off drugs or reduce frequency of use. Users talked of being immersed in drug dealing and consumption. For those on health programmes their journey to reduce consumption is much harder. Some users actively try to avoid dealers by staying housebound.

Case study with User 04

'I'm using at the moment. I got a habit at 15. Basically my dad died when I was young. He was murdered in [name]. I went into foster care in a children's home until I was 13. I've been on my own since then really. I tried heroin at 16 and had a habit since then. I've got a methadone script now. It's working out; I've been put on a tag. I'm trying to stay away from people. I'm trying to stay off it, now I've got this place. I've only had it a week. The people here have been brilliant.

'I normally only have to go to the chemist [for my script] down the road really and to Turning Point. Basically I'm trying to avoid the High Street, that's where most people are. You might see the odd dealer going past as you are going to score but I just tell 'em I've got an appointment, I'm late, quick, gotta go ... I stay in most of the day and play games or watch DVDs.

'I managed to get a new SIM card recently, but I was still getting text messages. Whereas I used to get them before, I used to look at them and think ... oh, maybe ... but now I'm all right as I'm not getting no phone calls as I've got a different number. In the past week since I've been here I've had a different number so.... When I did used to get them it did used to niggle at me a bit. Then I'd start thinking about it ... now I don't bother.

'It's more the users you see. The dealers you don't see. The odd one perhaps walks about, who's stupid. The majority of 'em are flatted up, know what I mean. However, if I do see 'em I try and avoid 'em. Or if they try and give me a number I say, "Yeah, yeah, I'll ring you" but I never do. I wanna get off it. I've been on it too long. I've had problems with my legs, with DVTs – I went to hospital and they said it nearly killed me, so I could lose my leg. It scared me, if I'm honest. I worry about it. It's one of the main reasons why I wanna stay away from it. If I'm not careful, I'll end up dead, I've been in prison all of my life, knowwhatImean. Turning Point give me good advice and the place down the road – a mental health place. So now I spend time buying DVDs.

'I never got robbed. I have run off from people a couple of times when I've sold drugs to people. Not long-term but I have sold for a short time, yeah. A couple of times people have done it, I've been threatened but I got offered a shot – a bag of gear like, to go and do it like. But I've never done it fully where I've gone out to do it. I can be a fast runner though. Not now since I have bad legs.

'That's all I know really. This is all new to me as I've never done anything else. I was talking to my key worker yesterday about filling out my day with something coz I get bored. When you do that you're running around all day. You've got something to do every day, ain't cha. But when you stop it, you've got nothing to do so you get bored. I'm stronger now, I'm not so bothered, I just sit in all day. It sounds silly but it's like prison, can't get [out] of the door [cos of the TAG]. So I stay in. Even though I can get to the door I tend to stay in that prison mode. I know I can't get drugs. I do my thing and get my methadone and stay in. That's what I plan to do until I get work.

'I had a job for six years. I was walking to work one day in [name] in the morning and I found nine deals, at half six in the morning across the road from the police station, So I picked them up, put 'em in my pocket, took 'em to work; didn't bother. Chucked 'em in a drawer, thought come the weekend I can sell all of 'em and make a hundred quid, knowthatImean. Then I had a big row with my missus. Four or five days later I ended up having a boot. Then when I used to snowball – brown and white together – obviously I went high and that ... then year and half later here I am again. I had to give up work. Won't get into it again, cos it was brilliant. I loved it.

'Me and [name] we've done £200 of drugs in one day. Before we went to prison a couple of times before we were just hammering it. At least £200 a day each. On black and white. We were snowballing and doing like three dark and one light, chucking in two or three in at a time. Then my habit was getting very bad. Since then I've come right down. I'm now on 60 mls of methadone. When I first got on it, I did use twice in the first week and once again. Then the day I got arrested I used as they mucked up my meth. That's the only time I used. Since then I've been on the script. I haven't used. If I was to be tested now I'd come up negative. I may be positive for cannabis but I do like a joint now and then.'

Coping

The multiple challenges of maintaining a drug habit, avoiding police detection, avoiding engagement with the criminal justice system, pervasive lack of trust in dealer transactions, and the constant need for risk mitigation and risk management generates anxiety and stress for many users. This is often coupled with stress arising from lack of employment, benefit changes, ill-health, debt, poverty and poor-quality housing. Such conditions contribute to/exacerbate the psychological stresses of unemployed users (Pearson, 1987a) leading some to limited life choices, aspirations and horizons to modest goals, for example getting through the day. They refer to this as 'coping'. In Bourdiouesian field theory, this is interpreted as practice and agency constrained by the habitus acting to limit or seal the social fate of the user:

> 'Apart from the house, everything is fine. We plod along, day to day. We have semi-regular visits from the boys in blue just to make sure that we're OK and that we haven't got people who are causing problems but it's all right, innit? We plod along. Do what we need to do. We do struggle and that. Sometimes drugs overtake and all that. Sometimes I end up itching all over. I haven't got the energy to sort it all out. So we tend to let things slide.' (User 02)

Views from the dealers

As with users, runner/dealers also operate within their own social field. Agency here might also be constrained by the rules of the drug dealing crew or USG. Actions are bounded by their habitus, determined by the gang operating rules and bounded by hierarchical status. Interactions with users are also governed by hierarchical position.

CL operatives were mostly disparaging about users, using comments laced with pity. Others viewed relationships as transactional:

'We call them Cats. So, you've got Cats, you've nitties, and there was another one as well, you had a Bitty.... There was another one as well. There's a few names that they call them. You'd call them vulnerable adults.' (USG 06)

Recognition and categorisation

CL operatives used acquired street capital to identify and categorise users with respondents differentiating between user 'types'. Opinions were formulated using key variables, including:

- repeated transactional interactions, that is, ease and speed, a 'hassle-free' deal, cash availability, 'lack of agro';
- longitudinal user engagement – visiting users homes, living with them in bandos;
- peer-group knowledge;
- previous county line experience;
- overall financial value of the user based upon introductions to other users;
- trust and reliability;
- presentation – chaotic, desperate or 'normal'.

Some respondents talked only of their 'clients', and were keen to demonstrate their business acumen. Others reserved 'clients' for the most 'normal' 'well-presented', with others referred to pejoratively:

'Trying to just recognise Cats? Well, there's a differen[ce] between homeless Cats and ones that are homeless and ones that actually smoke. You can tell by gestures, their hands, the way they move, their mouth, everything you can tell. You can actually tell who's just a normal homeless person, you can tell. When you've been seeing it for so long you know the difference. One hundred per cent, the user is the better client. They are the ones bringing you the money. A homeless person will come to you once in a while and he's short when he does come so it's different, cos he's got no money, always short.

'I would just walk past and give them a card and then when I get further down I would look back and I would wave my hand to tell them to follow me and I would take to him out of sight. I would give him a free shot right there and a little card, something that I would have the number written down on.' (USG 06)

An experienced CL manager is especially keen to secure a well-paying returning customer:

> 'You have black Cats, you have Asian Cats.... Mainly you had ... the rich Cats for me were the Asian Koreans or the Chinese that would come to me. They had money, man. They were chefs as well in their restaurants so they would always come with money. I remember when a shift would finish they would ring because I knew what time his shift finishes and he would ring me, and I know this guy would come straight, easily when he comes to me I know it's about £80, easy. And he always comes every day at a specific time, £80 he comes.' (USG 06)

Respondents viewed their client base as a captive market with little agency or choice. Where choice did exist runner/dealers viewed this as constrained by addiction, noting users 'have few options' and 'are desperate'.

> 'But then it's a choice to the user, the user is the one who chooses who he is going to call and to be honest, if the user goes to these guys and they treat him like shit, he will still always go to these guys.' (USG 06)

Some runner/dealers were disparaging of anyone who 'allowed themselves to get involved in brown [heroin]. Ah ... no one smokes that shit'. (Runner 03)

Looking for tick

Some transactions are reciprocal or based upon normal consumer practice, for example where users wish an extra 'rock' for being a 'good customer'. Such arrangements are initiated by either side. However, runner/dealers often measure 'desperation' by user desire to strike a deal when no money is present and they seek drugs 'on tick' (credit) (Taylor and Potter, 2013; Moyle and Coomber, 2015; Robinson et al, 2019). Occasionally this tactic is used by canny users shopping around before they switch to another, more favoured, supplier:

'Yeah, I could call the [Name] Boys and I could be like, "Look, I've only got £25, can I get three shots?" and they would be like, "No, come correct with £30". Then I would ring these guys, "I've got £25", "OK, come to us", do you know what I mean?' (USG 06)

Fake tick

Offering drugs 'on tick' is perceived differently by both sides of the transaction. Users view it as deferred payment, 'favour' or 'gifting' while suffering withdrawal effects but without any money to score. Often users forget, or overlook, credit has been extended. Dealers seldom forget and later call round for payment. Amounts are quickly inflated with added 'interest' to establish the process of debt bondage. Experienced users would only enter this transaction with a 'trusted' supplier:

'Yeah, or give it to you for nothing. It depends how much you spend, whether you're regular or whether they trust you. But normally it depends who it is. Yeah, we try not to. Besides they can give you something for nothing. And you don't realise it's happening and then they come to your door, or they come in and demand your money.' (User 02)

Dealers' views of the police

In conversation the young runner/dealers articulated feelings towards the police. The police were viewed as 'inconsequential', 'irrelevant' and an 'irritation'. Police were either deemed 'invisible' or a constant threat to operations, but this was a recognised part of the Game. Others viewed the police as 'entertainment':

'These lot? These lot are our entertainment. That's the realness, sitting chillin, they pull up and it's a chase, get me. They hassle us all the time.' (Runner 02)

A common trope was to view the police as a rival gang or 'Opps' – signifying their movements must be observed, monitored, surveilled and risk managed. Dealers source and collate intel from users in exchange for drugs. Risk mitigation involves collating car registration numbers and accessing officers' Facebook accounts for family details.

In Chapter 7 I take the opportunity to delve more deeply into the relationships that exist between users and dealers, one which is both exploitative and symbiotic. In Chapter 8 I look more closely at the outcomes, both perceptible and experiential, of county lines.

7

Ripples, Reverberations and Responses

This chapter moves on to consider the outcomes of involvement in CL networks and the wider consequences arising from it, often felt by non-participants including family members. Central to this is the violence needed to defend the line and control the line.

Family issues and familial reverberations

Runner/dealers often go missing from home for extended periods while going 'going cunch'. Families often are unaware of their whereabouts until they return.

At some point they make a decision to return to the parental home often triggered by events outside their control, for example their shift ended; they are replaced, temporarily or long-term; operations shift to another location; police 'heat' and so on. Unless they have a fall out with managers, they are paid return train fares or dropped off by car. Reappearance after weeks of disappearance usually brings parental relief followed by confrontation, anger and recriminations.

One young operative recounted such a scenario after going missing for two weeks:

> '[I'd say] Nothing. They'd ask me, they'd beg me, they'd cry, they'd scream, they'd be on the floor. Nothing. Nothing. You're not getting an answer from me. I was with my friend. And this is me looking like I had just come out of a concentration camp. I had to shave my hair because when we were staying in the crack house one time I got fleas from an animal in my hair and I had to shave my hair, so one time I

came back home, stinky and filthy, this was early days when we weren't able to use anybody's houses, my mum opened the door and she saw me and she said she felt her soul leave her body to see her child in that stage. I can still hear the scream. I can't imagine seeing my daughter now in that kind of state. No. Filthy stinking. And if you're a girl and it's that time of the month baby wipes can only do that much and a sink. It was awful. And this is how it still is now.' (USG 01)

Some parents try to control the domestic situation by actively intervening to prevent association with 'bad influences':

'My parents would try to keep me in the house. They'd lock me in. They'd stay in my room with me but I'd always go. I'd always find a way. I'd jump out of the window. I would say I was going to kill myself. I'd do all kinds of craziness and it wasn't fair. My dad had cancer at the time. My little sister had just turned one. It was awful.' (USG 01)

A common parental intervention is inviting support from the authorities, but opportunities for intervention are often missed:

'When I would go missing and come back, because obviously my parents would ring the police every time, the police would literally just come, you're here, we've seen you, tick, don't do that again, bye, bye. If somebody had asked me what was going on I would have said ... I wouldn't have said, "Excuse me, this is happening", I wouldn't have volunteered this information myself but that didn't happen.' (USG 01)

Reverberations

Street gang rules operate within a set of logical assumptions, though these have recently changed. The prevailing assumption (until recently) was that families should be left out of gang business unless actively involved. It was generally considered 'bad news' or trouble to involve them. This presumption has recently been overturned with the new rules being that the family are involved; know and possibly profit from USG activities; know and don't care; or don't know but telling them exerts greater pressure upon the young person, for example they could be ejected from the house and easily embraced by the gang.

Familial Reverberations occur when issues arising from criminal activity, or proximity to it, return to impact upon the domestic situation or wider family. Commonly this occurs due to: unpaid debts; teaching people 'a lesson'; revenge; intimidation; demonstration of power; as proxy method of reaching a gang-affiliate not personally locatable. In this way the physical violence is transferred by proxy to other family members as a substitute:

> 'In this time, in Essex, I was going back home occasionally for a day or two but my family was always threatened. We know where your mum lives, where your brother goes to nursery type thing, so as much as I hated it, and I was living in hell, I felt I needed to go back. I was scared for my life. I was scared for my family's life. I was scared that I would get in trouble with the police or they would go to the police and say that I had been dealing, or I was going to be identified. It was just constant fear and I wasn't eating. My mum and dad would do everything to keep me in the house. They had no idea where I was.' (USG 01)

The type of familial reverberation depends upon: the principal target; trigger motivation; role of target; relationship to USG. Actions range from mild, visible or easily communicated verbal threats, to physical attack (see Table 7.1). Delivery mechanisms vary depending but include by proxy. The severity, frequency, location and repeated nature of any targeting will be tempered by the type of message to be sent and the status level or importance of the targeted individual.

Reverberations to users' families differ from those towards families of runner/dealers. Again this illustrates a collision of two separate social fields: the criminal and legitimate; domestic family and street family.

Typically a user's family is aware of their status, including those living with parents, family or partners. It is the constant issue of debt which

Table 7.1: Type of reverberations towards wider family

Mild	• Threats delivered by text message • Denigration and disrespect on social media • Sitting in wait outside the house • Throwing stones at the property • Items pushed through the letterbox • Verbal assaults on family members, or witnessed by them
Serious	• Daubing the house with paint • Smashing windows • Physical assault
Life-threatening	• Kidnapping • Firebombing • Home invasion

most frequently ensures 'trouble can come back' to the family home. Users spoke of low-level threats made personally about parental homes. For some this is a normal part of life for users and some manage this risk through deflection. Domestic and family arrangements are commonly known among both users and dealers exacerbating potential threats.

One parent was adamant his family were targeted due to his son falling into debt with local dealers:

> 'Yes, years ago. A brick through the window, all the tyres let down on the car. I felt vulnerable. Yes, that would be the idea, just terrorise us, that's how they do it, you see? Go for the vulnerable, don't go for like the old man, he's a handful, so we go for the wife and the kids and smash the house and that sort of thing. Well, you would never catch them, would you? All these little scumbags run around at night and for whatever reason they want to do it, they do it no matter, what can you do? What can you do?' (User 07)

On this occasion the father paid off the debt after receiving a threat to life report from police. For users drug debt is a constant challenge, described by one user's father as 'never-ending'. Debt enforcement can generate fear and violence and is identified by all agencies as a key driver for violence towards users and families. One father stated that the dealers would easily now target families and 'they wouldn't think twice about it'. One parent ruminated on the impact upon the town:

> 'You've got to keep the dealers out. But once a town has got a good name, "keep away from there", they move on to the next one, and that is what happened in London. The police were so good in London, so, they're going into villages now. It would never end, would it? You always stop drugs for the time being, but then someone else would come. This generation of users ago, in the last few years, half a dozen would die and we'll keep going at that rate, and before you know it, the new lot coming up won't have heard of you.' (User 07)

Osman warnings (threat to life)

One young girl interviewed recently had to vacate London after receiving an Osman warning stating her life was in danger. Her account is testimony to the impact upon her family:

226

'I am not part of the gang but I know many of them as friends and I am connected to the boys in [Name] who are in beef with [Name]. People claimed I was part of it but really we were just friends. I went to a party and after that there were stories about me on social media – various group chats which caused trouble. Then a boy on the bus followed me. The police got involved, they had a word with my mum. There were pictures of knives sent to me on group chat – intimidating me. The police took the phone.

'Later, the police arrived and told us my life was in danger – it was [a] threat to life. We had one hour to pack and leave. We took a cab to Victoria to flee London. Our travel and our food was paid for. We stayed for one week in a small flat via the council. We were unable to go out. It was temporary accommodation – better than [Name]. We had to have six people in two beds, though it will settle down. Mum wanted to move. Brother and sisters got school here so we wanted to stay three, four months.

'I feel safer here as it's not [Name] [Crying]. It died down but it would burn up all over again if I saw them. In south London it can be beef – but then you're dead if they see you. Even if you are with friends then they would still come for you.

'The boys involved are around 17 years of age, but it was two girls behind the rumours. My friend then died – [Name] he was killed in [Name]. My name got tagged with it and there was no evidence at all. I was rumoured to be involved, so they had to shift me.

'We had to change my phone number and all my Facebook and Snapchat links and keep all our locations off grid. We have a sofa, a bunk bed, no cups or blankets and we were in there for three days. Now we have been moved to another flat it's more permanent.' (USG 04)

Case study: interview with User 06

This respondent was a white male, in his late twenties; recently ex-heroin user, now taking methadone and lives with his parents.

'I was using heroin, yes. I was about 15 years old and I had older friends and they were dabbling and I started to dabble with them, but they was all five or six years older than me. When they sort of pulled away from it, I was sort of … I sort of got stuck. I didn't even hit puberty when I first started taking drugs, you see. I smoked cannabis. I don't drink. I've actually stopped smoking now. I've started a[n] e-cigarette. Do I look better? I was very, very ill. I was about nine stone. I'm 12 stone now, so I was very skinny. Do you know, a lot of people do say "you don't look like an average user". If you saw me when I was using, then you'd see a difference.

'I was wasted. The police saw me … it must have been two months ago now, when I lapsed and he actually caught me. I was just about to score around the back of a church and he caught me right beforehand and he said I looked an absolute mess then. But when you see yourself every day you don't see it, you see? You don't see yourself looking worse. You lose your pride, you don't brush your hair as much, you don't care about your appearance, you just want your … hit.

'If I wanted to score I'd ring up or go looking for it, however. If I had somebody's phone number I'd call them. Or walk around the grounds, however. There's many ways of just … I'll give you an example. When I was 19, I had a court case on the go and I got put on tag. Because I was coming off the heroin for the first time properly, I moved with the intention of getting clean. On the first day up there, I said, "See you later, Mum, bye, Dad". I thought, "As soon as they're gone I'm going to go and score". I walked up the street and I thought I'll look out for the biggest wally.

'So I'd get the number and just put an order in, I don't know, "two brown" or whatever, they'll either tell you to go to them, or they'll come to you. However. Depends on … it works differently, it depends on who the supplier is or how high up they are. Say there's a dealer in the flat there, he might say to you, "Right, I'm going to meet you on X Street". Miles away and it might take him an hour to get to you, but they try and keep them all … the police as far as away from them or the deliveries as far away as possible. Or they might chance it and say, "Just walk past and I'll throw a tissue on the floor". That's another one, they just walk past and just chuck it. There's many ways but no physical exchange – no, that's old school. People are always going to want money, and they will always find new ways.

'They might only last a day. I've known people come down and last a day, half a day. But it's not the dealers that get caught, it's the addicts. It's the one who doesn't earn the money, the one who's been used by the dealers and it's them that gets the prison sentences. You know that's sort of what happened to me years ago. I weren't a dealer, anything but, and I was lying to Dad, just to get the money, and it's the addicts that get the short end of the stick. But yes, the dealers, they come and go. They might last a day, might last months. Look at mine from not long ago. He got done. From what I read.

'All the time you've got money the dealers are all right. If you haven't got money, you're no good to them, they don't care then. Or they try and make you feel … if they're … I want the word, not race, but I'm going to word them as blacks, OK. The blacks say to you they don't want to send out one of their own, so they might want to get an addict to do the running for them. And sometimes the addicts might be, "Look, it's getting a bit hot outside now, the police are floating about". The dealers will make them feel comfortable, "It's all right, buddy. You're all right really, you're my mate. We go back…" You know, they try and make you feel good and then … well, that's what they do. They try to buddy up to you. Get you feeling sort of like you'll do things for them and they'll look out for you and it's not a good world to be in.

'Sometimes you'd hear someone was down from London and serving up, usually by word of mouth. Normally you'd get a text, but to get the text, you've got to hear the word of mouth first, haven't you? So yes, normally, they always drop texts and stuff, that used to drive me mad, because I've changed my number so many times. My friend is dead now, he lived just over there. I knew him before he got on drugs and I grew up with him. He's dead now, he died not long ago of an overdose. And he would keep giving my number to people and I'd have a new number, and all of a sudden, I'd get a text saying "back on, best of both, free…", do you know, and all that rubbish, and then, before you know it, one number has got your phone number, then another number's got it and before you know it, you get all these texts. But nowadays, no one gets any texts, before, you had four or five numbers every day texting you, these numbers are on here "we're on here, we're on here". No one gets that any more because there's no one coming down, you know.

'OK, how does a drug deal work? Well, you could call up and they could say, "Just come to the house, or we'll come to you, or you wait where you are", or they'll send you to the middle of the park. Because they'll say, "Sit on the bench, make sure…" Sometimes they want to know who they're seeing. They'll say, "Are you wearing a hat?" or "What beer are you holding?" or "Do you have the top snapped off your beer?" You know it's however?

'You know, you could have a new number. Someone will say, "We're new down", and they can say, "Well, hi, I'm so-and-so, I just got your number of[f] so-and-so, do you mind if I meet you?" and they'll say, "Yes, come up here", and because you haven't seen them ... normally you know who the person is because you're not daft, but they don't always know who ... I mean, if they look like a gearhead ... for me, for example, sometimes they think because I.... So they're checking you and you're trying to work out who they are and...

'Most of the time people don't care, they just want to get their bit of gear and go home, don't they? Well, I never used on the streets. I have when I was seriously desperate, when I was withdrawing, where I couldn't physically walk home. I felt really bad doing that though, but normally ... well, I wasn't one for going in toilets and what not. That's not very secure or clean. I've never shared equipment or anything like that. But I stopped doing that because of my ... I messed up my circulation and I've caused myself many health problems doing it. Yes, bad things. I used to be really fit. I was at the gym, I was doing all sorts. I was ever so fit when I got off the drugs. Because I've got an addictive personality so when I stopped doing drugs I wanted something else to sort of turn my head, so I go into everything a 100 mile an hour.

'Violence has happened. Yes, ask Dad, years ago, he ... we had trouble with dealers before. Christmas Day we had stuff through the window, they duck taped me ... ask Dad ... my legs, my arms, put me in the boot. So yes, they do you ... because they wanted money. I didn't really owe it but every day that went by they would double it, and double it, and double it. I got into debt. But they'd know you'd be withdrawing, see, they see you withdrawing and they offer you 50 quid's worth and give it to you ... and for example, if they didn't think I could pay it, they wouldn't keep giving it. But when they knew I lived at home and know your dad always pays your debts, they've got collateral, you know? Dad's got family so they know how we can give him some because what car's his dad drive? They've got a house. Right, know what? They're all right.... When I used to knock around with a couple of individuals, that's how they used to operate. They wouldn't [give] tick [to] certain people. If they had holes in their shoes or rubbish clothes, they wouldn't do it. If someone had a nice tracksuit or come from a nice home, then they tend to [strap] them more.

'That caused difficulty at home. They pulled up outside, [Name] his name was, and they pulled up in a ... a Mercedes or something, ... big black sporty ... and they done the windows down and they called Dad ... Mum was on sleeping tablets and medication, so out for the count. They call my dad, so they look out the window. Dad would look out the window and they'd start showing their guns and stuff. They'd be like, "Go wake [Name] up. We want this amount of money," and Dad would not want to scare me or worry me, so he wouldn't tell me that he's been paying them, and then they'd be getting money or getting me to run for them on top of it as well. So they'd play [one] up against the [other], all sorts of stuff. Dad was paying them off.

'Overall, I probably owe Dad, since I was 17, about £230,000 or £220,000, something like that. Seriously, I'm not joking, about ... at least £200,000. It wasn't £200,000 worth of debt, it was through a ... I'd get on drugs, get in debt, then I might try and sort myself out and go to work. I might be at work a few months then I fall of[f] the wagon again, get in more debt, pay it off go back to work. I've done that. It's been like it for 12 years.

'It's tough ... do you know what? Dad had to knock the nail on the head, he said the families have it tougher than the addicts. I thought about it and thought, "Actually yes, they do." It can't be nice seeing a family member looking the way I looked or it can't be nice when Dad ... we was going to buy next door, that went out the window. We used to have a nice car, now that's ... so for years now, I'm paying Dad back. I'm still paying him back every week now. He paid off most of the debt to get these guys away. I was lucky. It's worrying that they would come and threaten the house, or come and threaten other people.

'I mean, it's pretty nasty. We had an Osman Notice? We had one. Years ago. I can't remember what that was ... I don't know what that was. I was only 18, 17, because I was ... well, I wasn't but I was meant to be a grass, a paid police informant, which is just another one of the stories to try and target me. But yes, so we've had it all. But then I still go back to it. Crazy life.

'Someone said if you put all the energy into getting off drugs as what you do to getting it, you know. Sometimes for me it wasn't the fix that I wanted, it was the chase, make the call, how do I get the money, who's on? So it weren't always the drug, it was sometimes the whole, how do I get the money, who's on the ... it's almost like an adrenaline thrill of chasing it which was more addictive than the drug.'

The ubiquity of violence

As CL business Models evolve and control of lines increases as does line competition, violence reverberates and ripples throughout the social field. There is a potential for increased violence due to:

- increased competition between rival county lines;
- local gangs reacting against changes to local drug supply;
- local dealers switching networks;
- local users switching networks;
- the County Line Control Repertoire.

For users, violence is anticipated and where possible, mitigated. Experienced users took pride in ability to identify risky situations or bad dealers:

> 'Yeah, yeah, we've been robbed, haven't we? I've been smacked in the face and that was somebody we already knew, a close friend. And you can't always be right in your judgement. And that is why we keep ourselves to ourselves, know what I mean.' (User 02)

Ever-present threats of violence dictate how users conduct daily business. They remain constantly aware of the presence of violence, making minor adjustments to their actions to mitigate risks, for example placing a phone in a side-room:

> 'I'm OK calling the police. The phone is always next door cos it's a bit hard if you're sitting here and I pick up the phone and call the police. But it's a bit hard doing that in front of you.' (User 04)

Previously cuckooed users assume violence will re-occur. When asked how they might defend their property one commented:

> 'Well, that depends upon how big their knife is! Don't open the door I guess, but they'll put their foot right through the door, yeah. I've had that happen on a couple of occasions.' (User 01)

Another user admitted limited ability to take action:

'Yeah, but you can't do nothing about it when they come in and then all of a sudden they bring a big thing like that out [stretches hands wide]. You don't know until they bring it out cos they're all nice to your face. They last time they did that, they took all the money.' (User 02)

Users admitted threats of violence were commonplace with survival predicated upon not reacting to each threat but developing the skill (street capital) of 'reading' the situation and identifying whether runner/dealers were edgy, tense, jittery or 'wound up'. Others felt resigned to the need to interact:

'Yeah, we see 'em, there's nothing really you can do about it. So you just get up, brush down and put it down to experience. You try to avoid that situation in the future.' (User 02)

As identified in Chapter 2 gang rules, habitus and normalised violence designate weapon-carrying as a normative part of the gang repertoire. Weapon-carrying among runner/dealers out delivering drugs is deemed a practical necessity and runner/dealers scoffed at the prospect that they might deal without carrying weapons. One respondent admitted to carrying but claimed he had never had to use it:

'Knife, screwdriver, hammer ... but the thing is I would never have even used it. I wouldn't have know how to, what do I do? I never did have to. I could have but I never did because I don't.' (USG 01)

Runner/dealers also admitted to secreting weapons within easy physical reach inside properties used for dealing, including cuckooed properties:

'In a property, yeah, all over the place. All over the place. Outside as well. Say the chalets, there used to be things like in the bins or whatever.' (USG 01)

In county lines drug supply networks knives and weapons were an expected element of any drug supply line:

'No, it's just, for instance, we'll get a bit of information that somebody's running from an address, we'll get in there by hook or by crook whether it be a warrant or whatever, and when we go through the door someone will be sitting there, either just wrapping their drugs, the startled look and generally there's, within reach somewhere, there's a knife.' (Police 02)

One police officer articulated how he felt the 'moral conscience' of young people had switched off regarding violence and that they were inured to feelings:

'I remember speaking to a young lad, [name], aged 15. He had scars all over his face, almost disfiguring him and on his arms and so on. I said, "What is the score with all these knives then?" He said, "Yeah, it's worrying". But when he spoke it was almost like a light went off in his brain. He said, "At school we used to give each other a dead arm, but now, it's cooler to stab. And it's better and it makes you look better if you've got these marks and scars". And he wasn't bullshitting. That was a real moment for me when I thought, Jesus Christ. A badge of honour and that is just playing around. And we've actually only just watched a video of two guys walking along and they took a sudden dislike to someone sitting on a railing and then suddenly it was tap, tap, tap, tap. Then they just walk off. It's a big worry. It seems as though they don't give a shit. It's the moral conscience light has just switched off. But then it promotes them among their peers.' (Police 02)

County Lines generate a vicious circle of potential violence (see Table 7.2) at all levels of the drug supply network. The illegal activity, coupled with absence of transactional trust, fierce levels of competition, the need to control/defend lines and the imperative to generate street capital channels behaviours supportive or directive of violence. Dominant here is the generally ubiquity of knives within CLs. Runner/dealers carry knives for fear of robbery by: rival dealers; rival gang members; their

Table 7.2: Location and rise in number of knife-related incidents

Force and location	Rise in number of knife-related incidents April 2010–September 2018	Percentage rise
Hertfordshire	272–513	89%
Essex	536–766	43%
Thames Valley	996–1,431	23%
Kent	346–873	152%

Source: Halliday and Parveen (2019) citing ONS

own gang members; non-drug-connected offenders – for example racial/casual; users.

User-dealers also carry knives for fear of robbery by other user-dealers; other users; rival gang members; their own gang members.

Given the totality and frequency of such use it is unsurprising knife-carrying is so ubiquitous (Violent Crime Taskforce, 2019). Harding (2020) has recently posited this increase relates to changes and unpredictability within the gang social field; asymmetrics of inter-gang rivalry; and increased use of the County Line Control Repertoire making knife-carrying, not only expected, but a logical action for street survival.

The ubiquity of weapons was widely recognised by police who all expressed anxiety regarding their own safety:

> 'Because it's getting more and more … the weapons have gone through the roof, zombie swords and so on.' (Police 13)

One reason for weapon-carrying among County Line operatives was their own fear of being robbed by rivals:

> 'It's generally quite uncommon now for someone not to have a weapon. And it's for protection against being robbed by users a lot of the time – as opposed to gang feuds. We recently spoke to one guy who we arrested and he said openly he'd take a Samurai sword and rob the dealers. Said, "I'd go in there and I don't care and they back down. So we'll take the drugs". Then they feed him back to their hierarchy and they come down here with packs looking for people on occasion.' (Police 13)

Knife crime fatalities in England and Wales have achieved a 70-year peak (ONS, 2019), sparking public alarm and political disquiet. The Crime Survey for England and Wales and the Office for National Statistics (ONS, 2019) report that between 2017 and 2018, 285 killings were carried out using a knife or sharp instrument (of which 55 occurred in London) – the highest level since commencement of Home Office records in 1946 (Violent Crime Taskforce, 2019). In the year ending March 2018, offences involving a knife or sharp instrument in England and Wales totalled 40,100 (Allen and Audickas, 2018).

Around 63 per cent of sharp instrument homicide victims were White; 25 per cent were identified as Black, representing the highest proportion of black victims since data collection commenced in 1997. One quarter of all victims were men aged 18–24 (an increase of 38 per cent), with one quarter killed by friends/acquaintances and one quarter killed by a stranger (ONS, 2019). Suspects too are mainly young men aged 16–24. While not all of these relate to county lines or drug dealing activity, data are suggestive of younger people and people of colour increasingly becoming victims.

Public debates are most acute in London where authorities recorded the highest rate of offences involving a knife (168 per 100,000) in 2017/18: an increase of 26 offences per 100,000 on the previous year (Allen and Audickas, 2018). In response the London Mayor has allocated £15M to establish a new MPS Violent Crime Task Force (VCTF). The VCTF victim profile indicates 81 per cent of London knife-enabled crime victims are male; 53 per cent are BAME; 38 per cent are white; and 33 per cent are aged 15–24. While offenders in London are 94 per cent male; 49 per cent aged 10–19; 17 per cent aged 20–24; 73 per cent BAME (MPS, 2019). The profile of victims/offenders in London are London-specific and are not reflected elsewhere in England and Wales, with young BAME men increasingly both victim and offender.

It is recognised that knife-enabled crime pertains to issues as variant as domestic violence, the night-time economy, alcohol-related interpersonal violence, gang violence and drug supply (Grimshaw and Ford, 2018; Holligan et al, 2016; ONS, 2019; Palasinski and Riggs, 2012; Traynor, 2016). For a recent analysis of contemporary evidence on knife crime, see Grimshaw and Ford (2018). Despite this, some of the national increase in knife-enabled crime is attributed to county lines (NCA, 2018) with emergence of home-grown urban gangs a recognised factor (Densley, 2014: Harding, 2014; NCA, 2017b; Pitts, 2008). Gang members are known to demonstrate a greater propensity to carry knives (McVie, 2010) compared to non-gang members. Controversially, however, recent data in London indicates gang-related knife crime is over-estimated accounting for 5 per cent of all knife crime with injury during 2016 (GLA: 15) (though definitions here remain contested).

Halliday and Parveen (2019) note that knife crime is rising most steeply outside London citing CL dealing as the main cause. In their analysis of official statistics they reported an average increase of 45.7 per cent in knife-related offences in 34 counties in England and Wales since 2010; compared to a rise of only 11 per cent in London. The Home Counties reported a rise of 44.8 per cent while Kent reported a rise of 152 per cent.

The Ministry of Justice (2019) noted that data for the year to March 2019 showed 72 per cent of those caught with knives and offensive weapons in England and Wales were first-time offenders. While fuller analysis is required, such data are suggestive of the use of 'clean skins' (people with no offending history to carry or hide weapons for others) as a partial explanation for this rise.

Massey and colleagues (2019) also reported that knife offences are often grouped locally with multiple offences occurring in small localised areas. This is suggestive of revenge attacks and tit–for–tat attacks.

Tackling knife crime is now being prioritised by the UK government via the Serious Violence Strategy (HM Government, 2018); the Metropolitan Police Service and the VCTF; and for the Mayor's Office for Policing and Crime (MOPAC) via its London Knife Crime Strategy (MOPAC, 2017).

Robbery among the wider community

Academics researching crime and drug markets have identified that within communities hosting local domestic drug markets, there are always individuals benefiting creating a local illicit economy. This economy provides markets for stolen goods and opportunities to generate additional income to purchase drugs (May et al, 2005). These illicit markets thrive in atomistic neighbourhoods characterised by poverty and deprivation and simultaneously provide help with basic needs for those in poverty. As noted by May and colleagues, the complex inter–twining of illicit economies with such communities is still not well understood, but their perceived value means localised domestic drug markets are 'tolerated'. Moreover deprived communities supporting embedded or well–established heroin markets are closely linked to acquisitive crime (Parker and Newcombe, 1987; Seddon, 2006). This can be viewed as a form of 'economic necessity' (Jarvis and Parker, 1989); a 'hustler' lifestyle (Preble and Casey, 1969); engagement in the 'fringe' economy of stolen goods (Auld et al, 1984); or as a criminal outcome of the need for material gain and attempts to alleviate the psychological stress of unemployment (Pearson, 1987a). Coomber and colleagues (2017: 7), however, note that user–dealers often prefer involvement in small–scale dealing as opposed to acquisitive crime such as shoplifting, burglary or theft which many view as 'morally shameful'.

County Lines networks are central to generating additional forms of crime in the host/target locations, including visible drug use and street dealing causing distress to local communities; house–breaking and burglary, but also robbery of brothels. As one respondent noted:

> 'My pal is now going to prison for three robberies. Robbing someone with a needle with blood on it. Yes, he'd gone into a shop, shoplifting and when he'd gone to leave the staff came out and he pulled it out. Now he's getting done for three, innit. And he was a nice fella. His mum died and then he just kept

doing more and more and more. He was my friend but he's run off with money of mine so he can get a hit. You can't trust no one. Everyone has lost their morals. You ain't got a friend who'll stick by you. None of that is out there now. Everyone is out for their new drug. It has ruined the area. It's ruined a lot of people I know. Decent people. Definitely.' (User 04)

Robbery, conducted individually, in duos or groups, represents a strategic action for advancement within the gang social field (Harding, 2014):

'No, you could go out on your own, or in a group. Most of the time with a group, it's easier with a group. When I would do something like that I'd only be with one person. Yeah, just one person, if I was to be honest back then.' (USG 02)

Local youth responses to the emergence of county lines

Appraisal and assessment processes

Emergence of CL networks in provincial towns are not formally announced so existing local dealers might be unaware this is happening until intelligence filters back that non-locals are dealing in town. From there things can move quickly. Established local dealers/local gangs need to quickly enhance their intel regarding: what is happening? Who are these new people? Will they provide new business opportunities to make more money? Will our profits be diminished/increased? Will my/our status be diminished/enhanced? Will my/our street capital be diminished/enhanced? Can they be trusted? Such queries initiate processes of local appraisal and assessment whereby local youth/dealers rely on users to make informal assessments and provide intel. Quickly their emergence will be construed as threat or opportunity.

Group consensus on the response to this new perceived threat/opportunity might not be achieved. Local gangs might have been acephalous up until this point; thus one response might be to appoint a head or Top-boy of their gang. Although in-group bonding and loyalty is strong among groupings of provincial youth, or might appear so when faced with an external advisory, framing of the issue as threat/opportunity will create division. Some individuals/pairs might move away from the group and, spying opportunities, establish their own early links with the emergent group.

Acquiescence and rejection-threat responses

Ability, or the willpower, for local youth to react/resist emergence of new networks is often determined by variables outside their control, for example if loosely based or recently convened they may be too 'weak' to offer resistance. Local isolation and lower group–identity, or frail/unsecure existing distribution networks, might determine how local youth now perceive the new arrivals. Internal dissatisfaction with the status quo can be an important consideration as a new CL operation heralds promise of greater professionalisation, organisation, opportunity and profit. Soon the local youth collective/gang will determine their response. Figure 7.1 illustrates the options available arising from appraisal and assessment – acquiescence and rejection.

For many local provincial youth/dealer groups, acquiescence might be a result of realistic assessment of current positions and future trajectories. It is perhaps the Opportunity model for many, offering possibilities of playing 'the real Gangsta Game'. This model is attractive to some while others will focus on increased opportunities, new roles, increased status and future potential dividends and profits. Those young people struggling to rise within the local hierarchy or frustrated and secessionist in outlook (Swartz, 1997: 124) might now support this approach which when turned into a narrative renders the 'old-guard' redundant or at least will deflate their status and power.

The rejection (or threat model) will focus on the established status quo retaining local market dominance. Here potential increased profits are largely over-looked in preference of retaining the perceived high status of the local gang or group. This model might also be called the Local Ego model as retention of long-acquired localised street capital is deemed primary, that is, local Top-boys or Top dealers do not wish to be usurped by outsiders. Sensing a power shift, shakedown or takeover, their instinct is to reject the emergence of an outside CL group, holding their ground, retaliate, and drive off outside insurgents. Again this might be informed by local user intel suggesting CL operatives are insincere; unaware of existing local structures; or ill-prepared. Local appraisals and assessments are now made at this juncture and low-level antisocial behaviour challenges emerge which brings police attention. Repudiation and rejection of insurgents takes place online as local youth attempt to demonstrate their local superiority and territoriality (Kintrea et al, 2011). Before long, a critical event occurs leading to reappraisal and re-assessment on both sides.

A more nuanced Adaptation model also can be identified for youth groups/gangs/dealer networks operating in provincial towns and how they adapt to CL emergence – see Table 7.3.

Figure 7.1: Local youth responses to arrival of county lines drug supply network

Awareness
The local gang/dealer network becomes aware of the appearance of other products/dealers in town via empirical data, local user intel and downturns in local sales or profits margins.

Appraisal, assessment and adjustment
The local gang/dealer network collate local user intel to assess emergent insurgents for strength, network links, potential, staff numbers, parent-gang links, market potential and enforcement capability

OPPORTUNITY	**THREAT**
Acquiescence	**Rejection**
• Acquiescence/acceptance of new opportunities • Take-up of new opportunities • Joint dealing • Market expands • Locals can be used to operate Domestic Satellite Hub • Possible integration/affiliation to London gang	• Arrival interferes with local distribution/perceived power balance/local kudos and status • Represents deflationary move regarding street capital • Can bring enhanced local bonding of local host groups and the (visible) emergence of a local gang • Retaliation and response both online and offline • **Critical event ensues** • Leads to reappraisal and reassessment
Comments:	**Comments:**
If the local grouping (gang) of young people is a looser network with a lower group identity or possibly a more ethnically diverse composition, then coercion might be used. In this scenario resistance might be limited and futile. Some ethnically based local youth might switch sides more readily. Other variables here include local isolation and distance from London or a metropolitan centre.	This might occur if the local youth (gang) are more established with a recognised or pronounced dominance or presence in local drug markets. Variables include local dominance, personal egos and loyalty of distribution networks. This scenario is more likely to be visible to the authorities as the critical event is likely to be public, involving anti-social behaviour, knife crime and possibly homicide.
Market: Expansion and Acquisition	**Market:** Shakedown or Takeover

The steps in Table 7.3 illustrate a spectrum of different modes through which a local domestic gang/dealer network might pass once confronted with emerging CLs. While some modes overlap, others can be viewed as developmental stages in the acceptance of change. Timelines for each step remain undetermined and await further exposition. Locally based drug

Table 7.3: Spectrum of local adaptations post-emergence of county lines

Acceptance	Some local domestic gangs/dealer networks simply accept that they are out of their depth and give in quickly to these new emergent arrangements
Adjustment	Local adjustments are made by the local gang/dealer network to improve supply or product quality. Emergent CLs become viewed as opportunities to freshen up and step up. Initial market entry might be slow, difficult or unproductive, leading the emergent CLs to disengage
Accommodation	Local gang/dealer networks find ways of reconciling differences with the emergent group, including possible agreements to divide the town by area or by product supply, for example emergent CL operatives supply Class A while existing group supply recreational drugs
Acclimatisation	Existing local gang/dealer networks become accustomed to a different climate or business environment, for example in some cases working alongside emergent CLs
Absorption	The emergent CL may absorb/assimilate the local domestic gang/dealer network offering protection and improved upline networked links. This has great potential for fast future market expansion offering localised increased protection from rivals (in reality this promise might be untrue)
Adaptation	The local domestic gang/dealer network fully adapts to the new emergent group, possibly deciding to disengage with key markets or user groups; to shrink their market share; to aggressively reclaim their market share or work collaboratively with the emergent CL group
Affiliation	The local domestic gang/dealer network might choose to connect or associate with the emergent county line or the parent street gang and affiliate openly and publicly with them, thereby adopting the gang brand or CL brand
Acceleration	The above steps seek to accelerate the local CL market as the local gang/dealer network now effectively joins forces opening up and diversifying new markets, doubling intel and local knowledge, generating and filling new roles, and faster market expansion

dealing crews may differ from existing localised gangs in how they react to emergent CLs. They may in fact operate with a moderated spectrum as potential impacts with emergent CLs might differ, for example more easy absorption and less likely to reject or challenge their emergence.

Moreover the above spectrum will be influenced and possibly compromised in situations where strong competition exists between competing lines. In this scenario, some issues will be exacerbated and others curtailed or heightened.

The similarity or co-terminosity of social fields between the parent gang from London (or other metro centre) and the local domestic or host gang will also influence the progression (or otherwise) of this spectrum.

It stands to reason, however, that local host markets which have sought accommodation with and assimilation by emergent County Line networks will emerge from this change process faster and fitter than those resorting to struggle for dominance. Thus they accelerate more quickly becoming more profitable and productive. Again this process indicates a different experience for each line and for engagement with each local domestic gang/dealer network. Yet again as each is determinant upon multiple variables over an elastic time-frame, each CL experiencing divergent relationships with local gangs and existing local dealer networks. This further adds to the kaleidoscopic presentation of county lines.

In such ways county lines networks become fully established within an area. Table 7.4 identifies what occurs in terms of relationships with local gangs/dealer networks post-establishment of a county line and once the market has settled down in a new state of (relative) equilibrium.

Once the CL is established and new professional business (and social) arrangements are in play, local youth who previously operated within the local gang or local dealer network are recruited and utilised. This process is sometimes coercive and sometimes agentic but can amount to a series of abstractions of local youth from their hometown. Unlike London gang-affiliated youth being trafficked to provincial areas, this involves local provincial youth being used as runner/dealers on other lines. Occasionally they become local Satellite Hub managers as their localised knowledge of users and police movements is highly valuable. Some youth are ready and prepared for these new roles.

Through a process of employee/staff line management, adoption of gang rules, adherence to the County Line Control Repertoire and a desire to fit in, local youth now adapt to new cultural norms and values. This process of acculturation is fully supported by social media, peer affirmation and a dramatic increase in weekly wage or profits.

Table 7.4: Local gang relationship changes post-establishment of county lines

Abstraction	Local youth previously working with the existing local gang/dealer network seek roles outside their area as CL operatives/managers for the new CL gang
Acculturation	Eventually the existing gang/dealer network becomes adapted to a different set of cultural norms and values. The social field of the emergent CL gang has assimilated the existing local domestic gang/dealer network.
Adhesion	The values and rules of the social field of the parent USG become normalised and fully adopted by local gang/local dealer network

The final element of this troika of post-CL emergence changes relates to adherence of parent gang values. Here new opportunities of horizontal and vertical movement across and within the gang hierarchy becomes available (more in promise than in reality, however). Constant grinding and acculturation of CL work brings experience, generating new and exciting street capital. The value of this street capital is only truly realised (and converted into economic capital) within the social field of the USG or CL crew. Thus greater skill and experience becomes the cultural bedrock for greater embeddedness within the USG. The doxa and illusio (Bourdieu 1991: 22) not only still apply but are enhanced and made real via tangible results and advancement. Such activity, in frequency, regularity and embedded criminality generates ever-greater adhesion to the social field.

The emergence of a new CL network can forge increased cohesion among local/domestic youth group into an identifiable street gang – the Sprouting model – whereby local gangs emerge as a response. A second, often more immediate potential outcome, is a violent response by a local criminal gang already active in the area. Here an active and established group seeks to confront the emergent CL operatives leading to an asymmetric clash.

The Sprouting model

In this study, respondents held different perceptions about the existence of local groups of youth involved in criminality and drug dealing with some viewing them as 'an emergent street gang', and others 'an established street gang'. This lack of consensus illustrates wider perceptional variance across all stakeholders and practitioners which arises in part from practitioner 'bias' or remit. Some pertains to conflicting views of gang definitions/descriptions. When asked if the local youth group was developing into an USG all answered in the affirmative:

> 'I think that characteristics of it are here, the videos and all that kind of stuff. So, I think that the culture of it has breathed in.' (Stakeholder 05)

Local stakeholders and practitioners gradually became more aware of the changing nature of localised offending:

> 'Like under our nose ... happened over five years ... we can identify individuals coming in and certain events happening and the change in pattern of offending... A definite

influence from London. I know county lines is steeped from gangs.' (Stakeholder 05)

On occasion changes in offending patterns and local youth group presentation is traced back to handful of individuals with disproportionate effects upon local youth:

'It was almost their level of sophistication, given their age and their offending and their outlook on offending and attitudes towards it, seeked [sic] to then tip the scales, as it were. They then met and became a force to be reckoned with. They had kind of celebrity status and it was then that we really began to see things speed up in the process of others joining...' (Stakeholder 06)

One local stakeholder articulated local concerns:

'Yes, it's on our radar, cause it's going on and we're concerned about it. Vulnerable young people are aware of potential grooming into drugs networks. Our district is an ideal hunting ground for vulnerable young people. Mostly cos there is a lot of poverty. Big issues of placing those people here from outside the county. Geography means we are close to London and we don't have the resources to deal with this or to tackle organised crime, so it's a perfect storm.' (Stakeholder 09)

One possible response to emergence of CLs is for local youth (or low-level locally active drug dealers) to form into a local street gang. Often some local criminal elements have maintained criminal activity and low-level dealing unhindered by competition. Only when outside competition emerges do things change and young people group up for protection (Thrasher, 1927). It is logical this protection principle was dormant until an outside 'threat' emerges whereupon territoriality is viewed as the town itself rather than a metropolitan ward or postcode. Here group esteem (Vigil, 1988) is challenged with perceptional expectations that local youth must step up to meet any challenge.

It is possible that some local youth have viewed themselves as a gang for sometime or been labelled as such by local police. It might be the process of gang formation is accelerated as a threat response from outside insurgency. Several respondents in this study identified that local groups have taken CL emergence as the trigger to consolidate and brand themselves as a street gang, sometimes referred to as them 'rising up':

'I think there's a lot of kudos in that, but I think that's fuelled by social media. I think there's a lot on social media if you look for it that revolves around the kudos of the gang culture from London.' (Police 04)

This process of gang formation is essentially protective against outside insurgency offering strong bonding narratives for young people keen to demonstrate in-group loyalty and 'see off' external threats. In this way a local street gang might 'sprout' as a result of emergent competition.

Sprouting can occur, or is quickened, through appearance of a 'catalyst' serving to direct local youth or bond them more tightly while offering a vision of the future. A common view expressed was that the rehoming into the locality of young London gang-affiliated boys with existing offending histories created the catalyst for increased local offending leading to local USG development. Respondents talked commonly about London Boys having 'increased sophistication' and experience and were able to re-commence USG activity or dominate less sophisticated local boys:

'Yes, and again, black boys, so self-identify, safety in numbers, they came together, but one of them had come from a gang situation up north, like significantly [involved]. He had been shot and all… So, he came here having lived the gang life and within three months, was involved in a murder. But he was not part of a gang situation here, so I think that there is a movement of people around the country, disaffected young people and when they get to areas, they come together…' (Stakeholder 05)

One YOT practitioner suggested that currently the local existing 'gang' was more a youth group involved in anti-social behaviour and low-level criminality, but she noted CL crews from London offered structure and hierarchy:

'Well, my perception of it is that it wasn't a gang, as like a business enterprise that uses violence. I think it was a kind of hodgepodge of different kids who had aspirations to make a lot of money and were trying their luck at dealing, used to be into violence, but after the murder, it all seems to have died down a bit. I can tell you now who is supposed to be in [gang name]. It changes every day as to who is… So, it seems to have gone down to a level of kids on the corner, maybe. But I think it is right, if somebody was to come in who did offer that level of organisation and structure, I think people would be ready to jump in…' (Stakeholder 06)

One local police officer articulated the evolving local situation as follows:

'And this is a massive problem. We've got a thing around different gangs – so you've got your group from London who came down here solely to make money whether they are using vulnerable boys from London or willing participants in it – that's one gang. Then there are gangs that are down here but are formed via connections in London but are rehomed down here but they think, "Oh, this is a good place to make some money". And they keep doing that. Then you've got your local gangs – we've got a couple of local gangs – predominantly white lads but they reintegrate with the rehomed London arrivals.' (Police 10)

Asymmetric clash: when local youth misread London boys

The arrival of a new external gang or crew presents challenges and opportunities both socially and in terms of business for local youth including potential reputational damage and street capital deflation. This model might also equate to pre-county lines/traditional drug supply model in Table 2.2 (Chapter 2).

Arrival or emergence of a CL network into a provincial town creates a sudden collision between two social fields – the local domestic gang/group and the London-based CL crew. Often the latter London group are present in the new location by proxy – meaning CL managers supported by runner/dealers. Critically CL operations are underwritten by London-based parent gangs located only an hour or two from the host town location and always on call.

The Rejection–Threat model (see Figure 7.1) sets up a focussed rivalry between insurgent CL crews and incumbent local youth. In terms of social field theory (Bourdieu, 1984; Harding, 2014), the CL crew present as insurgent sucessionists – new entrants into the social field – pitted against conservationists (local youth keen to maintain their status-quo grip on local drug market, profits and hard-won reputation). A loss of any element equates to massive street capital deflation. The sucessionists view moving into a new town as an investment strategy calculated to generate fresh profits and high volumes of street capital. Their aim and goal is driven by money and the underpinning reputation accredited to those who make it mounds.

Increased engagement with local dealers and user-dealers generates considerable intel for the London-based parent gang. By operating a local satellite Hub their local intel is greatly enhanced giving heightened knowledge of local players, their networks, movements and behaviours. The local domestic youth have failed to take full account of this and critically underestimated the nerve, earnestness and professionalism of the London-based parent gang. The London-based parent gang have been thoroughly schooled in generating street capital and are hyper-vigilant in ensuring they protect against street capital deflation. They have access to enforcers and guns which will be used if necessary.

Emergence of the London-based CL crews generates a local dilemma for the host town youth: what should their response be locally? Do they retaliate and respond, coalesce and join in, or do they give up and roll over? Crucially they do not want to be seen as fake.

When the critical event arrives it bears more resemblance to a football game between a Premier League division and a Third Division team. With the arrival of violence local boys are untested and loyalties can evaporate quickly when faced with serious violence.

Critical to any potential or inevitable conflict between the sucessionists and the conservationists are the logistical, practical and behavioural characteristics of each other's gang/group. Community intelligence will be garnered to permit an assessment of the Opps (opposition) and their capabilities – either to hold on to their territory/market or to take it. Judgements will be made and sources, both online and offline, scourged for information and opinion. The gang characteristics, which are up for assessment, are, however, both manifest and latent.

Manifest characteristics of a gang/group include:

- numbers of youth involved or affiliated to the gang/group;
- ability, time taken to group up in numbers if required;
- local presence, visibility and numbers, in the area;
- age and physicality of members;
- weaponry available and visibly present;
- online presence and reputation.

These characteristics are largely empirically determined and visible to other youth or rival gangs/groups. Opinions will be formed quickly regarding how many people affiliate to the gang/group; who they are? their ages?; their stature and ability to engage in a fight?; who is 'on their side'?; will they will win a fight?; will they fight fair?

247

Assessments are transformed into a Fakery Integer, signifying how fake/authentic the gang/group is (Fakery being the gang slang antonym to authentic). Such assessments are openly discussed among both sides, and those seeking strategic advancement will position themselves to strike out against the rivals. Emergent crews are placed upon an imaginary spectrum of Agile–Fragile indicating ability, skills, numbers, capabilities and so on.

Seasoned USG members are aware that manifest characteristics only represent part of the picture. The other half remains hidden below the water line as latent characteristics including:

- acquired street capital and skilled experience in 'The Gang Game';
- habitus – history, tradition, street socialisation and so on;
- future trajectory – horizons, direction, strategic aims;
- velocity and potential – the earnestness, desire and intent to carry through with actions;
- perceptional vantage point – ability to read the Game based upon street capital skill and experience;
- loyalties and networks – links to wider groups and backers;
- authenticity – ability to demonstrate embeddedness and adherence to gang rules and values.

These latent gang characteristics are what really determines the inner core of a USG member, underscoring their true authenticity. A local gang/group without these latent characteristics is quickly dismissed a fake or wannabee.

While manifest characteristics favour local youth, the latent characteristics favour the London-based USG. Different rules from different social fields now apply with London-based USGs practised in calling in enforcers to 'teach the locals a lesson in gang life'. Increased weaponisation includes guns, machetes, acid throwing.

While the local host town youth can quickly group up furnished with local on-site knowledge to proudly cite their localised reputation for aggro, they are quickly mismatched in terms of pedigree and provenance by London-based USGs whose latent characteristics are laden with hardened gang violence and seasoned experience.

An asymmetric clash ensues with the balance in favour of hardened London-based youth who bring quite different levels of understanding and determination. Local youth are now 'out of their depth'.

The asymmetry involved here is much more than simply the size of the gang, numbers involved, length of time involved in gang culture or propensity for violence. It involves asymmetry of aspirations, expectations, adherence, belief and immersion. The local domestic youth 'act out' gang cultural and gang life by way of local performance to generate localised respect making them 'big guns in the community'. This permits acquisition of street capital by being publicly seen as anti-authoritarian. For many this is a transitory phase before settling into paid employment. Expectations and horizons might be limited and most aim to settle down in the local community. This is not comparable to the established career trajectory of more sophisticated USGs from London who are seasoned gang affiliates managing CLs.

Potential gains in street capital are available via early take-out or win against the Opps. If local youth succeed in driving off insurgent sucessionists they will most likely progress to dominate the local market until the next critical event.

For insurgent CL crews, success brings reputational enhancement and street capital inflation. They are seen to be 'true to their word' and able 'to follow through'. Both accolades enhance citations of professionalism. Indeed such asymmetric clashes are an integral part of the professionalisation strategy by 'clearing the decks' competitor eradication, market dominance and reputation building:

> 'Well, basically, threats being made from [name] and his peer group to people in the other gang. This was the time when the [town] [gang name] and the rival [gang name] were firing insults on social media … threats to stab people – I'm going to do this or that… It was immediately apparent that the [gang name] guys were all empty words – being big and strong in their own bedroom with the curtains drawn. For the other gang – it wasn't empty words. They were prepared to follow it through and then some. We did a lot of community work after the stabbing in [town name]. There was a lot of shock and tears, how could it happen, but no realisation it was because they were all on social media in the build-up to it. All those on social media who are now crying were the ones making the threats. Well, now this happened.' (Police 09)

The clash of social fields and asymmetry of engagement between the two gangs is expressed movingly by one police officer who recounted the recent murder:

> 'To him he thought he was getting beaten up and not stabbed. But to the guys doing the stabbing they thought, "No, this isn't enough, you don't get it. Enough is enough when you are dead. We're not here to mess around". For him it was, "OK,

I get it. That's enough, you've made your point". He didn't
realise he was being stabbed and they were in the process of
murdering him. It just shows the mindset – he didn't realise
it wasn't enough for them. They were not like your average
[district name] kids, making silly threats on FB. To them it
was a loss of face. It's "I've threatened to do something and if
I don't follow through with it then I've lost face in front of my
peer group", so it was a clash of two different worlds re the
level of violence. The extent they were prepared to go [to],
and they don't think or care about consequences.' (Police 09)

An asymmetric clash essentially pits together two rival groups mismatched
and unequal in size, numbers, experience and purpose. Violence escalates
pre-critical events. The emergence of CL crews supported by a London-
based parent USG signifies significant shifts: firstly, in local offending
rates; secondly, in perceptions of local youth involvement in drug dealing;
thirdly, changes and moderation in what is deemed to be a credible or
permissible action among young people. It poses new questions and alerts
them to new boundaries. Local youth reflect on what it means to play
the gang game in this new way and they ruminate upon their current
and future involvement.

Such asymmetric clashes are a regular feature in towns across England
where local youth interface with London-based or metropolitan-based
gangs with greater experience, drive and purpose. It is likely that this has
generated considerable levels of offending and is partially to account for
the upswing in knife-enabled crime and violence currently witnessed
across the country.

Critical events

Figure 7.1 identifies that the Rejection-Threat model of response will
ultimately lead to a showdown or point of conflict which can be viewed
as a critical event. This event is often preceded by low-level antisocial
behaviour, street fighting, public disorder, interpersonal violence which
can escalate either quickly or over time. Knife-enabled crime at this
juncture is not uncommon. The critical event is essentially a 'wake-up call'
for those in the domestic youth gang/group bringing home the reality of
the violent social field they have entered. The critical event also acts as a
signal event (Densley, 2012; Densley and Pyrooz, 2017; Innes, 2014) for
other practitioners in the local authority, police or local agencies working
with the local youth.

A true critical event is more violent and severe and can arrive calibrated in terms of numbers, experience, history and so on, and this generates an asymmetric clash. In this study one of the local towns experienced a murder of young 17-year-old male. A subsequent review identified months of tit-for-tat exchanges culminating in the critical event.

Trigger events include incidents which appear or can be perceived as relatively unimportant or low-level but which generate immediate street capital deflation, for example the theft of a necklace or valuable item. This can lead to a ramped-up response from one group to another. On occasion such incidents are deliberately overplayed by one side as a cited reason for taking violent action against the rival side. Retaliation is viewed as restorative strategic action aimed at restoring and re-inflating damaged street capital:

> 'I think it got very real when we had the murder last year, I think it got very real for a lot of people and we started to see a slip back, a sort of reaction kicking back against that. But we've still got those hardcore, wannabe gang members out there who are still insisting on behaving in that way.' (Police 04)

Post-Critical Event, one police officer reflected upon the impact the event had had on the local existing gang:

> 'The day [name] was murdered, it just stopped overnight. We were obviously out patrolling for all sorts of repercussions, revenge attacks and so on. We thought, "Who could they go for? Who are the key players that [gang name] might go for?" But the entire [gang name] side went, "OMG, this is not what I thought we were getting into. I thought we were hanging around [place name] Park in a group of 50 with all our peer group, you know, trying to be all hard, and this no … you know, I didn't actually think anyone would actually get stabbed". It just literally stopped overnight and even now it's never really raised its head.' (Police 09)

Two years after the murder local stakeholders identified local trends had shifted:

> 'An acceptance now of violence, it seems; a high level of violence is almost normal. There is an acceptance of and an expectation of violence.' (Stakeholder 06)

Getting out of the trap

Although our knowledge of CL supply is still forming through research, how exactly young people desist from county lines remains unexplored. Criminal desistence is often theoretically linked to 'maturational reform' (Matza, 1964: 22) whereby criminals 'mature out' of crime and open up their lives to new experiences (Farrington, 2003). When asked why he might wish to cease working a County Line, one street gang member responded:

> 'Well, the fact that a lot of my friends are going to university. The fact that they are seeing other things.' (USG 03)

Gang embeddedness (Pyrooz et al, 2013), spirituality (Deuchar, 2018), interaction with the criminal justice system, trigger events (McNeill, 2012) and individual choice and situational context (Laub and Sampson, 2003: 145) are all cited as rationales for desistence. Desistence from crime is not the same as desistence from gangs and while daily interactions diminish, connections mostly endure (Densley, 2013: 137; Moule et al, 2013). When connections are strongly linked to income generation, as with county lines, desistence might be further tempered or even shelved completely. Others find the line too much to handle:

> 'I started the line and got out of there. I wasn't there, I never stayed there. I ended up giving the line to two little boys at the end. It just became hot. They kept getting arrested and just driving up there to sort shit out was just becoming long. So, I just gave them the line and said "Do you know what? If you want it, it's yours." because the houses were getting raided, getting kicked in and the police were coming in there with cameras and stuff. You were on TV when they were doing their raids. It was crazy. I just gave the kids the line and I just said, "Look, do your thing". They were over the moon.' (USG 06)

Despite such challenges there were several respondents self-identifying as street gang members or CL operatives who wished to leave the life behind them. As one CL operative pined:

> 'I don't want to be involved. We call it trapping. It's not just because we're trapping the person with the drugs, but because we're trapped as well. They had to call it trapping – we can't get out of the cycle. It's very hard to leave the cycle because

you get used to that kind of income, or that income actually pays for your lifestyle, your rent, your car, for so many different things that when you try to leave you're going to have nothing if you leave. So, you are kind of trapped into that cycle. Usually what happens is something drastic has to happen to that person for them to decide to just cut their losses.' (USG 03)

The concept of the trap and double meaning of 'trapping' as a commonly expressed term for drug dealing was spontaneously identified by several respondents. Also mentioned, by an older street gang member, was the cyclical nature of youth involvement in running drugs:

'I've seen a cycle. What I've explained to you, it happens to every generation about five years apart, it happens again, and again, and again.' (USG 03)

Another respondent talked of county lines as being like a trap but his emphasis was more on loyalty to the dealing crew he had been working with and his wish not to let them down:

'Well, this road life thing, it's fucked how it's set up, man, cos it's a bit of a trap. Once you're in it, you can't really come out of it, and when you come out of it, you don't want to let your family down, you understand, your little team, your little gang, you don't want to let them down, you understand? So you're being loyal to everyone, loyalty is key and I want to make money the same way, like the same speed, if there's a [pagan] or whatever, we have to beat them.' (USG 09)

Other more traditional forms of desistance were expressed such as life changes and maturing out (Matza, 1964). When asked, 'What would you have to do to exit the county lines life?', some respondents cited further education, or entrepreneurship, as key future routes.

Another CL operative had reflected upon desistance, but decided the Game offered more opportunity and benefits than desistance at this stage:

'Well, eventually, when the money is dying off, then eventually, yes, I've got to get out, but right now, I see this as the long-term future. It's clear to see that this is a life that, once you're in, it's very hard to get out of.' (USG 09)

When asked if he would exit county lines one respondent commented:

'Of course I would, bruv, of course I would, cuz, but chief is mans been coming up all year, so come up to do what? It's all I know, fam. Do what, bruv? Man's a trapper, fam. Man's an old fucking G blood, know what I'm saying? I've burnt myself. I put the work in. Now I'm getting the rewards. And it comes with consequences. This is what you don't understand – the consequences. You have all this … you watch these children get gassed thinking that they're trappers.' (USG 11)

For another, survival and adherence to the Game were paramount:

[Question: Are you happy with that life?]

'Well, it's the only life I know and it's the life I'm gonna keep on living and until I get a free pass out of here, I've got to survive.' (USG 10)

The link between survival, the Game and the concept of being trapped in the Game came out most strongly for one young CL operative who commented:

'I don't care how you analyse this shit, but this is what it is, and these [young dealers] are touched, these are lost and this is all I knows. N****rs are trapped, n****rs are lost.' (USG 10)

Trigger events for desistance

Desistance is often an evolving process, as highlighted by McNeill (2012), and can involve the interplay between social/personal identity, peer group and family influences and are reflexively viewed following a crisis point or 'trigger event' (Deuchar, 2013). One female CL manager ruminates how trigger events propelled her exit from CLs:

Case study – USG 01

'We were in [town], not far from [town]. But that line went on for a while. I ended up becoming pregnant – I'd just turned 17 – by this same guy. I remember when I was in labour the phone was still going, he still had the [name] line, and he's answering it every two seconds while I'm in active labour so it was still going on. Then I thought, "What the hell is this? Yes, we're getting money and I have everything for my baby, and I have my hostel and I have my sofa and all that kind of stuff but I don't want to be part of this any more. I am having a child". I didn't want to have a child anyway at that age at all, it wasn't in my plans at all but that was an eye opening for me where I was kind of drifting. At this point I was holding the phones and stuff, up until I had my daughter, I was holding the phones, I was organising everything.

'When I had my baby and I was in London, because we were staying up in [name] quite a lot, I was in London, my daughter she was quite a sick baby, she was six weeks and I was in my little hostel by myself and had just got off the phone to my friend. Suddenly the door has gone in, four people with balaclavas took my little baby into another room, I was there [at] gunpoint, they trashed the whole house looking for someone, I don't know what they were looking for, there was never anything in my place there. They had my daughter in the other room for an hour so you can imagine what that was like, she's a newborn baby, she's a girl, have no clue. The worst day of my life. And then from that point on – they were looking for something, I found out only a couple of years ago, that came from my best friend who I just got off the phone to obviously knew what we were doing, knew that we had money blah, blah, she told her boyfriend, "My friend [name] has got this, that and the other in her house", so it was him and his friends. So, that came from my best friend. It's always someone, it's never random, it's always someone close to home. It's not your enemy. So, from that point on I was "no, no", and I ended up literally walking into the police station with my baby and saying, "I need help".

'They ended up relocating me. They ended up getting restraining orders, prohibited steps, non-molestation orders against my daughter's dad and all of that kind of stuff. I never went into detail about what I was, drug wise or anything like that, I just wanted to be safe and leave that lifestyle. So, that's how I exited it and it was really hard. I know it is really hard and I know one of the girls who we had working up there she's in prison now because she started using, they had encouraged to do so and her life just went, she was a care leaver, didn't have any family. I know I've left mass destruction in my path but that's how I got out of everything. I was extremely lucky (a) not to lose my life and (b) not to get locked up, I've been arrested for other things but nothing to do with drugs but you don't hear that often.'

Dealers views change

Respondents varied in their biographies of how and why they became involved in CLs. Most had prior or ongoing involvement with USGs.

CL managers and Olders identified rapid change focussing on the age of those involved, their motivation, ubiquity and prevalence of multiple lines, increased sophistication, and the levels of violence and control now deemed required as central to operations.

One CL manager commented the 'youth of today' are significantly different from 'Old School days' of even five years ago and drew clear distinctions between the altruistic principles of supporting his family which motivated his earlier involvement in CL, and the more materialistic motivations now prevalent among younger CL operatives. A second CL manager noted a new precocious entrepreneurial spirit among Youngers:

> 'It's different because now you've got young kids being groomed. In my time little kids didn't have the balls to do this. They didn't have the balls. But now it's different. This age group now, you've got 15-year-olds going country and starting a line, 16-year-olds and they are using other kids like themselves making them grind and they are paying them.' (USG 06)

The image of a new toxic version of CL was endorsed by runner/dealers, vocal in issuing Cassandra-like warnings about future trajectories of CL in the UK:

> 'It's gonna get a lot worse, it's gonna get a lot worse, man, before it gets better, it's gonna have to get a lot worse cos no one is listening, so before it gets better, it's gonna get a lot worse.' (USG 09)

> 'Yeah, you can't stop the youth. You can't stop the young ones. The young ones are the real ones you need to fear because they have no remorse. They're not thinking. They're just off. And the scary thing about it is that there are certain children out there that are young, wild, and don't know how to control it. That's dangerous. That's a good dangerous, it's not a bad dangerous, if they have both personalities then you can control them perfectly. People like that, these brothers don't have anything on them and these are just children. Thinking like this, having this mentality. I know someone younger than me so smart, so wise, dangerous wise and good wise.' (USG 02)

The youngest and most embedded operatives expressed nihilistic views that they would 'die on streets' and not be around to see it. Stakeholders expressed concerns that things would continue to 'get worse'.

Chapter 8 moves on to consider the role of agencies, including the police and local stakeholders, in addressing and tackling county lines.

Conclusion

In advance of summarising how county lines might be more effectively addressed in terms of policy and practice, and before outlining the unique contribution of the book, it is perhaps useful to consider how this study is now positioned within the current research agenda.

Positioning the study

As illustrated earlier in Chapter 1, the academic understanding of county lines has been slow to emerge over the past decade. This is partly due to the fact that drug markets are not homogenous and structural alterations are not easily identifiable. Earlier work on drug markets at the turn of the century focussed more on social context, market segmentation and internal supply systems. The last five or more years has seen the nexus of criminology/drug misuse/public health scholarship focus more on the emergence of county lines distribution networks.

This study can now confidently affirm much of the work of colleagues with regards to the principle learning on CL drug markets thus far, notably: that the majority of CLs involve USGs (NCA 2016; 2017a; 2019a, 2019b); that dealers migrate and commute out of town to new markets (Coomber and Moyle, 2017; Densley, 2013; Disley and Liddle, 2016; Hallworth, 2016; Harding, 2014; Harding and Cracknell, 2016; Johnson, 2015; Johnson et al, 2013; Windle and Briggs, 2015b); that drug markets are altering in the UK (Andell and Pitts, 2017; Coomber, 2015; Disley and Liddle, 2016; Hay et al, 2019); that despite the impact of information technology, face-to-face transactions remain favoured for dealing heroin and crack cocaine (Coomber, 2015, Coomber and Moyle, 2017); that younger people are exploited by USGs and drug dealing crews within CLs (Andell and Pitts, 2018; Firmin 2018; Robinson et al, 2019; Pepin, 2018; Windle and Briggs, 2015a, 2015b); that some young people enjoy their role in CLs and that vulnerability is contested (McLean et al, 2020; Moyle, 2019; Robinson et al, 2019; Spicer et al, 2019; Windle et al,

2020); that some young people prefer independent dealing (Briggs, 2012; Coliandris, 2015; Hales and Hobbs, 2010; Windle and Briggs, 2015a); that user/dealers are present within CLs (Coomber and Moyle, 2014; Coomber et al, 2015); that CLs represent increased professionalisation and occupational culture (Andell and Pitts, 2018; Hesketh and Robinson, 2019; McLean et al, 2020; Whittaker et al, 2019); and that CLs impact locally upon host towns (Andell and Pitts, 2018).

This study, however, raises some challenges to current thinking in regard to some key issues. On 'vulnerability', supporting views of McLean et al (2020), Moyle (2019), Robinson et al (2019), Spicer et al (2019), this work identifies greater evidence of agency operating among users. While Decker and Pyrooz (2013) note that violence associated with drug dealing is both expressive and functional, this study identifies that it is also instrumental and utilised as a control mechanism. While violence associated with drug dealing can be overstated (Coomber, 2015), this study identified that within CL networks, violence is prolific, endemic, normalised and mostly under-reported. While dealers in the crack scene are often claimed to be crack users (Coomber, 2015; Jacobs, 1999), this study identified that the use of young people as migrating dealers has altered this position. Crucially in terms of USGs merging into organised criminal network and organised crime, Decker and Pyrooz (2013) argue that as USGs present with high levels of violence, volatility, fluidity and a lack of organisational structure, they are unlikely to be involved in organised crime. Findings from this study suggest that this is perhaps an ill-fitting American perspective in contemporary Britain.

Aside from these unifying observations of academic alignment or otherwise, I wish to set out the more unique contributions to the field and to the research agenda arising from this study.

Convergence of social fields

This study argues that the current rise in youth violence in the UK arises from a convergence of three social fields (markets or domains): an evolution of urban street gangs; profound evolutionary changes in drug markets and drug supply networks; and the profound alteration, adaptation and amendment of both of these by information technology and social media. While the statistical verification of this proposition might well be elusive, the over-arching narrative is, I think, a convincing one illustrated by several components.

Street gang evolution

UK USGs have evolved quickly and significantly since the millennium (Densley, 2013; Harding, 2014; Pitts, 2008, 2010). Austerity has sharpened the edges of deprivation, reducing the opportunities available to young people and widening the Pool of Availability, leaving more young people ready, willing and waiting to step into the social field of the street gang. More young people view USGs as the logical response to their personal ambitions and circumstances or the *only* logical response to a perceived need for survival. For many in such predicaments, the USG logic now has greater appeal so its rules become more widely adopted, or at least more widely comprehended. Austerity also increases real and perceived vulnerability of individuals, which must be countered by generating respect and reputation. For many young people, the USG therefore offers the best or most immediately available route to build respect and reputation – and thus reduce their perceived vulnerability. As more young people gravitate towards USGs, Olders and now Youngers seek to expand their power base by utilising ever-younger age groups to do their bidding. This further acts as risk mitigation. USG age ranges now expand downwards. The reduced opportunities propelling people towards USGs also reduces opportunities for gang exit, and for many the USG becomes more adhesive and difficult to leave (Harding, 2014). Thus older gang-affiliated youth often 'get stuck' in the street gang. The age range for some USGs is now 10–30 years. Overall, this means more people are now affiliated to USGs, their extended networks, their rules and their logic. Greater numbers in USGs means it is more difficult to rise above peers in either respect or status and achieve distinction (Bourdieu, 1984).

Increased competition

The effect of greater USG affiliation is an increase in numbers now seeking to use USGs as their route to distinction. Critically, this means greater and more serious levels of competition within the social field as each affiliate jostles with peers to generate more street capital, to get noticed, build respect and reach the top (or at least survive). Increased levels of competition within the field bring new players daily into the Game, further diluting levels of trust. New working relationships must be built amid growing suspicions. Loyalties and skills are tried and tested by all actors in the field. Overall, it's now a more competitive social environment, leading to increased turbulence within the social field of the USG. Old established ways of being are usurped by new young radicals. New more aggressive and strident methods (strategies) are proposed and enacted. These often include reputational extravaganza, which lower the benchmark of what is a permissible and credible action within the gang. This in turn changes normalised practices and outcomes – the most significant being the emergence of ultraviolence. It is ultraviolence that now offers a competitive edge in the endless quest to generate street capital in this social field.

Field flux

This study offers the concept of 'field flux' – energised turbulence within a social field. This is now evident and experienced as a result of multiple dramatic contentions within the social field, namely increased numbers of affiliates (both younger and older); increased hierarchical competition; new field rules and sudden changes, and disruption to the field settlement. Field flux is further exacerbated by changes to new emergent fields, such as that of the county lines dealing crew and also that of the user. Alterations to their internal structuration simultaneously cause turbulence with the social fields. The boundaries of these social fields are relational rather than fixed. They interconnect with each other, generating fresh locales of contention and lacuna to be filled. This leads to rapid repositioning within the internal field structure, as actors strive to position themselves for advantage while Elders struggle to avoid a void.

In summation, the social fields of USGs, drug dealing and drug using are all changing and evolving, generating friction internally but more noticeably also along the relational boundaries of each field.

The imperative of competitive advantage

Arising from increased competition within the social field of the gang actors now must find new ways to define themselves and their hierarchal position. This process commands the imperative of competitive advantage. Establishing competitive advantage will now define success (empowered advancement) or failure (vulnerability) within already violent environments: that is, using acid and corrosive liquids as weapons, the extended reach of a knife or sword, ability to 'mob up' quickly using social media – all increase competitive advantage. Individually, interpretations of this imperative include 'strike first, ask questions later'; overpowering rivals with frenzied attacks; trust no one; develop a reputation for overwhelming force. Once acquired, these advantages cannot be allowed to slide. If in doubt, 'Take the player out the Game', 'Kill the competition!'

Recent examples of competitive advantage include the use of cars as weapons to 'hunt down' then 'mow down' rivals before stabbing them to death while they lie prostrate on the pavement. The ubiquitous insistence of competitive advantage demands an alarming escalation of brutality and overall desensitisation to violence and its impacts. Increasingly, actors embedded within the social field become inured to this and the propinquity of violence is normalised.

It is now competitive advantage that drives the acquisition of street capital and which underpins all aspects of youth violence. This is most keenly witnessed in the development and expansion of county lines drug supply networks.

The accelerant role of social media in current youth violence

Alongside offering obvious multiple benefits for all communities, social media has impacted upon the USG and upon youth violence in various ways. Notably, it acts as an accelerant to all ongoing and developing turbulence within the social field of the gang, including, business transactions, personal relationships, petty disputes, unwelcome opinions and strategic moves. It amplifies feelings and has the potential to erode trust, and to birth insecurity and vulnerability.

Significantly it brings strong emotional proximity to any event whereby images of physical violence can now be live-streamed to viewers, into classrooms or on to mobile phones. This generates heightened anxiety, feelings of emotional propinquity and empathy, and it further generates overwhelming desire for involvement and response. Personal posts and grime videos generate further involvement, soliciting multiple opinions from ever broader groups of young people. Additionally, social media is used to market and trade drugs, groom new USG recruits, build personal biographies and brands; increase exposure to gang life and gang rules, all of which in turn expand the orbit of the gang to young people never previously exposed to it. Where once gang life was bounded by the territorial confines of estate life, social media has expanded it into a new online landscape where gang-life can thrive anew, raising tensions, leading to multiple reverberations, revenge attacks and retaliation. For young people this world is unpoliced, ungoverned and, for some, unsafe.

County lines as a business model

This study has adopted a fresh insight and perspective into the emergence and development of county lines as a formative criminal enterprise and business. The application of marketing and business principles permit us to view this as a fundamental reorientation of drug supply to the end user. From this fresh perspective, concepts emerge of product placement, branding, customer value, loyalty and satisfaction, pricing strategies and customer relations. Successful CLs now adopt and follow the marketing mix. It is these insights offered by marketing principles that now help us to illuminate new strategic actions for actors within the social field of the gang and the drug dealing crew. Moreover, it permits the instant realisation of competitive advantage and ascendant street capital generation.

Competitive advantage drives this social field and is established in several ways. Above all, is the imperative to get your drugs to the end user first. A 24-hour-dial-a-dealer operation is most effective. As a logical interpretation of the 'gig economy', this business model sees door-to-door delivery via moped following requests enabled by mobile phones – now central to all aspects of the customer/business model. This drug supply model now permits effective drug dealing beyond gang postcodes into more distant and more profitable markets. These new markets are sourced by USGs who then respond to market conditions by expanding their drug supply networks accordingly.

As competitive advantage propels this social field, the CL networks operate increasingly sophisticated business models, marketing principles and techniques to orient illegal drug products to existing and new markets. Effective line managers will use creative pricing strategies and market-entry techniques. County line networks are not static but constantly evolving business models.

This study acknowledges the evolution of drug supply from the traditional family firms operated at the lower end of criminal networks (Hobbs, 2001; Pearson and Hobbs, 2001) which involved local drugs for local people. In a break from often prosaic iterations of how CLs form and shape, this study offers a spectrum of evolutionary stages, each identifiable as a separate business model differentiated by key characteristics, products and target users. These four models operate in a spectrum that moves from the status quo through formalisation to professionalisation and to diversification. A series of push factors propel CLs from urban centres and, similarly, pull factors operate as gravitational magnetism into host towns. The variation of these push and pull factors, each evolving against different timescales, means county lines present differently or at least present as different evolutionary stages right across the UK, creating a kaleidoscopic presentation of county lines, often indistinguishable to many. This cloaked similarity inhibits local police, local leaders and local communities from a shared consensus as to what is happening and why their town differs from the next.

Professionalisation

County lines drug supply networks now present us with the professionalisation of the subterranean tier. Previously professionalisation was only truly available to those who secured a place in OCNs either through skill, longevity or family/kinship links. In some ways, OCNs operate as a further education bracket of criminal activity, offering high stakes but high dividends. County lines drug supply networks represent a deregulation of drug distribution and a democratisation of drug supply as seen in moves away from traditional local family cartels supplying middle markets in provincial UK towns. County lines networks now offer routes in and roles for all levels, imbued with a spirit of entrepreneurialism. This, however, comes with much violence and more to come.

Exploitation

The increased Pool of Availability, the evolution of USGs and the imperative for competitive advantage now provides the opportunity, and necessity, to expand drug markets by exploiting the young and vulnerable.

The key driver for this is, of course, the constant quest for competitive advantage, which this study illustrates as a move from migrating and commuting dealers (Hallworth, 2016; Johnson, 2015; Coomber and Moyle, 2017; Windle and Briggs, 2015b) to one of establishing Satellite Hubs and user-dealers. The utilisation of user-dealers with newer models of CL networks cuts costs and overheads while increasing control and generating increased profits. Dividends of improved localised knowledge assist in customer profiling, customer service and police avoidance. The supply of vulnerable users is met by exploiting young people, often those 'going missing' from home or from care and coercing them to 'go county', 'muling' drugs internally, to distant towns. Other techniques include exploiting people with disabilities or the user community as free accommodation via cuckooing.

While confirming the broad findings of McLean et al (2020), Spicer et al (2019) and Coomber and Moyle (2017), the four-point typology from Spicer et al (2019) is now enhanced in this study by a more detailed typology. This new cuckooing typology illustrates how such exploitation works, though interpersonal relationships between users/dealers that are often more nuanced than reported. These exploitative business models can amount to human trafficking and modern-day slavery and are advanced through violence, threat, intimidation and control. Females are subject to sexual exploitation and degradation and many young people who fall into debt are tethered to the gang via debt bondage. Recent market evolution sees local substance misusers coerced into becoming user-dealers operating from local Satellite Hubs. These vulnerable victim/offenders are now often the active runner/dealers, further cutting business costs for CL managers but fracturing local user communities.

The County Line Control Repertoire

Maintenance of a fully operational county line with multiple staff necessitates tight control to ensure maintenance of competitive advantage, profit margins, professionalism and customer service. This study also advocates the Control Repertoire alongside the conception of more agentic responses from 'vulnerable' tenants. A County Line Control Repertoire operates as a menu of sanctions to be exercised by managers both internally to runner/dealers and externally to users. This can include fake debt, robbery, intimidation and violence. The local calibration of this repertoire varies but in places can be vicious and brutal. In a further unique contribution to the research field, this study details how threats are now expanded to include family members, and reverberations of county lines can ripple back into communities extending lines of influence, control and fear.

Asymmetric clash

Arrival of county lines into a local provincial town can be gradual or sudden, but it is seldom long before their consequences become noticeable. Over time arrival leads to profound changes in drug supply and distribution markets, but it can also lead to clashes with local youth or criminal networks already active in drug supply. This study offers the conceptualisation of localised responses to CL emergence from local youth in a typology of possible responses culminating in asymmetric clash. Various responses within the typology posit that numerous options are available but asymmetric clashes can erupt between inexperienced vocal, local youth and the more sophisticated experienced hardcore USGs from urban centres. Many UK towns are now experiencing this problem and its attendant rise in localised violence and knife crime. In places, this can lead to local gangs sprouting to match the arrival of new market insurgents.

Criminal confidence and local change

This study found that police and stakeholders voiced concerns that USGs and CL drug dealing crews had not only evolved recently but significantly increased in levels of confidence and sophistication over the last two years. Many also lamented cuts to policing, youth services and local authority budgets, which they felt had hindered opportunities for addressing county lines and USGs while giving the impression that the governing authorities were absenting. In some communities, criminal elements have viewed this with enthusiasm and now present with increasing confidence and disdain for authority. The arrival of CL networks also heralds the rapid development of adjunct issues such as drug supply to pop-up brothels; emergent and strengthening links to organised criminal networks (OCN) such as Albanian links to the cocaine supply routes. In places, policing tactics may not have evolved to deal with new emergent migrant communities with community penetration hampered by staffing shortages and diminishing intelligence and analytical capability.

Rupturing of user community equilibrium

A further unique contribution of this study is articulating the hidden voice of the user community and their families and detailing the impact of CLs upon them. Worryingly, the impact upon user communities is significant, changing them from rather downtrodden soporific communities to something more fractured and divergent. This study found that the emergence of CLs have upended traditional supply routes generating huge uncertainty and mistrust among user communities coupled with greater levels of violence than ever before. New opportunities are also created for users: however, only to increase and deepen their own involvement in drugs supply and criminal activity by becoming full-time commercial user-dealers (as opposed to social supply dealers) – an activity previously only taken by a few, more agentic, individuals. County lines now offer more integral involvement for some users. A key finding from this study is affirmation that CLs have upset the equilibrium of local domestic user communities, sending ripples of mistrust and confusion among a previously often hidden and reasonably compliant community. While criminal activity was always open to some users, engagement was intermittent to generate funds for purchasing drugs. County lines now present opportunities for much closer symbiosis with criminal elements, further complicating the fragile local dynamics of user communities. In some local user communities, a fracturing of the homeostasis has appeared, leading to greater isolation, greater exploitation with increasingly vulnerable users drawn deeper into criminal activity from which they cannot escape. This bleak outcome can only be avoided by de-coupling the user community from the criminal activity elements of drug supply. This will require a refocus on the vulnerabilities and isolation of user communities in conjunction with a paradigmatic shift in how such communities are viewed and perceived. This means moving away from perceptional classification as quasi-criminal 'addicts' and 'junkies', with re-classification of user communities as vulnerable and exploited victims under a public health model. This in turn will open up debates about decriminalisation of drugs and state involvement in future health provision. This will require a major tectonic shift in public attitudes and social policy; however, it is overdue and must start soon to avoid further disastrous outcomes for user communities in terms of ill-health, criminalisation, violence and other negative outcomes.

Fresh theoretical insights

Aside from the above unique insights into the daily practice of running and managing county lines, this study seeks to theorise differently about the social field of the USG and that of CLs. The central theoretical perspective builds upon previous iterations of street capital and social field outlined in my previous book, *The Street Casino* (2014). Advancing these theoretical concepts, I now seek to move the research agenda on further by postulating a series of fresh theoretical insights emerging from this study. I shall return to the originating theorisation of social field and street capital and foreground the conceptualisation of employability, purpose and value for those involved in CLs; their manifest and latent motivations for joining; the search for authenticity and realness; and the ability to be fast-streamed to distinction, are set out below.

Employability

Retaining the concept of business principles for county lines, it is important to view this from the perspective of the actors involved. Thus a central feature of county lines drug supply networks is what it offers both young people and those willing to enter it – employability.

County lines is compelling for many young people, notably those with limited or zero work experience other than having their CV rejected and their applications unanswered. This offer is essentially unmatched elsewhere in the current economy. It offers tax-free profits and working hours to suit yourself (once reaching the higher ranks). Mirroring the gig economy in structure, it is familiar to young people and permits travel outside estate boundaries or gang turf. It offers a clear hierarchical structure for advancement, a set of codified rules and behaviours, a client base and rules of engagement. It teaches skills in marketing, customer satisfaction and crafting market share. It builds loyalty and teamwork and covert skills in surveillance, monitoring and avoidance of authority. It offers opportunities for staff management, recruitment and selection. It is an equal opportunity employer with opportunities equally available to all. They operate as a series of mini franchises where successful employees can now take their transferable skills. These skills also provide the 'pay-off' – demonstrable assets and profitable returns. Consumerism is now achievable and immediate – with rewards no longer deferred. It offers opportunities for personal fast-tracking and elevated profits for hard work. It builds entrepreneurial flair and provides rewards of immediate satisfaction. Success is validated and reified beyond the immediate location as CL operatives secure status and benefits beyond the workplace, on their own estate. It offers pathways out of poverty, out of the estate, out of hardship and deprivation. It offers the possibility of contributing to society, helping your mother, your family. It generates adrenaline, gives excitement and designates you as an 'authentic playa' in the Game, one of the street gang alumni. Cleverly county lines offer similar outcomes to some in the drug using community. Here the value of elevated status is equally attractive. Moreover, it offers a regular supply of quality cut-price or free drugs and a regular income: for some this will be the first time. It reduces the necessity to beg or engage in survival sex or engage in wider criminal activity such as burglary. It offers hope and relative stability and the reminder of a normal life. County lines offers and gives all this – if only you can survive the Game. This seductive offering – which can be remodelled into a recruitment drive – helps to validate the USG and drug dealing crew as a credible strategy offering fast and visible (not deferred) returns. Once seen as a credible and legitimate strategy for young people, the USG no longer becomes viewed as a choice for survival: it segueways to become 'the choice'. Those who have sought employment or succeeded in their CL employment constitute a pool of human resources who have demonstrated they are prepared to work in a particular (criminal) way. Forming a Pool of Resources, they are ripe for further exploitation by further criminal enterprises operated by USGs and OCNs, such as money laundering operations (for example, barber shops, hairdressers, nail bars and tanning shops). In this way, this cohort of employees constitutes an emerging criminal professional cohort, skilled (at least on the surface) with corporate management skills but in reality having been subjected to violent manipulation and control, and now prepared to use it in their own personal repertoires. This cohort becomes a training ground for OCNs and its increased UK size and presence offers opportunities for expansion of these OCNs. In this way, it reaffirms the validity of the social field of the gang or drug dealing crew.

Latent and manifest motivations: realness and success

Motivations for CL involvement are identifiable as both latent and manifest. These narratives help position actors into easily comprehensible meta-narratives aimed at global understandings of poverty and survival, including responsibilisation and taking control to survive; making money through entrepreneurism; and working together with family support. Each narrative is universal, appealing and self-justifying, especially to those outside the gang social field. The 'survival' narrative is most widely articulated by respondents identifying as USG affiliates. As social competition has sharpened, those 'on road' within the gang social field view their strategic actions as logical and necessary arising from a need to 'survive the streets': 'Survival, man, that is straight survival, man' (USG 11). Taking forward the above narratives for many, county lines is a natural evolution for USGs and involvement in county lines is now a normalised expectation of USG members. Running CLs becomes a normative expectation and status-definer within the gang social field. However, not all motivations for CL involvement are manifest and the various latent motivations constitute powerful forces.

Realness and the search for authenticity

In his book *Real Gangstas* (2012: 38), Tim Lauger rightly identifies that the gang social field is characterised by widespread disagreement and uncertainty that shapes internal and interpersonal interactions, leaving members to develop individuated understandings of what it means to be a gang member. These perceptional understandings are then used to accept/reject those claiming gang-member status. This process is most keenly contested when authenticity is questioned, generating queries over legitimacy. Suchman (1995: 574) defines legitimacy as 'a generalised perception or assumption that the actions of an entity are desirable, proper, or appropriate within some socially constructed system of norms, values, beliefs, and definitions'.

Returning this definition to USGs, Lauger (2012: 38–40) refers to the paradox of legitimacy, noting that given a failure to achieve 'fieldwide agreement about the norms, values, beliefs and definitions needed to establish legitimacy, each claimant is left without a clear method to attain legitimacy. This is the paradox of legitimacy. A dubious intergang environment forces gang members to seek out legitimacy, but it does not provide any objective criteria for establishing legitimacy'. It should also be noted that this issue also arises intra-gang and helps to perpetuate ongoing turbulence within the social field. Lauger continues advocating that 'this pursuit of legitimacy reflects a continuous and enduring cultural process whereby gang members create and negotiate various cultural artefacts that provide meaning to daily life'. Behavioural expectations between fake and 'real' gang members are routinely discussed by all within the gang social field. Lauger also notes that 'these culturally proscribed expectations then shape their interpretations of situations and cause them to "do gang" or act in a manner that real gang members are supposed to act, so that they are not labelled fake' (2012: 40). Concurring with these findings, I have termed this the search for authenticity.

Authenticity therefore becomes *the* defining characteristic for USG members which instantly validates, designates and then reifies a bona fide street provenance. To be deemed 'authentic' is to be simultaneously authenticated as a bona-fide player in the Game whose presence is certified by other bona-fide 'playas'. Authenticity concurrently confers a passport to act within the social field of the gang, conferring both permission and authority. Once designated and conferred it removes questions of legitimacy and deems all actions 'credible'. It supports and reinforces the doxa and illusio (Bourdieu, 1991). In this way authenticity becomes a kite-mark of gang habitus, both designating and verifying 'realness'. Interactions with the gang social field provide spaces and avenues through which assessments of authenticity are then made. These interactions help to establish the aims, values, shared beliefs and current definitions which then become established within the social field in what Fligstein and McAdam term 'the settlement' (Fligstein and McAdam, 2012: 88). In short 'the settlement' means a shared understanding of what is happening and the stakes involved; the actors involved and their broad governing rules of play; and a 'broad interpretive frame that individuals and collective actors bring to make sense of what others within the strategic action field are doing' (Fligstein and McAdam, 2012: 88). If a majority of actors within the field understand, share, then reproduce this settlement then the social field stabilises and actors default to this position as it then aligns with their own strategic interests. Within the gang social field, the settlement is unstable and still evolving, meaning consensus about what makes a 'real' gangsta, or gang member, is still not fully established. If this definitional standard is not wholly agreed it remains open to individuated interpretations and evaluations. Narrowing this concept into the gang social field, alongside a highly competitive world for USG members there is also a parallel competitive struggle for legitimacy and authenticity. As a central core of street capital (Harding, 2014; Sandberg and Pederson, 2011) authenticity is conferred by others who adjudicate actions and then credit, or discredit, them accordingly. Those who self-adjudicate, self-designate or self-claim positions that are unconferred are destined to ridicule and exclusion as wannabees. This in turn positions them as vulnerable with diminished street capital. Within the current USG social field, behaviours, actions and artefacts have become increasingly legitimised and now act as compass points for orienting gang members in search of authenticity. The search for authenticity gives purpose to bored isolated young people struggling to see how they will advance. At this point in time this is self- (or gang-)representation on social media; participation/representation in drill music; and participation/representation in county lines. Visible or successful presence in any, or all, of these elements is now seen as *the* defining feature of authenticity and, as such, young USG members, or those seeking this lifestyle, strive to demonstrate proximity to, adherence to, or embeddedness within each element. This therefore represents the royal flush of authenticity in early 21st-century gang life in the UK. As identified in Chapter 3, some of the prerequisites for joining a CL crew include demonstrable aptitudes, attitudes, aspirations and also authenticity. Within the struggle for authenticity, CL participation is now the pre-eminent assessment criteria. While social media presence and drill music bring wider reputational enhancements, only CLs can generate true economic returns and visible lifestyle enhancements. Being a 'trapper' not only generates income but does so in ways visible to others – and is deemed authentic and legitimate by them. County lines becomes a 'fast-track to authenticity' – an aspect further enhanced by starting up one's own line. 'Trapper' becomes a moniker of distinction and kitemark of authenticity. Street gang conversations routinely revolve around the county lines, trapping and drug supply, creating a simulated world construct and endless conversational centrepiece. To sit outside county lines removes an entry point into such conversations, thus diminishing opportunities to construct a personal biography or to raise street capital. To summarise: 'you are either in it, or you nobody'.

Fast-streaming of street capital

A further theoretical insight to emerge from this study is the proposition that county lines now operates as a way to fast-track street capital generation. Indeed, within this social field it is now widely acknowledged an essential and valued rudiment of CLs is providing opportunities to fast-track street capital. In *The Street Casino* (Harding, 2014: 123) such opportunities included use of pit bulls and weapon dogs. From 2015 in the UK the use of noxious substances (acid) as weapons joined the list – each being essentially a situational or short-lived strategy for advancement. County lines, however, takes strategic advancement to a different level, offering a holistic sub-world of possibilities where one can endlessly build street capital and rise through the hierarchy of the social field, generating reputation, status and income. In this way agentic involvement in CLs far outstrips selling weed on street corners as it offers routes to power, wealth and status that previously took years to accumulate. This then is a 'fast-stream' approach to building street capital and distinction. In a social field marked now by increased social competition among participants, getting to the top quicker (and richer) than your competitors generates a distinct advantage. Not only does involvement in CLs signify authenticity, achieving peer-approval propels you to a position of authority, independence and experience far beyond what's achievable skulking around the estate on a BMX bike or moped. Furthermore, the criminal repertoire of CLs offers multivariate sub-menus of violence, control, expansion and recruitment, all offering additional opportunities for generating street capital. Rapid fast-track accumulation of street capital therefore becomes a powerful latent motivation for engagement in county lines. Entry into CL networks also offers multiple entry levels not dependent upon age, where success can be measured by one's bottom line. Respondents working CLs talked glowingly about their independence and avoidance of zero-hour contracts, sneering at those grafting on those contracts.

As a fast-stream approach to distinction, CLs activity is both persuasive and proven to be effective. Respondents talked animatedly how they had gone from being a relative 'innocent' to being super street-wise, from 'zero to hero'. To achieve this learning curve, CL operatives must learn quickly on the job; fortunately, the variant CL business models provide differentiated roles and hierarchical positions through which one must pass to reach the top level. Again this organisational format replicates that of gaming and thus is recognisable by many young people. Rapid expansion of street skill and street capital accumulation becomes the goal and CLs the playing field upon which this journey takes place. Actors can find suitable skill levels within this game, for example by specialising in recruitment, cuckooing or staff/line enforcement. As with any fast-stream employment, CL operatives must demonstrate their acumen quickly and regularly to validate advancement. They recognise this as an imperative to build the line, keep control and defend the line. Failure here indicates unworthiness to progress as a fast-streamer. Success generates instant street capital return which is then used to bolster field position and accumulate more street capital. Violence becomes the credo through which this is achieved. Instant returns of street capital are now much welcomed due to increased competition among gangs. A bankable credit line of street capital prevents victimisation by others keen to take your winnings, and it acts as a strong disincentive to those seeking to take over your line.

In essence, for young USG members, CLs offer rapid experiential learning rather than grafting for years on the street, selling weed, defending turf and territory to gain street capital. This fast-stream approach means acquiring street capital is now expedited, sharp-edged and narrow in its focus. With CL business models still relatively novel, few Olders are experienced to carefully instruct Youngers; thus normal behavioural moderators are absent. This too escalates the levels of violence currently pervading CLs nationally. This newer, sharper way of generating fast-tracked street capital suggests capital accumulation methods are not fully rounded, nor based on the experience of 'old heads' citing 'old school' learning. Rapid learning does not suit everyone equally well and in a social field where field rules are still under development, extravagant actions are not uncommon. Taking all of this into account it is possible to identify how and why the UK is witnessing an increase in certain forms of violence arising from: the evolution of UK USGs; increased social competition within USGs; the increased volume of CL networks; the fast-tracking of street capital accumulation; the individuated rules still developing within the social field; the search for authenticity; the need for increased control of lines; the development and gradation of different CL models; all these are contributory factors. The sheer volume of existing and emergent USGs and county lines now means this process is multiplied and accelerated across the UK.

Tactical and regional variations among USGs and CL crews make this process even more volatile contributing to further violence escalation, for example when a CL operative, accustomed to field rules operating in one area, moves elsewhere, only to fall foul of different field rules, expectations or behaviours. Here mis–reading or mis–interpreting rules can be fatal. Conversely, CL operatives simply impose their tougher, more violent forms of control upon less sophisticated, unsuspecting locals.

Replicative reinforcement

The imperative to build status and reputation via street capital accumulation is stronger than ever in this more competitive social arena of the street gang. County lines networks now provide the prime loci for this to occur. Simultaneously CLs provides a locus for certification of authenticity. Through such motions a virtuous circle emerges where street capital = the search for authenticity = a role in county lines = street capital. This process of replicative reinforcement creates an immersive subterranean world of increased isolation from reality and from the common values of ordinary society. It reinforces tropes of 'street justice', 'survival' and 'winning at all costs'. Ultimately, it creates the conditions for deeper embeddedness of those involved in this world. Increasingly this subterranean tier is being professionalised and increasing in confidence.

Gang proliferation and propagation

One significant outcome of CL models is the national expansion of drug dealing crews and USGs across the country (BBC News, 2014). Opportunities are created and realised for USGs to establish satellite bases (dealing Hubs) in seaside and county towns. This creates a 'gang ripple effect' whereby metropolitan USGs establish spheres of influence well beyond their home territory. In this way USGs are 'seeded' or 'franchised' by the parent gang. This method of increased proliferation mirrors the experience of the USA from the 1970s to the 1990s when youth gangs dramatically expanded across the United States (Miller, 2001). One outcome of this 'gang ripple' model, if left unchallenged, will be the propagation of street gangs (or at least street gang culture, logic and rules) in smaller towns and cities outside the metropolitan pockets of deprivation traditionally more often associated with street gang emergence.

Propagation of USGs brings two immediate challenges: a) retaliation from local youth groups or criminal networks leading to increased violence and associated gang crime; b) extended distribution networks, more embedded structures and greater linkages between USGs and local organised crime groups.

Proliferation of CL networks now extends UK-wide with some parent gangs running multiple lines. Increasing numbers of young people and users are now actively involved and this involvement will likely expand. As the skills base of CL operatives expands and becomes more sophisticated and skilled, their involvement becomes deeper. Many will seek to advance to distinction by running their own line/s. Competition among lines and among those running the lines will increase. Andell and Pitts (2018) have already acknowledged the co-opting or elimination of competing distribution systems and local crime families into CL networks. Expansion of drug dealing crews and the USGs behind them is not simply about geographical expansion; it is also about a downwards expansion into a more embedded gang structure. A skilled criminal network will seek alternative criminal income if their primary market is removed. Current moves by parent gangs towards consolidating CLs suggests future winners and losers in terms of overall market share. Those playing to win in this game will be connected to, and backed by, bigger players in the Game – organised crime networks. In terms of *The Street Casino*, players linked to the house have the house advantage and as we know, the house always wins (Harding, 2014). Of interest to the OCNs will be a cohort of skilled CL operatives already experienced in the gig economy of running county lines.

As USGs and drug dealing crews expand across the UK via CLs, the gang social field always expands. As Bourdieu tells us, the social field is not bounded physically but relationally. Thus it is not so much the physical expansion of CL operatives that matters here but the expansion of the rules and codes of the gang social field such that they become familiar and normalised by wider groups of society and those never previously exposed to them. This is already underway via social media. Soon it will be possible to affiliate to the Woolwich Boys of London but live in Coventry or Edinburgh. The gang social field, once limited to those occupying its habitus and turf, will become familiar conceptual territory for those seeking alternative routes to advancement. County lines will have provided the schooling, and elevated their skill base from elementary and routine to sophisticated and niche. Local domestic groups of youth will continue to challenge emergent CLs until they themselves retain a stake in its profits. Violent flashpoints have already emerged and locals continue to jostle for position with runner/dealers and parent USGs. One effective outcome of utilising local users has been to undermine local domestic youth in terms of market coverage and domination. Local USGs continue to emerge in smaller UK cities and towns now that austerity has created the preconditions making them both possible and attractive. County lines can become the touchpaper for such home-grown gangs to emerge as a localised response to emergent county lines 'insurgency'. This is further inflamed (or seeded) by relocation policies for gang-exit programmes and rehousing and settlement programmes for ex-prisoners. Housing policies whereby deprived families exit London for provincial towns further exacerbates this development. Thus USGs, once the limited preserve of the most hardened/deprived metropolitan communities, are an emerging feature of local criminality. Where conditions are ripe for seeding the only logical outcome is propagation of street gangs.

Walter Miller (1980, 2001) noted similar evolutionary outcomes in the USA in the 1970s to 1990s, noting how USGs, unheard of outside urban centres with a population of 2–3 million, suddenly began to emerge in smaller cities and towns across the USA. In the early 1970s, Miller reported only six US cities with established youth gangs, rising to 2,550 cities by the 1990s, representing each US state. Notable was the 'migration' of USGs from larger metro-cities to smaller towns and rural counties. Miller (1992) notes that the most common explanation for this expansion was increased availability and widening markets for illegal drugs. He further cites immigration, federated relationships, exploitation of new markets, government policies, a rise in female-headed households, gang subculture and the media as contributory factors to this rapid expansion.

Future outlooks

Left unchallenged the future possibilities look bleak. In the short-term increased CL competition will bring increased control of CLs followed by attendant violence. CL managers and parent gangs will seek to cut costs and develop their competitive edge by ensuring their drugs reach end users faster and more securely than others. Delivery will match Uber Eats and Amazon for speed and efficiency becoming increasingly inventive and sophisticated. Detection will become more difficult and might move beyond the realm and ability of traditional policing and local communities. Deregulated drug supply markets have the potential to create a greater diversification of lines with a greater diversification of product. Product diversification will most likely lead to specialisation with key groups looking to dominate key sides of the market – for example, the increasing domination of the UK cocaine trade by Albanian criminal networks. Emergent new communities, such as Eastern Europeans, will utilise family, kinship and community networks to open new international supply lines into the UK. Thriving markets and thriving profits will always attract big business. The obvious outcome of multiple CL networks operating throughout the UK will be greater involvement of OCN seeking to control the markets and secure profits. Upline, this means larger international operations and cartels seeking involvement.

Once new CL supply lines are fully established, running 24/7 with sophisticated high-end delivery, the market will be ripe for new products. New synthetics will then most likely appear and due to the highly efficient sophisticated supply routes now operating, will reach the market in great quantities and with greater impact than before, for example opioids. Throughout this scenario local policing will become increasingly ineffective as it remains geared to the arrest and detention of lower-end runner/dealers who by now will be mostly user-dealers. The cycle of arrest/conviction/imprisonment/return will become even more pointless than it presently is. Within this dynamic social field once settlement is closer to being achieved, it is possible that violence for local youth will decrease. OCN tend to eschew violence as 'not good for business' – however, when it does come, it is bigger and more violent than before. From the perspective of a young person, CL risks and dangers exist but they can be managed and mitigated. Young people also see dangers in normal society but admit to having little, if any, control over these dangers and risks, be that their Experian credit checks, their schooling, their access to banks and mortgages or rental property. At least in county lines you can (eventually) have greater agency and control and the risks can be deflected, downplayed and ignored. Without considerable investment and commitment, central government may now struggle to turn this around – as this is a world which always delivers, it works.

How do we get ahead of this?

We do not have the policing/partnership structures to address this successfully now or over the long-term. We face a 21st-century problem with 20th-century structures, policies and organisations. These are culturally siloed, operationally slow, unresponsive, unmodernised, unadjusted, technologically ill-equipped, inefficient and unsuitable.

We need a radical new way of working to address this.

Towards fixing the problem

County lines are evolving and increasingly complex to understand, not least the many manifest and latent motivations now being surfaced through research which move the topic beyond that of simply business marketing and profiteering. Moreover the county lines phenomena is beset with multiple inter-agency challenges, for example, how do we address the nuanced relationships between victim/offender; the contested meanings of vulnerability; definitional shortcomings of key terms; inter-regional variance in gang matrices; short-term funding arrangements; and even national, regional and local political interference.

It will need cooperative multi-agency work to address this at national, regional and local levels. There are no short-term or single solutions to the challenge of county lines and criminal exploitation. Only by working in concert across a range of disciplines will these possible solutions have any chance of realistic effect (see for example the range of solutions recommended by the New Bletchley Network, 2019).

Policy and practice solutions

This book has focused presentation of the issues of county lines and creating a series of underpinning theoretical perspectives. It has also focused on articulating the voices of the actors involved while detailing the internal practices and behavioural dynamics present. Much more context was collated throughout this research in terms of policing and partnership working to tackle and address county lines. This partnership agenda is an increasingly busy forum and some promising practice is emerging. Limited space, however, prevents a more fulsome exposition here of how CLs might be tackled, though it is useful to close the book by pointing to some key policy options and practice interventions that could be adopted (often without need of funding or legislative change) to help us address the challenges now faced by CLs and criminal exploitation. I list some of these here, though not in any order of merit or importance. They represent key groupings of focus which are either broad or specific, urgently required, or more suggestive.

People

- A national youth conversation: let's ask young people for their views and ideas on solutions; we need to find solutions 'with' young people not 'to' young people.
- Community mobilisation: we must inform our communities of the current situation then actively seek their help by unleashing the community energy of volunteering.
- Community champions: we must identify and build new leaders in our communities and, where possible, vibrant and inclusive community hubs that welcome young people and their views.

- Reporting apps: let's create new ways for young people to report crime and alert us to tensions.

Partnership

- Community Safety: a reinvigorated community safety approach will share the burden of delivery and ownership and widen expertise. Though much withered away as a profession, Community Safety offered a robust and effective approach towards crime reduction. The roles, job descriptions and structures for auditing, strategy development, reporting, scrutiny and so on all still exist. The full legislative structure for community safety is still on the statute books – let's use it.
- Integrated partnership working: partners need to be co-located and fully integrated to work effectively. Old town hall departments and executive fiefdoms need reconfiguring and refocussing, not least to avoid duplication of service provision.
- Displacement: we must ensure effective action in one borough does not simply push problems into the next borough. Coordination and regional joint working is key.
- Gang research: more research is needed into all aspects of USGs, knives and drug markets to allow academia to improve our understandings and then to contribute to solutions.

Provision

- Drug misuse services/reduce demand: we must tackle the demand side for drugs and dramatically upgrade provision for drug misuse services. This should include a wide-ranging review of current data but also new methods of service delivery including peripatetic service delivery. This should include a national revisiting of how we view pejoratively and criminalise the drug-using community, and extending the public health model to include them as vulnerable participants in solutions.
- Statutory youth services: all youth services should be placed on a statutory footing with improved service provision, inventive engagement and fresh innovative service delivery.
- Contextual safeguarding – This approach expands the objectives of child protection systems, recognising young people are vulnerable to abuse in multiple social contexts. It should be adopted as national policy and best practice.
- Schools early intervention: we need to vastly increase our early intervention programmes with schools, developing innovative

classroom engagement to build awareness, build capacity and improve resilience among young people.

Strategy

- Leadership: leaders at all levels across all stakeholders must now recognise and understand this issue; and give strong strategic direction and lead collaborative work across all partners.
- Prevent/intervene/enforce: all three elements are needed for a balanced strategy. Over-reliance on one single element will only alienate communities and weaken the overall effectiveness of any response.
- Threat, risk, vulnerability: policing and public policy must be informed by this approach to assessment so we can better recognise the violence and exploitation underpinning this issue.
- Prisons: we need to tackle emergent USGs in UK prisons and open prisons to academic research. We need to better understand the interconnectivity between the street and the prison and tackle issues such as community resettlement and lack of rehabilitation.
- Credibility and consistency: all programmes, actions, policies and efforts must be credible, coordinated, consistent and bespoke if possible to their local community.

Analysis

- Data-sharing: too often this is inhibited by concerns over DPA/ GDPR. We need more robust ways to ensure effective data-sharing supports partnership efforts (see Fuller, 2015 and HMICFRS, 2020). Common platforms to share partner data often do not exist.
- Data quality: often partner data is of poor quality, out of date, not coterminous, incomplete or simply not worth sharing. This is an area which needs speedy improvement.
- Mapping: we need to use high-quality analytical products from each partner to create multi-layered mapping of themes, groups, people and places which will then inform our practice (see Cullen et al, 2016).
- Creation of up-to-date area profiles. This should include contemporary research and data collation to identify new drug misuse patterns and changes among user groups.
- Social media: more active tracking and analysis of social media posts is needed to give early warnings to police and partners of any rising local tensions among local youth.

Policy

- School exclusions/PRUs/support teams: we also need to end school exclusions and the damaging isolation and stigma of PRUs. Schools must retain responsibility for the performance/attendance of children they exclude. We must resource PRUs to reduce the pipeline effect of young people entering gangs and county lines. Schools need to establish safeguarding teams and parent support teams and more accurately report CL and USG issues with the support of Ofsted.
- Trauma-informed approach: all our interventions must take account of vulnerability, exploitation, ongoing trauma and mental health implications for participants in USGs and CLs. This provision should be long-term, with greater investment in bereavement counselling, mental health provision for young people and ongoing support.
- Fix the sustaining policies: let's address those housing policies that sustain county lines and street gangs, including children's homes and looked-after children, and ban placing children in unregulated homes.
- Pathways out: we need to identify those young people wishing to exit USGs and CLs and then provide effective pathways out.
- Sustainable funding: it's not all about money, but let's recognise the magnitude here and then resource this more effectively by allowing local groups to future proof their action and delivery plans.

Local issues identified by respondents

In addition to the broader points listed above a number of more localised solutions were offered by respondents in this research:

Policing

- A need to increase visible community and neighbourhood policing to avoid the police being viewed in a negative way as only a rapid-response group.
- More neighbourhood policing to build enduring community relationships and to generate community intelligence and comprehension. This could possibly include greater use of PCSOs, but must definitely include great community engagement of newly arrived migrant communities.
- Greater analytical capacity and ability: more skills, more staff, more training and better use of all data products. This should include a

police/partner Vulnerability Assessment Score to sit alongside any gang matrix to monitor those at risk of gang affiliation or involvement.
- More covert tactics might be needed to secure policing success upline and gain access into the organised criminal networks.

The above approaches should be governed by some underpinning principles:

- collaboration and involvement of young people;
- trauma-informed solutions, evidence-based but also inventive and creative solutions;
- a focus on gender to ensure bespoke solutions are available for young women;
- a focus on parenting, domestic violence and abuse.

Last word

As this study illustrates, it is clear that in the UK the social fields of the urban street gang and of drug distribution markets, and the actors involved in each, are rapidly evolving and changing. We need now to consider, through wider research, how the relational boundaries of these social fields are interacting with the social field of organised crime. This study, and others, report a blurring of these lines and morphing of criminal activity that was once more clearly defined. New interpretive models are needed to explore these relational social field boundaries which are shifting, dynamic, temporal and situational. We need new glasses to bring this blurred landscape into focus. Only once we fully understand this new landscape can we begin to comprehend its new challenges and then address its morbid symptoms.

References

Agar, M. (1973) *Ripping and Running: A Formal Ethnography of Urban Heroin Addicts*, New York: Seminar Press.

Aldridge, J. and Medina, J. (2010) *Youth Gangs in an English City: Social Exclusion, Drugs and Violence*, ESRC End of Award Report, RES-000-23-0615, Swindon: ESRC.

Aldridge, J., Medina-Ariza, J. and Ralphs, R. (2008) 'Dangers and problems of doing "gang" research in the UK', in F. van Gemert, D. Peterson and I. Lien (eds) *Street Gangs, Migration and Ethnicity*, Cullompton: Willan Publishing, pp 31–46.

Allen, G. and Audickas, L. (2018) *Knife Crime in England and Wales, Briefing Paper No. SN4304*, House of Commons Library.

All-Party Parliamentary Group for Runaway and Missing Children and Adults (2016) 'Inquiry into the safeguarding of "absent" children: "It is good when someone cares"', Final Report, https://www.childrenssociety.org.uk/what-we-do/resources-and-publications/inquiry-into-the-safeguarding-of-absent-children

All-Party Parliamentary Group on Runaway and Missing Children and Adults (2017) 'Briefing report on the roundtable on children who go missing and are criminally exploited by gangs', https://www.missingpeople.org.uk/files/PandR/APPG%20Missing,%20Gangs%20and%20Exploitation%20Roundtable%20Report.pdf

All-Party Parliamentary Group for Runaway and Missing Children and Adults (2019) *No Place at Home*, London: The Children's Society.

Andell, P. (2019) *Thinking Seriously about Gangs*, London: Palgrave Macmillan.

Andell, P. and Pitts, J. (2017) *Preventing the Violent and Sexual Victimisation of Vulnerable Gang-Involved and Gang-Affected Children and Young People in Ipswich*, University of Suffolk.

Andell, P. and Pitts, J. (2018) 'The end of the line? The impact of county lines drug distribution on youth crime in a target destination', *Youth & Policy*, www.youthandpolicy.org/articles/the-end-of-the-line

Anderson, E. (1999) *Code of the Street: Decency, Violence, and the Moral Life of the Inner City*, New York: NY: W.W. Norton.

Attia, M. and Edge, J. (2017) 'Be(com)ing a reflexive researcher: a developmental approach to research methodology', *Open Review of Educational Research*, 4(1): 33–45.

Auld, J., Dorn, N. and South, N. (1984) 'Heroin now: bringing it all back home', *Youth & Policy*, 9: 1–7.

BBC News (2014) 'London gangs expanding across UK, Met Police warns', www.bbc.co.uk/news/uk-25974360

Beckett, H., Brodie, I., Factor, F., Melrose, M., Pearce, J., Pitts, J., Shuker, L. and Warrington, C. (2013) *'It's wrong but you get used to it': a qualitative study of gang-associated sexual violence towards, and exploitation of, young people in England*, Luton: University of Bedfordshire.

Bennett, T. and Holloway, K. (2004) 'Gang membership, drugs and crime in the UK', *British Journal of Criminology*, 44(3): 305–23.

Bennett, T. and Holloway, K. (2009) 'The causal connection between drug misuse and crime', *British Journal of Criminology*, 49(4): 513–31.

Berelowitz, S., Clifton, J., Firimin, C., Gulyurtlu, S. and Edwards, G. (2013) *'If only someone had listened'*, Inquiry into Child Sexual Exploitation in Gangs and Groups, Office of the Children's Commissioner.

Black, C. (2020) 'Review of Drugs, Executive Summary', https://assets.publishing.service.gov.uk/government/uploads/system/uploads/attachment_data/file/868438/2SummaryPhaseOne+foreword200219.pdf

Bourdieu, P. (1984) *Distinction: A Social Critique of the Judgement of Taste*, Cambridge, MA: Harvard University Press.

Bourdieu, P. (1985) 'The genesis of the concepts of habitus and field', *Sociocriticism*, 2(2): 11–24.

Bourdieu, P. (1986) 'The forms of capital', in J. G. Richardson (ed) *Handbook of Theory and Research for the Sociology of Education*, New York: Greenwood Press, pp 241–58.

Bourdieu, P. (1990) *The Logic of Practice*, Cambridge: Polity Press.

Bourdieu, P. (1991) *Language and Symbolic Power*, Cambridge: Polity Press.

Bourdieu, P. and Wacquant, L. (1992) *An Invitation to Reflexive Sociology*, Chicago, IL: University of Chicago Press.

Bourgois, P. (1995) *In Search of Respect: Selling Crack in El Barrio*, Cambridge: Cambridge University Press.

Braun, V. and Clarke, V. (2006) 'Using thematic analysis in psychology', *Qualitative Research in Psychology*, 3(2): pp 77–101.

Briggs, D. (2010) 'Crack houses in the UK: some observations on their operations', *Drugs and Alcohol Today*, 10(4): 33–42.

Briggs, D. (2012) *Crack Cocaine Users, High Society and Low Life in South London*, Abingdon: Routledge.

British Transport Police (2019) 'Annual report and statistical bulletin 2018/19', https://www.btp.police.uk/about_us/your_right_to_information/publications/annual_report_2018-19.aspx

Brown, C. (1965) *Manchild in the Promised Land*, New York: Signet Books.

Bryman (2004) *Social Research Methods* (2nd edition), Oxford: Oxford University Press.

Butera, J. (2013) *Cuckooing: Home Takeovers of Vulnerable Tenants*, Department of Criminology, University of Ottawa.

Centre for Social Justice (2009) *Dying to Belong*, London: The Centre for Social Justice.

Children's Commissioner (2019) *Keeping Kids Safe*, Children's Commissioner for England.

Children Act (1989) http://www.legislation.gov.uk/ukpga/1989/41/contents

Christopher, M., Payne, A. and Ballantyne D. (1991) *Relationship Marketing: Bringing Quality, Customer Service and Marketing Together*, Oxford: Butterworth-Heinemann.

Coliandris, G. (2015) 'County lines and wicked problems: exploring the need for improved policing approaches to vulnerability and early intervention', *Australasian Policing: A Journal of Professional Practice and Research*, 7(2): 25–36.

Coomber, R. (2004) 'Drug use and drug market intersections', *Addiction Research & Theory*, 12(6): 501–05.

Coomber, R. (2006) *Pusher Myths: Re-Situating the Drug Dealer*, London: Free Association Books.

Coomber, R. (2015) 'A tale of two cities: understanding differences in levels of heroin/crack market-related violence – a two city comparison', *Criminal Justice Review*, 40(1): 7–31.

Coomber, R. and Turnbull, P. (2007) 'Arenas of drug transactions: adolescent cannabis transactions in England – social supply', *Journal of Drug Issues*, 37(4): 845–65.

Coomber, R. and Moyle, L. (2012) *A Rapid Appraisal of the Illicit Drug Market in Southend-on-Sea, Essex*. Full Report. Plymouth University, Drug and Alcohol Research Unit.

Coomber, R. and Moyle, L. (2014) 'Beyond drug dealing: developing and extending the concept of "social supply" of illicit drugs to "minimally commercial supply"', *Drugs: Education, Prevention and Policy*, 21(2): 157–64.

Coomber, R. and Moyle, L. (2017) 'The changing shape of street-level heroin and crack supply in England: commuting, holidaying and cuckooing drug dealers across "county lines"', *The British Journal of Criminology*, 58(6): 1323–42.

Coomber, R. and Pyle, E. (2015) *A Rapid Appraisal of the Illicit Drug Market in the Unitary Authority of Torbay, Devon*. Full Report. Plymouth University, Drug and Alcohol Research Unit.

Coomber, R. Moyle, L. and South, N. (2015) 'The normalisation of drug supply: the social supply of drugs as the "other side" of the history of normalisation', *Drugs: Education, Prevention and Policy*, 23(3): 255–63.

Coomber, R., Moyle, L. and Knox Mahoney, M. (2017) 'Symbolic policing: situating targeted police operations/"crackdowns" on street-level drug markets', *Policing and Society*, 29(1): 1–17.

Coomber, R., Moyle, L., Hatton, Z. and Gavin, J. (2014) *A Rapid Appraisal of the Illicit Drug Market in the City of Plymouth, Devon*. Full Report, Plymouth University: Drug and Alcohol Research Unit.

Creswell, J. W. (2007) *Qualitative Inquiry and Research Design: Choosing Among Five Approaches*, Thousand Oaks: Sage Publications.

Cullen, P., Moore S., Rye, J., Balcombe, M. and Clarke, M. (2016) *Local Analysis Tool: County Lines*, London: Home Office.

Daly, M. (2016) *Killing the Competition*, New Brunswick: Transaction Publishers.

Davis, M. (2006) *Planet of Slums*, London: Verso.

DeBeck, K., Shannon, K., Wood, E., Li, K., Montaner, J. and Kerr, T. (2007) 'Income-generating activities of people who inject drugs', *Drug and Alcohol Dependence*, 91(1): 50–6.

Decker, S. H. and Lauritsen, J. L. (2002) 'Leaving the gang', in R. C. Huff (ed), *Gangs in America*, Thousand Oaks, CA: Sage, pp 51–7.

Decker, S. and Pyrooz, D. (2013 online) 'Gangs: another form of organized crime?', in L. Paoli (ed) *The Oxford Handbook of Organized Crime* (2014), Oxford: Oxford University Press.

Deighton, J. (1992) 'The consumption of performance', *Journal of Consumer Research*, 19(3): 362–72.

de Munck, V. C. and Sobo, E. J. (eds) (1998) *Using methods in the field: a practical introduction and casebook*, Walnut Creek, CA: AltaMira Press.

Densley, J. (2012) 'Street gang recruitment, signalling, screening and selection', *Social Problems*, 59(3): 301–21.

Densley, J. (2013) *How Gangs Work: An Ethnography of Youth Violence*, London: Palgrave Macmillan.

Densley, J. (2014) 'It's gang life, but not as we know it: the evolution of gang business', *Crime & Delinquency*, 60(4): 517–46.

Densley, J. and Pyrooz, D. (2017) 'A signaling perspective on disengagement from gangs', *Justice Quarterly*, 36(1): 31–58.

Densley, J., McLean, R., Deuchar, R. and Harding, S. (2018a) 'An altered state? Emergent changes to illicit drug markets and distribution networks in Scotland', *International Journal of Drug Policy*, 58: 113–20.

Densley, J., McLean, R., Deuchar, R. and Harding, S. (2018b) 'Progression from cafeteria to à la carte offending: Scottish organised crime narratives', *The Howard Journal of Crime and Justice*, 58(2): 161–79.

Densley, J., Deuchar, R. and Harding, S. (2020) 'An Introduction to Gangs and Serious Youth Violence in the United Kingdom', *Youth Justice*, 20(1): 1–8.

Dent, J. (2017) *Modern Slavery Act 2015: Recent Developments (Commons Briefing Papers CBP-7656)*. Available at: http://researchbriefings. parliament.uk/Research Briefing/Summary/CBP-7656

Denzin, N. (1978) *Sociological Methods: A Sourcebook*, London: Butterworths.

Department for Education (2014) *Statutory guidance on children who run away or go missing from home or care*. https://www.gov.uk/government/publications/children-who-run-away-or-go-missing-from-home-or-care

Desroches, F. (2007) 'Research on upper level drug trafficking: a review', *Journal of Drug Issues*, 37: 827–44.

Deuchar, R. (2009) *Gangs, Marginalised Youth and Social Capital*, Stoke-on-Trent: Trentham Books.

Deuchar, R. (2013) *Policing Youth Violence: Transatlantic Connections*, London: IOE Press.

Deuchar, R. (2018) *Gangs and Spirituality: Global Perspectives*, Basingstoke: Palgrave Macmillan.

Deuchar, R., Harding, S., McLean, R. and Densley, J. (2018) 'Deficit or credit? A comparative, qualitative study of gender agency and female gang membership in Los Angeles and Glasgow', *Crime & Delinquency*, https://doi.org/10.1177/0011128718794192

DeWalt, K. M. and DeWalt, B. R. (2002) *Participant Observation: A Guide for Fieldworkers*, Walnut Creek, CA: AltaMira Press.

Disley, E. and Liddle, M. (2016) 'Local perspectives in ending gang and youth violence areas: perceptions of the nature of urban street gangs', Research Report 88. London: Home Office. Available at: www.gov.uk/government/uploads/system/uploads/attachment_data/file/491802/horr88.pdf

Duluth Domestic Abuse Intervention Project, Duluth Power and Control Wheel, https://www.theduluthmodel.org/wheels/

Dorn, N. and South, N. (1990) 'Drug markets and law enforcement', *British Journal of Criminology*, 30: 171–88.

Dorn, N., Murji, K. and South, N. (1992) *Traffickers: Drug Markets and Law Enforcement*, London: Routledge.

Drugwise (2017) Shapiro H., Daly M., Highways and Buyways, *A Snapshot of UK Drug Scenes*. https://www.drugwise.org.uk/highways-and-buyways-a-snapshot-of-uk-drug-scenes-2016/

Dunlap, E., Johnson, B. D., Kotarba, J. A. and Fackler, J. L. (2010) 'Macro-level social forces and micro-level consequences: poverty, alternate occupations, and drug dealing', *Journal of Ethnicity in Substance Abuse*, 9(2): 115–27.

Edmunds, M., Hough, M. and Urquía, N. (1996) *Tackling Local Drug Markets*, Volume 80, London: Home Office Police Research Group.

Elias, N. (1994) *The Civilising Process*, Volume 2, Oxford: Blackwell.

Farrington, D. (2003) 'Developmental and life-course criminology: key theoretical and empirical issues – the 2002 Sutherland Award address', *Criminology*, 41(2): 221–5.

Fligstein, N. and McAdam, D. (2012) *A Theory of Fields*, Oxford: Oxford University Press.

Fields, A. and Walters, J. (1985) 'Hustling: supporting a heroin habit', in B. Hanson, G. Beschner, J. Walters and E. Bovelle (eds) *Life with Heroin: Voices from the Inner City*, Lexington, MA: Lexington Books, pp 49–73.

Fine, M. (2002) *Disruptive Voices: The Possibilities for Feminist Research*, Ann Arbour, MI: University of Michigan Press.

Firmin, C. (2010) *Female Voice in Violence.* A study into the impact of serious youth and gang violence on women and girls, London: Race on the Agenda.

Firmin, C. (2011) *Female Voice in Violence.* Final report on the impact of serious youth violence and criminal gangs on women and girls across the country, London: Race on the Agenda.

Firmin, C. (2018) *Abuse Between Young People*, Abingdon: Routledge.

Fraser, A. (2015) *Urban Legends*, Oxford: Oxford University Press.

Fukuyama, F. (1995) *Trust: The Social Virtues and the Creation of Prosperity*, London: Hamish Hamilton.

Fuller, I. (2015) 'Sharing information to safeguard against "County Lines" gang activity', Centre of Excellence for Information Sharing, http://informationsharing.org.uk/sharing-information-to-safeguard-against-county-lines-gang-activity/.

Gambetta, D. (2009) *Codes of the Underworld: How Criminals Communicate*, Princeton, NJ: Princeton University Press.

Gilbert, N. (2008) *Researching Social Life* (3rd edition), London: Sage Publications.

Goffman, I. (1974) *Frame Analysis: An Essay on the Organisation of Experience*, Cambridge, MA: Harvard University Press.

Goldstein, P. J. (1985) 'The drugs/violence nexus: a tripartite conceptual framework', *Journal of Drug Issues*, 39: 143–74.

Green, J. and Thorogood, N. (2004) *Qualitative Methods for Health Research*, London: Sage.

Griffiths, P., Gossop, M., Powis, B. and Strang, J. (1993) 'Reaching hidden populations of drug users by privileged access interviewers: methodological and practical issues', *Addiction*, 88(12): 1617–26.

Grimshaw, R. and Ford, M. (2018) *Young people, violence and knives – revisiting the evidence and policy discussions*, London: Centre for Crime and Justice Studies.

Hagedorn, J. (2007) *Gangs in the Global City: Alternatives to Traditional Criminology*, Urbana, IL: University of Illinois Press.

Hagedorn, J. (2008) *A World of Gangs*, Minneapolis, MN: University of Minnesota Press.

Hales, G. and Hobbs, D. (2010) 'Drug markets in the community: a London borough case study', *Trends in Organized Crime*, 13(1), 13–30.

Halliday, J. and Parveen, N. (2019) 'Knife crime up most steeply outside London as county lines dealing spreads', *The Guardian*, 11 March 2019.

Hallworth, J. (2016) 'County lines: an exploratory analysis of migrating drug gang offenders in North Essex', Unpublished master's thesis, Institute of Criminology, University of Cambridge, UK. Available at: https://www.crim.cam.ac.uk/global/docs/theses/john-hallworth.pdf/at_download/file

Hallsworth, S. (2013) *The Gang and Beyond: Interpreting Violent Street Worlds*, New York, NY: Palgrave Macmillan.

Harding, S. (2012a) 'The role and significance of street capital in the social field of the violent youth gang in south London', Doctoral thesis for University of Bedfordshire.

Harding, S. (2012b) 'Street government: the role of the urban street gang in the London riots', in D. Briggs (ed) *The English Riots of 2011: A Summer of Discontent*, Hook, Hampshire: Waterside Press, pp 193–215.

Harding, S. (2014) *The Street Casino*, Bristol: Policy Press.

Harding, S. (2015) 'The cybergang: gangs and social media', Conference presentation at British Sociological Association Conference, Glasgow, 16 April 2015.

Harding, S. (2016) 'The evolution of London gangs', The National Gangs Conference, Conference presentation Hendon Police Training School, November 2016, London.

Harding, S. (2020) 'Getting to the point? Reframing narratives on knife crime', *Youth Justice*, https://doi.org/10.1177/1473225419893781

Harding, S. and Cracknell, (2016) *Ending Gang and Youth Violence Programme: Independent Review*. London: Home Office.

Harding, S., Deuchar, R., Densley, J. and McLean, R. (2018) 'A typology of street robbery and gang organization: insights from qualitative research in Scotland', *British Journal of Criminology*, 59(4): 879–97.

Hay, G., Rael dos Santos, A., Reed, H. and Hope, V. (2019) 'Estimates of the prevalence of opiate use and/or crack cocaine use, 2016/17: Sweep 13 report', https://bdoc.ofdt.fr/index.php?lvl=publisher_see&id=4445

Hernandez, V. P., Kanabar, R. and Nandi, A. (2018) *Low income dynamics among ethnic minorities in Great Britain*, Colchester: Institute for Social and Economic Research.

Hesketh, R. and Robinson, G. (2019) 'Grafting: "The boyz" just doing business? Deviant entrepreneusrship in street gangs', *Safer Communities*, 18(2): 54–63.

HM Government (2011) 'Ending gang and youth violence: a cross-government report', https://www.gov.uk/government/publications/ending-gang-and-youth-violence-cross-government-report

HM Government (2016a) 'Injunctions to prevent gang-related violence and gang-related drug dealing', https://www.gov.uk/government/publications/injunctions-to-prevent-gang-related-violence-and-drug-dealing

HM Government (2016b) 'Ending gang violence and exploitation', https://www.gov.uk/government/publications/ending-gang-violence-and-exploitation

HM Government (2018) 'Serious violence strategy', https://www.gov.uk/government/publications/serious-violence-strategy

HMIC (2016) 'Missing children: who cares? The police response to missing and absent children', www.justiceinspectorates.gov.uk/hmic/wp-content/uploads/missing-children-who-cares.pdf

HMICFRS (2017) 'Stolen freedom: the policing response to modern slavery and human trafficking', https://www.justiceinspectorates.gov.uk/hmicfrs/wp-content/uploads/stolen-freedom-the-policing-response-to-modern-slavery-and-human-trafficking.pdf

HMICFRS (2019a) 'County lines', https://www.justiceinspectorates.gov.uk/hmicfrs/glossary/county-lines/

HMICFRS (2019b) 'Cuckooing,' www.justiceinspectorates.gov.uk/hmicfrs/glossary/cuckooing/

HMICFRS (2019c) 'Urban street gangs', https://www.justiceinspectorates.gov.uk/hmicfrs/glossary/urban-street-gangs/

HMICFRS (2020) 'Both sides of the coin: an inspection of how the police and National Crime Agency consider vulnerable people who are both victims and offenders in "county lines" drug offending', https://www.justiceinspectorates.gov.uk/hmicfrs/publications/both-sides-of-the-coin-county-lines/

Hobbs, D. (2001) 'The firm: organisational logic and criminal culture on a shifting terrain', *British Journal of Criminology*, 41(4): 549–60.

Holligan, C., Mclean, R. and Deuchar, R. (2016) 'Weapon-carrying amongst young men in Glasgow: street scripts and signals in uncertain social spaces', *Critical Criminology*, 25(1): 137–51.

Home Office (2012) 'Ending gang and youth violence report: one year on', London: The Stationery Office.

Home Office (2013a) 'Ending gang and youth violence: review 2012–13', https://www.gov.uk/government/publications/ending-gang-and-youth-violence-review-2012-to-2013

Home Office (2013b) 'Ending gang and youth violence: annual report 2013', https://www.gov.uk/government/publications/ending-gang-and-youth-violence-annual-report-2013

Home Office (2014) 'Review of the operation of injunctions to prevent gang-related violence', https://www.gov.uk/government/publications/review-of-the-operation-of-injunctions-to-prevent-gang-related-violence

Home Office (2016a) 'Ending gang violence and exploitation', https://www.gov.uk/government/publications/ending-gang-violence-and-exploitation

Home Office (2016b) 'Drug misuse: findings from the 2015–16 Crime Survey for England and Wales', 2nd edition, https://www.gov.uk/government/statistics/drug-misuse-findings-from-the-2015-to-2016-csew

Home Office (2017a) 'Criminal exploitation of children and vulnerable adults: county lines guidance', https://www.gov.uk/government/publications/criminal-exploitation-of-children-and-vulnerable-adults-county-lines

Home Office (2017b) 'Drug misuse: findings from the 2016 to 2017 CSEW', https://www.gov.uk/government/statistics/drug-misuse-findings-from-the-2016-to-2017-csew

Home Office (2018) 'Criminal exploitation of children and vulnerable adults: county lines guidance', https://assets.publishing.service.gov.uk/government/uploads/system/uploads/attachment_data/file/741194/HOCountyLinesGuidanceSept2018.pdf

Home Office (2019) 'Child exploitation disruption toolkit: disruption tactics', https://www.gov.uk/government/publications/child-exploitation-disruption-toolkit

Hope, T. (1994) 'Communities, crime and inequality in England and Wales', Paper presented to the 1994 Cropwood Round Table Conference Preventing Crime and Disorder, 14–15 September, Cambridge.

Hough, M. and Natarajan, M. (2000) 'Introduction: Illegal drug markets, research and policy', in M. Natarajan and M. Hough (eds) *Illegal Drug Markets: From Research to Prevention Policy*, Volume 11, Monsey, NY: Criminal Justice Press, pp 1–18.

Hudek, J. (2018) *County Lines Scoping Report, May 2018*, JM Consulting.

Innes, M. (2014) *Signal Crimes: Social Reactions to Crime, Disorder and Control*, Oxford University Press: Oxford.

Irwin-Rogers, K. and Pinkney, C. (2017) *Social Media as a Catalyst and Trigger for Youth Violence*, London: Catch 22.

Jacobs, B. (1999) *Dealing Crack*, Boston: Northeastern University Press.

Jacques, S. and Allen, A. (2015) 'Drug market violence: virtual anarchy, police pressure, predation, and retaliation', *Criminal Justice Review*, 40(1), 87–99.

Jarvis, G. and Parker, H. (1989) 'Young heroin users and crime: how do the 'new users' finance their habits?', *The British Journal of Criminology*, 29(2): 175–85.

Jewkes, Y. (2004) *Media and Crime*, London: Sage Publications.

Johnson, L. T. (2015) 'Drug markets, travel distance, and violence. Testing a typology', *Crime and Delinquency Journal*, 62(11): 1465–87.

Johnson, L. T., Taylor, R. B. and Ratcliffe, J. H. (2013) 'Need drugs, will travel?: The distances to crime of illegal drug buyers', *Journal of Criminal Justice*, 41(3): 178–87.

Katz, J. (1988) *Seductions of Crime: The Moral and Sensual Attractions of Doing Evil*, New York: Basic Books.

Kawulich, B. (2005) 'Participant observation as a data collection method', *Forum: Qualitative Sozialforschung/Forum: Qualitative Social Research*, 6(2): Article 43.

Kenway, P. and Palmer, G. (2007) 'Poverty among ethnic groups: how and why does it differ?', London: New Policy Institute.

Kintrea, K., Bannister, J. and Pickering, J. (2011) '"It's just an area – everybody represents it": exploring young people's territorial behaviour in British cities', in B. Goldson (ed) *Youth in Crisis?: 'Gangs', Territoriality and Violence*, London: Routledge, pp 55–71.

Kotler, P. and Armstrong, G. (2018) *Principles of Marketing* (17th edition), Harlow: Pearson Education Ltd.

Krisberg, J. (1974) 'Gang youth and hustling: the psychology of survival, *Issues in Criminology*, 9(1): 115–31.

Landman, R. A. (2014) '"A counterfeit friendship": mate crime and people with learning disabilities', *Journal of Adult Protection*, 16(6): 355–66.

Laub, J. and Sampson, R. (1993) 'Turning points in the life course: why change matters to the study of crime', *Criminology*, 31(3): 301–25.

Laub, J. and Sampson, R. (2003) *Shared Beginnings, Divergent Lives: Delinquent Boys to Age 70*. Cambridge, MA: Harvard University Press.

Lauger, T. (2012) *Real Gangsters*, New Brunswick: Rutgers University Press.

Lloyd, C. (2010) *Sinning and Sinned Against: The Stigmatisation of Problem Drug Users*, London: Drug Policy Commission.

Locum Today (2019) '70 per cent rise in children placed in unregulated accomodation', http://locumtoday.co.uk/article.php?s=2019-06-03-70-per-cent-rise-in-children-placed-in-unregulated-accommodation#.XmpCKUB2t9A

Maffesoli, M. (1996) *The Time of the Tribes: The Decline of Individualism in Mass Society*, London: Sage Publications.

Maher, L. (1997) *Sexed Work: Gender, Race and Resistance in a Brooklyn Drug Market*, London: University Press.

Maher, L. and Dixon, D. (1999) 'Policing and public health: law enforcement and harm minimization in a street-level drug market', *British Journal of Criminology*, 39(4): 488–512.

Marsh, S. (2019) 'Councils "unwittingly helping drug gangs recruit children"', *The Guardian*, https://www.theguardian.com/uk-news/2019/sep/16/councils-unwittingly-helping-drug-gangs-recruit-children-inquiry-says

Martin, J. L. (2003) 'What is field theory?' *American Journal of Sociology*, 109(1): 1–49.

Massey, J., Sherman, L. and Coupe, T. (2019) 'Forecasting knife homicide risk from prior knife assaults in 4835 local areas of London, 2016–2018', *Cambridge Journal of Evidence-Based Policing*, 3(1–2): 1–20.

Matrix Knowledge Group (2007) 'The illicit drug trade in the United Kingdom, http://drugslibrary.wordpress.stir.ac.uk/files/2018/01/rdsolr2007.pdf

Matza, D. (1964) *Delinquency and Drift*, New York, NY: John Wiley and Sons.

May, T. and Duffy, M. (2007) *Drug Dealing in Local Communities*, London: Nacro.

May, T. and Hough, M. (2004) 'Drug markets and distribution systems', *Addiction Research & Theory*, 12(6): 549–63.

May, T., Duffy, M., Few, B. and Hough, M. (2005) *Understanding Drug Selling in Local Communities, Insider or Outsider Trading*, York: Joseph Rowntree Foundation.

McLean, R. (2017) 'An evolving gang model in contemporary Scotland', *Deviant Behavior*, 39(3): 309–21.

McLean, R. (2019) *Gangs, Drugs and (Dis)organised Crime*, Bristol: Bristol University Press.

McLean, R., Densley, J. and Deuchar, R. (2018a) 'Situating gangs within Scotland's illegal drugs market(s)', *Trends in Organized Crime*, 21(2): 147–71.

McLean, R., Robinson, G. and Densley, J. (2020) *County Lines: Criminal Networks and Evolving Drug Markets in Britain*, Springer Briefs in Criminology, Springer: Cham, Switzerland.

McLean, R., Deuchar, R., Harding, S. and Densley, J. (2018b) 'Putting the "street" in gang: place and space in the organization of Scotland's drug selling gangs', *The British Journal of Criminology*, 59(2): 396–415.

McNeill, F. (2012) 'Four forms of "offender rehabilitation": towards an interdisciplinary perspective', *Legal and Criminological Psychology*, 17(1): 18–36.

McSweeney, T., Turnbull, P. J. and Hough, M. (2008) *Tackling drug markets and distribution networks in the UK: A review of the recent literature*, London: Institute for Criminal Policy Research.

McVie, S. (2010) 'Gang membership and knife carrying: findings from the Edinburgh study of youth transitions and crime', Edinburgh: The Scottish Centre for Crime and Justice Research.

Merton, R. (1938) 'Social structure and anomie', *American Sociological Review*, 3(5): 672–82.

Messerschmidt, J. W. (1993) *Masculinities and Crime: Critique and Reconceptualization of Theory*, Oxford: Rowman and Littlefield.

Miller, W. B. (1958) 'Lower class culture as a generating milieu of gang delinquency', *Journal of Social Issues*, 14: 5–10.

Miller, W. B. (1980) 'Gangs, groups, and serious youth crime', in D. Shichor and D. H. Kelly (eds) *Critical Issues in Juvenile Delinquency*, Lexington, MA: Heath, pp 115–38.

Miller, W. B. (1992) *Crime by Youth Gangs and Groups in the United States*, Washington, DC: U.S. Department of Justice, Office of Justice Programs, Office of Juvenile Justice and Delinquency Prevention.

Miller, W. B. (2001) *The Growth of Youth Gang Problems in the United States: 1970–98*, Office of Juvenile Justice and Delinquency Prevention, Washington DC.

Ministry of Justice (2019) 'Knife and offensive weapon sentencing statistics: October to December 2018', https://www.gov.uk/government/statistics/knife-and-offensive-weapon-sentencing-statistics-october-to-december-2018

Missing People (2016) 'The absent category – safeguarding children and vulnerable adults?' https://www.missingpeople.org.uk/latest-news/762-the-absent-category-safeguarding-children-and-vulnerable-adults.html

Missing People (2017) 'APPG on runaway and missing children and adults', https://www.missingpeople.org.uk/about-us/about-the-issue/policy-parliamentary-work/90-missing-children-and-adults/16-all-party-parliamentary-group.html

Missing People (2018) 'Still in harm's way: a report by Missing People and ECPAT UK', https://www.missingpeople.org.uk/latest-news/1061-still-in-harm-s-way-a-report-by-missing-people-and-ecpat-uk.html

Missing People (2019) 'New research: all of us were broken', https://www.missingpeople.org.uk/latest-news/1086-new-research-all-of-us-were-broken.html

Moore, J. W. (1990) 'Gangs, drugs, and violence', in M. De La Rosa, E. Lambert and B. Gropper (eds) *Drugs and Violence: Causes, Correlates, and Consequences*, pp 160–75.

MOPAC (2017) 'The London knife crime strategy', https://www.london.gov.uk/sites/default/files/mopac_knife_crime_strategy_june_2017.pdf

Moule J. R., Decker, S. and Pyrooz, D. (2013) 'Social capital, the life-course, and gangs', in M. Maguire, R. Morgan and R. Reiner (eds) *Handbook of Life-Course Criminology*. New York: Springer, pp 143–58.

Moyle, L. (2019) 'Situating vulnerability and exploitation in street-level drug markets: cuckooing, commuting, and the "county lines" drug supply model', *Journal of Drug Issues*, 49(4): 739–55.

Moyle, L. and Coomber, R. (2015) 'Earning a score: an exploration of the nature and roles of heroin and crack cocaine "user-dealers"', *British Journal of Criminology*, 55(3): 534–55.

Moyle, L. and Coomber, R. (2016) 'Bourdieu on supply: utilizing the "theory of practice" to understand heroin and crack cocaine user-dealing', *European Journal of Criminology*, 14(3): 309–28.

Moyle, L., Coomber, R. and Lowther, J. (2013) 'Crushing a walnut with a sledge hammer? Analysing the penal response to the social supply of illicit drugs', *Social & Legal Studies*, 22(4): 553–73.

MPS (Metropolitan Police Service) (2010) '"Confident, safe and secure": MPS drugs strategy 2010–2013', http://policeauthority.org/Metropolitan/committees/sop/2010/100304/06/index.html

MPS (Metropolitan Police Service) (2019) Violent Crime Task Force: Tackling Violent Crime across the Capital. C. S. Ade Adelekan presentation to Tackling Gang and Youth Crime. Westminster Insight Conference, 23 January.

Murji, K. (2007) 'Hierarchies, markets and networks: ethnicity/race and drug distribution', *The Journal of Drug Issues*, 37(4): 781–804.

NCA (National Crime Agency) (2015) *NCA Intelligence Assessment: County lines, gangs and safeguarding.* National Crime Agency publications, https://www.nationalcrimeagency.gov.uk/who-we-are/publications/359-nca-intelligence-assessment-county-lines-gangs-and-safeguarding-2015/file

NCA (National Crime Agency) (2016) County Lines Gang Violence, Exploitation and Drug Supply 2016 *National Briefing Report NCA:* National Crime Agency publications, https://www.nationalcrimeagency.gov.uk/who-we-are/publications/15-county-lines-gang-violence-exploitation-and-drug-supply-2016/file

NCA (National Crime Agency) (2017a) *National Strategic Assessment of Serious and Organised Crime.* National Briefing Report, NCA.

NCA (National Crime Agency) (2017b) *County Lines Violence, Exploitation and Drug Supply 2017*: National Briefing Report, NCA, https://nationalcrimeagency.gov.uk/who-we-are/publications/234-county-lines-violen-ce-exploitation-drug-supply-2017/file

NCA (National Crime Agency) (2017c) *UK Missing Persons Bureau: Missing Persons Data Report 2015/16.* NCA.

NCA (National Crime Agency) (2018) *Crime threats: Drugs.* Available at: https://www.nationalcrimeagency.gov.uk/what-we-do/crime-threats/drug-trafficking

NCA (National Crime Agency) (2019a) *Intelligence Assessment – County Lines Drug Supply, Vulnerability and Harm 2018*, NCA: National Crime Agency publications, https://nationalcrimeagency.gov.uk/who-we-are/publications/257-county-lines-drug-supply-vulnerability-and-harm-2018/file

NCA (National Crime Agency) (2019b) *National Strategic Assessment of Serious and Organised Crime: Speech by DG Lynne Owens.* NCA, https://nationalcrimeagency.gov.uk/news/181-000-uk-offenders-fuelling-chronic-and-corrosive-threat-from-serious-and-organised-crime

New Bletchley Network (2019) *Knife Crime: Effective Strategies and Coordination (a second report from the New Bletchley Network)* New Bletchley Network, https://www.newbletchley.org/

Newcombe R. (2007) *Trends in the Prevalence of Illicit Drug Use in Britain. In Drugs in Britain: Supply, Consumption and Control*, London: Palgrave.

OHCHR (2000) *Protocol to Prevent, Suppress and Punish Trafficking in Persons Especially Women and Children, Supplementing the United Nations Convention against Transnational Organized Crime*, https://www.ohchr.org/en/professionalinterest/pages/protocoltraffickinginpersons.aspx

O'Malley, L. (1998) 'Can loyalty schemes really build loyalty?' *Marketing Intelligence and Planning*, 16(1): 47–55.

ONS (Office for National Statistics) (2019) *Homicide in England and Wales: year ending March 2018*, ONS.

Palasinski, M. and Riggs, D. (2012) 'Young white British men and knife-carrying in public: discourses of masculinity, protection and vulnerability', *Critical Criminology*, 20(4): 463–76.

Parker, H. and Newcombe, R. (1987) 'Heroin use and acquisitive crime in an English community', *British Journal of Sociology*, 38(3): 331–50.

Parker, H., Bakx, K. and Newcombe, R. (1988) *Living with Heroin*, Milton Keynes: Open University Press.

Parkin, S. (2013) *Habitus and Drug Using Environments: Health, Place and Lived-Experiences*, Farnham: Ashgate.

Pearson, G. (1987a) 'Social deprivation, unemployment and patterns of heroin use', in N. Dorn and N. South (eds) *A Land Fit for Heroin?* London: Macmillan, pp 62–94.

Pearson, G. (1987b) *The New Heroin Users*, Oxford: Basil Blackwell.

Pearson, G. and Hobbs, D. (2001) *Middle Market Drug Distribution*. Home Office Research Study 227. London: Home Office.

Pepin, S. (2018) *County lines exploitation in London* (Commons Debate Packs CDP-2018-0009). Available at: https://researchbriefings.parliament.uk/ResearchBriefing/Summary/CDP-2018-0009

Perri 6, (1997) *'Social exclusion: time to be optimistic'*, Demos Collection, 12, pp 3–9.

Pitts, J. (2008) *Reluctant Gangsters*, Cullompton: Willan Publishing.

Pitts, J. (2010) 'Mercenary territory: are youth gangs really a problem?', in B. Goldson (ed) (2011) *Youth in Crisis? 'Gangs', Territoriality and Violence*, London: Routledge, pp 161–82.

Pitts J. (2013) 'Drifting into trouble: sexual exploitation and gang affiliation', in M. Melrose and J. Pearce (eds) *Critical Perspectives on Child Sexual Exploitation and Related Trafficking*, London: Palgrave Macmillan, pp 23–37.

Polsky, N. (1967) *Hustlers, Beats, and Others*, Chicago: Aldine.

Potter, G. (2009) 'Exploring retail-level drug distribution: social supply, "real" dealers and the user/dealer interface', in Z. Demetrovics, J. fountain and L. Kraus (eds) *Old and New Policies, Theories, Research Methods and Drug Users across Europe*, Lengerich, Germany: PABST Science Publishers, pp 50–74.

Potter, G. and Taylor, M. (2013) 'From "social supply" to "real dealing"; drift, friendship, and trust in drug-dealing careers, *Journal of Drug Issues*, 43(4): 392–406.

Preble, E. and Casey, J. J. (1969) 'Taking care of business: the heroin user's life on the street, *International Journal of Addictions*, 4(1): 1–24.

Presdee, M. (2000) *Cultural Criminology and the Carnival of Crime*, London: Routledge.

Presser, L. (2009) 'The narratives of offenders', *Theoretical Criminology*, 13(2): 177–200.

Public Health England and Department of Health (2017) *Adult substance misuse statistics from the National Drug Treatment Monitoring System (NDTMS)*. Available at: https://assets.publishing.service.gov.uk/government/uploads/system/uploads/attachment_data/file/658056/Adult-statistics-from-the-national-drug-treatment-monitoring-system-2016-2017.pdf

Pyrooz, D., Sweeten, G. and Piquero, A. (2013) 'Continuity and change in gang membership and gang embeddedness', *Journal of Research in Crime and Delinquency*, 50(2): 239–71.

Pyrooz, D., Turanovic, J., Decker, S. and Wu, J. (2016) 'Taking stock of the relationship between gang membership and offending: a meta-analysis', *Criminal Justice and Behavior*, 43(3): 365–97.

Razzall, K. (2019) 'Action needed against "rogue" homes for teenagers, says minister', BBC 18 July 2019.

Rees, G., Pople, L. and Goswami, H. (2011) 'Understanding children's well-being', The Children's Society, https://www.childrenssociety.org.uk/sites/default/files/tcs/promoting_positive_well-being_for_children_economic_factors_march.pdf

Reuter, P. (2009) 'Systemic violence in drug markets', *Crime, Law and Social Change*, 52(3): 275–84.

Ritchie, J. and Lewis, J. (2003) Qualitative Research Practice: A Guide for Social Science Students and Researchers. London: Sage

Robinson, I. and Flemen, K. (2002) *Tackling Drug Use in Rented Housing: A Good Practice Guide*, London: Home Office.

Robinson, G., McLean, R. and Densley, J. (2019) 'Working county lines: child criminal exploitation and illicit drug dealing in Glasgow and Merseyside', *International Journal of Offender Therapy and Comparative Criminology*, 63(5): 1–18.

Rubin, H. and Rubin, I. (2005) 'Listening, hearing and sharing social experiences', *Qualitative Interviewing: The Art of Hearing Data*, Sage Publications.

Ruggiero, V. (2010) 'Unintended consequences: changes in organised drug supply in the UK', *Trends in Organized Crime*, 13(1): 46–59.

Ryan, G. and Bernard, H. (2000) 'Data management and analysis methods', in N. K. Denzin & Y. S. Lincoln (eds) *Handbook of Qualitative Research* (2nd edition), Thousand Oaks, CA: Sage Publications, pp 769–802.

Safer London Foundation (2016) 'County lines: what do I need to know?', Blog, https://saferlondon.org.uk/2016/09/county-lines-i-need-know/

Safeguardinghub.co.uk (2019) *Even residential care for children have 'rogue traders'*.

Sandberg, S. (2008) 'Black drug dealers in a white welfare state: cannabis dealing and street capital in Norway', *British Journal of Criminology*, 48(5): 604–19.

Sandberg, S. (2010) 'What can "lies" tell us about life? Notes towards a framework of narrative criminology', *Journal of Criminal Justice Education*, 21(4): 447–65.

Sandberg, S. and Pederson, W. (2011) *Street Capital*, Bristol: Policy Press.

Sanders, T., O'Neill, M. and Pitcher, J. (2017) *Prostitution: Sex Work, Policy & Politics*, London: Sage.

Sanders, T., Scoular, J., Campbell, R., Pitcher, J. and Cunningham, S. (2018) *Beyond the Gaze: Summary Briefing on Internet Sex Work*, London: Palgrave Macmillan.

Sanghani R. (2018) 'Sex workers are setting up "pop-up brothels" around the UK', BBC, www.bbc.co.uk/bbcthree/article/1e40a4e9-5206-4c10-9d76-d5423471db5e.

Schank, R. C. and Abelson, R. P. (1977) *Scripts, Plans, Goals and Understanding: An Inquiry into Human Knowledge Structures*, Hillsdale, NJ: L. Erlbaum.

Seddon, T. (2000) 'Explaining the drug–crime link: theoretical, policy and research issues', *Journal of Social Policy*, 29(1): 95–107.

Seddon, T. (2006) 'Drugs, crime and social exclusion: social context and social theory in British drugs-crime research', *British Journal of Criminology*, 46(4): 680–703.

Shiner, M. (2013) 'British drug policy and the modern state: reconsidering the criminalisation thesis', *Journal of Social Policy*, 42(3): 623–43.

Sibley, D. (1995) *Geographies of Exclusion*, London: Routledge.

Smithson, H., Ralphs, R. and Williams, P. (2013) 'Used and abused: the problematic usage of gang terminology in the United Kingdom and its implications for ethnic minority youth', *British Journal of Criminology*, 53(1): 113–28.

Social Research Association (2003) *Ethical Research*, www.the-sra.org.uk.

Spicer, J. (2018) '"That's their brand, their business": how police officers are interpreting county lines', *Policing and Society, An International Journal of Research and Policy*, 29(8): 873–86.

Spicer, J., Moyle, L. and Coomber, R. (2019) The variable and evolving nature of 'cuckooing' as a form of criminal exploitation in street level drug markets, *Trends in Organized Crime*, https://link.springer.com/article/10.1007/s12117-019-09368-5

Stephens, P., Leach, A., Taggart, L. and Jones, H. (1998) *Think Sociology*, Cheltenham: Stanley Thornes.

Stevens, A. (2011) *Drugs, Crime and Public Health*, Abingdon: Routledge.

Stewart, T. (1987) *The Heroin Users*, London: Pandora Press.

Storrod, M. and Densley, J. (2017) '"Going viral" and "going country": the expressive and instrumental activities of street gangs on social media', *Journal of Youth Studies*, 20(6): 677–96.

Stuart, J., Barnes, J. and Brodie, I. (2002) *Conducting Ethical Research*, London: NESS.

Sturrock, R. and Holmes, L. (2015) *Running the Risks: The Links between Gang Involvement and Young People going Missing*, London: Catch 22.

Suchman, M.C. (1995) 'Managing legitimacy: strategic and institutional approaches', *Academy of Management Review*, 20(3): 571–610.

Sutherland, E. H. (1947) *Principles of Criminology* (4th edition), Philadelphia: J. B. Lippincott.

Swartz, D. (1997) *Culture and Power: The Sociology of Pierre Bourdieu*, Chicago: University of Chicago Press.

Sykes, G. and Matza, D. (1957) 'Techniques of neutralization: a theory of delinquency', *American Sociological Review*, 22(6): 664–70.

Taylor, S. (2008) 'Outside the outsiders: media representations of drug use', *Probation Journal*, 55(4): 369–87.

Taylor, M. and Potter, G. (2013) 'From "social supply"' to "real dealing": drift, friendship, and trust in drug-dealing careers', *Journal of Drug Issues*, 43(4): 392–406.

Thomas, P. (2013) 'Hate crime or mate Crime: disablist hostility, contempt and ridicule', in A. Roulstone and H. Mason-Bish (eds) *Disability, Hate Crime and Violence*, London: Routledge, pp 135–46.

Thrasher, F. (1927) *The Gang: A Study of 1,313 Gangs in Chicago*, Chicago IL: University of Chicago Press.

Tita, G., Cohen, J. and Engberg, J. (2005) 'An ecological study of the location of gang "set space"', *Social Problems*, 52(2): 272–99.

Toy, J. (2008) *Die Another Day: A Practitioner's Review with Recommendations for Preventing Gang and Weapon Violence in London in 2008*, London: MPS Research and Analysis Unit.

Traynor, P. (2016) *Closing the 'security gap': young people, 'street life' and knife crime,* Submitted PhD, University of Leeds School of Law.

Turner, A., Belcher, L. and Pona, I. (2019) *Counting Lives*, London: The Children's Society.

Turner, V. (1974) *Dramas, Fields, and Metaphors*, Ithaca, NY: Cornell University Press.

Vigil, J.D. (1988) 'Group processes and street identity: adolescent Chicano gang members', *Ethos*, 6(4): 421–45.

Violent Crime Task Force (2019) *Tackling Violent Crime across the Capital*. PowerPoint presentation by Detective Superintendent Sean Yates at MPS briefing, Gang dynamics and knife crime, Operation Sceptre, National Force Briefing, 1 March.

Wacquant, L. (1992) 'Decivilisation and demonization: la mutation du ghetto noir americain in decivilizing and demonizing: the remaking of the Black American ghetto', in S. Loyal and S. Quilley (eds) *The Sociology of Norbert Elias*, Cambridge: Cambridge University Press 2004, pp 95–121.

Wacquant, L. (2008) *Urban Outcasts: The Sociology of Advanced Marginality*, Cambridge: Polity Press.

Wakeman, S. (2015) 'The moral economy of heroin in "Austerity Britain"', *Critical Criminology*, 24(3): 363–77.

Walklate, S. (2018) *Handbook of Victims and Victimology* (2nd edition), Abingdon: Routledge.

Webb, E., Campbell, D., Schwartz, R. and Seehrent, L. (1996) *Unobtrusive Measures: Non-Reactive Research in the Social Sciences*, Chicago: Rand McNally & Company.

Wessells, B. (2010) *Understanding the Internet*. New York: Palgrave.

Whittaker, A., Cheston, L., Tyrell, T., Higgins, M., Felix-Baptiste, C. and Havard, T. (2019) *From Postcodes to Profit: How Gangs have Changed in Waltham Forest*, London: London South Bank University.

Williams, T. (1992) *Crackhouse: Notes from the End of the Line*, London: Penguin Books.

Windle, J. and Briggs, D. (2015a) 'Going solo: the social organisation of drug dealing within a London street gang', *Journal of Youth Studies*, 18(9): 1170–85.

Windle J. and Briggs D. (2015b) 'It's like working away for two weeks', *Crime Prevention and Community Safety*, 17(2): 105–19.

Windle, J., Moyle, L. and Coomber, R. (2020) '"Vulnerable" kids going country: children and young people's involvement in county lines drug dealing', *Youth Justice*, 1–15. doi: 10.1177/1473225420902840

Yates, J. (2006) '"You just don't grass": youth, crime and "grassing" in a working-class community', *Youth Justice*, 6(3): 195–210. NAYJ: Sage Publications.

Young, J. (1971) *The Drugtakers: The Social Meaning of Drug Use*. London: Paladin.

Young, J. (1999) *The Exclusive Society*, London: Sage Publications.

Žižek, S. (2009) *First as Tragedy Then as Farce*, London: Verso.

Index

Note: page numbers in italic type refer to figures; those in bold type refer to tables.